LIBERATING GRACE

LIBERATING GRACE

Leonardo Boff

Translated by John Drury

ORBIS BOOKS
Maryknoll, New York 10545

Sixth Printing, February 1990

Library of Congress Cataloging in Publication Data

Boff, Leonardo.
  Liberating grace.

  Translation of A graça libertadora no mundo.
  Bibliography: p.
  1. Grace (Theology)   I.   Title.
BT761.2.B6313   234'.1   79-4206
ISBN 0-88344-282-5

First published as *A graça libertadora no mundo,* copyright © 1976 by Editora Vozes Ltda., Rua Frei Luís, 100, 25.600 Petropolis, RJ, Brazil

English translation copyright © 1979 by Orbis Books, Maryknoll, NY 10545

Manufactured in the United States of America

To Cardinal Evaristo Arns,
Cardinal Archbishop of São Paulo,
friend and teacher,
for his apostolic and prophetic service
to the whole Brazilian church

Contents

PART TWO
EXPERIENCING GRACE

PART THREE
THEOLOGICAL REFLECTIONS
ON THE GRACE EXPERIENCE

PART FOUR
GOD AND HUMANKIND
AS REVEALED IN THE GRACE EXPERIENCE

Abbreviations

AA	*Apostolicam Actuositatem*
AG	*Ad Gentes*
DS	Denzinger, *Enchiridion Symbolorum*, ed. Adolf Schönmetzer
ETL	*Ephemerides Theologicae Lovanienses*
GS	*Gaudium et Spes*
LG	*Lumen Gentium*
NA	*Nostra Aetate*
PL	*Patrologia Latina*
RB	*Revue Biblique*
REB	*Revista Eclesiástica Brasileira*

Preface

Qui ante nos scripserunt
Non domini nostri
Sed duces fuerunt.
—Guilbert of Tournai,
Franciscan, died 1288,
De modo addiscendi.

A train is hurtling swiftly toward its destination. Its gleaming body cuts through the fields like an arrow. Crossing rivers and cities, it slips through the landscape like a thread in motion. Nothing can stop it. It is perfect in form, in color, and in speed.

Inside the whole human drama is going on. Inside there are people of all sorts. Some are talking; others are silent. Some are at work on something; others are resting. Some are looking out on the landscape; others are preoccupied with their own business affairs. Some are just being born; others are on the point of dying. Some quietly go on loving or hating. Some are arguing about the train: it is going in the wrong direction. Some think they have taken the wrong train. Some are opposed to the idea of any train at all. We should never have made trains at all; they pollute the atmosphere. Others accept the train and its advantages gratefully or even envision faster trains. Still others question nothing. They know that they are moving in some direction and will reach some point of arrival. Why fret about it? Some people run nervously toward the front cars. They want to get there more quickly. Others oppose the movement of the train and head toward the back, trying to flee from the train altogether.

The train goes on indifferently, following its certain destiny. It patiently carries all, whether they are excited about it or bored with it. It is even willing to carry its detractors, offering all an opportunity to take a splendid, joyous trip.

All the passengers are traveling for free, gratis. No one can step off the train or flee. They find themselves there inside the train. Freedom is exercised there. They can go toward the front or toward the back. They can alter the train cars or leave them as they are. They can enjoy the passing landscape or get aggravated at their companions. They can accept the train joyfully or reject it bitterly. Yet the train continues on toward its inevitable destiny and courteously carries all of them.

And some people really do accept the train wholeheartedly. They delight in its existence and enjoy its speed. They take pleasure in the passing landscape and make friends with their traveling companions. They try to make sure that everyone feels good and they stand up to those who try to damage the coaches or inconvenience their fellow passengers. They do not let quarrels or delirium obscure the whole sense and purpose of the journey. To them it is wonderful that such a train exists and that it can carry us so quickly back home, where others anxiously await us, where the embraces will be long and love never ending.

Liberating grace at work in the world is like such a train. The destination in this case is God, and so is the route. For the route is the destination anticipated, the goal slowly turning into a reality and carrying human beings along.

Grace carries all, giving all the opportunity to have a good trip. It does not reject the lazy, the rebellious, or the intriguers. Like a train, grace does not change the face of negations. Only human beings change, spoiling their journey. But they are still carried along gently and steadily. God, who is grace, "is good to the ungrateful and the wicked" (Luke 6:35).

When we accept the train, enjoy its course, and wish our fellow travelers well, we are already anticipating the festive joy of our arrival at our final destination. Traveling in that way is like going home. It is grace. Grace is "glory in exile," just as glory is "grace in its homeland." It is heaven.

When we spurn the train, disturb the journey, and ruefully run in the opposite direction trying vainly to flee, we are already anticipating absolute frustration. But the train continues on its course, carrying its opponents inside. God does not change or alter his gratuitousness, but human beings can. Their frustration will be all the greater when they realize that they are being kindly carried along in spite of everything. That is hell.

And you, reader, which direction are you traveling?

PART ONE

POSING THE THEME
OF GRACE TODAY

CHAPTER 1

Grace and the Task of Theology

"Grace" and the Essential Christian Experience

The word "grace" refers to the most basic and original Christian experience. It is an experience of God, whose sympathy and love for human beings run so deep that he has given himself. It is an experience of human beings, who are capable of letting themselves be loved by God, of opening up to love and filial dialogue. The result of this encounter is the beauty, gracefulness, and goodness that is reflected in all of creation—but especially in human beings and their history. Humanity is good, gracious, grateful, beautiful, cordial, and merciful because it was visited by a God who is the same; and this God has made humanity what it is.

Grace signifies the presence of God in the world and in human beings. When God chooses to be present, the sick are made well, the fallen are raised up, the sinners are made just, the dead come back to life, the oppressed experience freedom, and the despairing feel consolation and warm intimacy.

Grace also signifies the openness of human beings to God. It is the ability of human beings to relate to the Infinite, to enter upon a dialogue that wins them their humanity day by day and rewards them with deification.

Grace is always an encounter between a God who gives himself and a human being who does likewise. By its very nature grace is the breaking down of realms or worlds that are closed in upon themselves. Grace is relationship, exodus, communion, encounter, openness, and dialogue. It is the history of two freedoms, the meeting of two loves.

For this reason grace signifies the reconciliation of heaven and earth, of God and humans, of time and eternity. Grace is something more than time, more than history, more than humanity. It is ever something *more* which happens with unexpected gratuitousness. As Leonardo Coimbra put it so well:

Grace is always something extra, above and beyond what is useful at the moment. . . . It is an excess, above and beyond all time, all space, all forms, and all lives.[1]

God the Father realizes himself continually for all eternity as a Mystery that offers himself as the Son and the Holy Spirit. He prolongs his communion and self-giving in worldly terms. Once the world is established, he penetrates more deeply into it with a superabundant and astonishing outpouring of love and self-giving. He himself becomes the world under the name Jesus Christ, who is saving grace for all humans (Titus 2:11). "When the kindness and love of God our Savior appeared, he saved us" (Titus 3:4). Grace is the name for God himself insofar as he is always communion, exodus from self, love for others, and sympathy with those that are different from him. Grace is not a quality of God; it is the essence (*divinitas*) of God. God does not possess grace; he is grace.

As persons, human beings ever remain open to the possibility of being something more and relating to others. They are not just a being-there; they are an ex-istence. They always are living an encounter with what is different from themselves. They are always a something more. Thus grace is the supreme reality that envelops them insofar as it signifies encounter, limitless openness, and communion. Humans live in the divine atmosphere insofar as divinity signifies the fullness of communion and self-giving. Indeed, human beings are truly human only in that atmosphere of grace, of something more than themselves. Thus humans are always something more than "human," more than what we can see and define as human.

When we talk about grace, we are trying to grasp this phenomenon that breaks down all the narrow barriers which we use to describe realities, dimensions, and worlds. Grace establishes one single world where opposites meet: God and humans, Creator and creatures. Grace is oneness and reconciliation; hence it is synonymous with salvation, with perfect identity between humans and God.

Grace Coexisting with Dis-grace

If grace is all that we have described above, then it is ever threatened by what we can call dis-grace, i.e., lack of encounter, refusal to dialogue, and closing in upon oneself. Grace and dis-grace are two possibilities of freedom. This is the mystery of creation, an absolute mystery to which reason does not have access.

Grace is the absolute meaning that brings fulfillment to everything. It is a light that illumines everything and makes all comprehensible. Dis-grace is absolute absurdity, sheer darkness without a trace of light. It has no rationale. There is no logical argument for dis-grace and sin, which cannot be understood in any way. Dis-grace is a brute fact, which can only be realized. It forces itself upon us as the absurd, and yet it exists as a fact and an experience.

For a created being grace is grace amid the possibility of dis-grace. The human being is always a threatened being who can be dis-graced. As a history of evil, violence, destruction, and cruel inhumanity, history itself is a history of dis-grace in the world; and it is fleshed out in the closing up of beings in themselves.

Concrete human beings live out this drama of being simultaneously graced and dis-graced: *"Omnis homo Adam, omnis homo Christus."*[2] They are both Christ and Antichrist, openness and closedness. Their concrete experience is a paradoxical one of both grace and dis-grace.

The aim of my reflections in this book is to deal with the experience of grace. While I shall take account of the experience of dis-grace, sin, and perdition also, I shall do so from the standpoint of grace. I shall try to shed the light of the grace experience on the dark corners of our life.

Theology's Relationship to Grace

In dealing with grace we can approach the subject in two different ways. We can talk about grace in the same terms that Christian experience has used throughout its long history. In other words, we can talk about grace in the same way that theology manuals have done in the tract on grace. The manuals show us how grace had been dealt with by theologians and the church when they confronted heterodox doctrines that could not be accepted by the church community. Scholarly theology created a whole system about grace, using a whole terminology of its own and creating a well-defined doctrine. The whole emphasis was on the doctrinal aspect, and so we got talk *about* grace. There was almost no evidence of grace itself, of the grace experience and its presence in the world.

In such a framework theology has little to think about. It simply administers a line of thought that has already been worked out and officially approved. That is of no little importance, of course, because it does provide us with information and put us in contact with the experience of grace as it took place in the history of the church and found semantic expression. But important as that task is, theology has another inescapable task within the community of faith. It must *ponder* and think about the experience of grace that is taking place today in the world and in the church. Thus theology prolongs an experience that is ever present in the church and the world, creating an idiom that embodies and expresses this experience.

So there is a second way to approach the theme of grace. We can try to articulate the present-day experience of grace, expressing it in a way that is appropriate for our time, accessible, and acceptable to the community of faith. In this way the Christian community can identify with its past tradition while also feeling that it is creatively prolonging it. Here the emphasis is not on talking *about* grace but on letting grace do the talking (though all talk is *about* something). In other words, we want to create an idiom and a line of reflection which will make us conscious of the divine grace in which we now live, which will help us to detect the presence of God and his love in the world, quite apart from the fact that we may be thinking and talking about it.

Grace does not begin to exist when we talk about it. We talk about it because it first exists in our lives. We may experience real grace and the presence of God without ever using those terms. The function of theology is not to create the realities about which it speaks; it is to talk about realities which exist prior to its talk and which are encountered in human life.

We already live in the *divine milieu* of grace. The problem for theology is how to deal with that fact thematically, how to speak about grace in a meaningful way today. We do not want an outdated idiom to keep people from taking cognizance of the full depth and meaning of something that they are actually living. The fact is that human beings are living the experience of grace; but they may not know it or reflect on it. Theology is reflection on this reality. Its aim is not to monopolize grace but to make human beings aware of the grace that is visiting their lives.

Omnipresence of the Experience of Grace

Here we encounter another danger that should be pointed out. In our talk about grace we may erroneously think that grace becomes present and operative only where it is talked about. The true relationship is quite the opposite. We can talk about grace only because it actually exists prior to any such talk. Talk is a moment of grace insofar as we try to make explicit the reality of grace as human beings. We must make every effort to avoid a mistake that has often been made by theology. Too often it has sought to ensnare grace in the meshes of theological language. This illusion finds expression in many forms. People say that grace comes into the world only through the church; or that human beings can get to Christ only through the church; or that salvation comes to us only through the church. Thus the church is turned into a monopoly over something that really cannot be monopolized. It is not the church that contains grace but rather grace that contains the church within itself. All authentic grace reveals an ecclesial character in the sense that it tends to manifest itself visibly and to form a community.

God, Christ, and grace are always free. They manifest themselves in the world through many mediations. The church is one such mediation—an explicit, conscious, and communitarian one—but it is not the only one. Thus theology must be careful when it attempts to talk about grace and let grace talk. It must never presume to limit the activity of grace to the confines of its talk. To do that would be to make grace a ghetto affair and restrict it to human dimensions. Stripped of its divine character, it would no longer be God's grace. But grace is divine, so it is present in everything and nothing can escape its influence. Theology must constantly remind itself of that fact.

In systematic terms, then, our task here is twofold. We want to reflect on the experience of grace as we encounter it in the circumstances and limitations of our own day. Then we want to talk about grace in such a way that this experience can be adequately translated for the ecclesial community.

Since we are historical beings, however, we are immersed in a current of life that flows down to us from the past. We are products of the past to some extent, and that has its impact on our own experience of grace. We must be aware of the theological legacy which we have inherited from the past and which may still be present in the collective unconscious of the Christian community. In the next two chapters, then, I shall take a look at the past theology of grace in order to gain some perspective on where we are today. This may help us to see how we should articulate the experience of grace for the days ahead.

CHAPTER 2

Past and Present Doctrines About Grace

When we examine the articulation of grace on the level of theological reflection, we notice a fairly prominent development in the choice of semantic tools. This development should not be viewed solely in speculative and formal terms. It is the expression of cultural changes that took place in history, and of various forms of Christian praxis that were associated with a given point in the societal structure. Such changes and modifications were reflected in the choice of linguistic instruments, though often it was an unconscious process. Among the cultural changes, for example, two obvious factors are the socioeconomic dimension and the relative distribution of power, or access to power, among those who elaborated theological positions.

My overview here does not purport to trace the history of critical, theological reflection on grace. That is done in the history of dogmas and doctrines. I simply want to pick out certain dominant elements that gave direction to this reflection.

The Old Testament

The Old Testament talks of the experience of grace and reflects on grace in terms of history, e.g., the liberation from Egypt, the fact of creation, and the election of Israel. Grace is experienced as God's attitude and way of acting, which includes fidelity, justice, uprightness, and magnanimity above and beyond any human legalistic criteria. It is the benevolence that humans experience in their struggle to survive and to create a meaningful life.

The theme of the covenant, in particular, expresses the experience of something *more* that is bound up with grace. Out of pure benevolence God chooses the lowliest people of all to proclaim and bear witness to the one God. Israel experiences the reality of its singular place in history as a grace that goes beyond the fact of creation common to all peoples. Grace is always lived as the merciful goodness of God, not in abstract but in historical terms. It is political peace, social well-being, liberation, security amid the pressure exerted by the great powers, an upright life, and an openness to the future that God promised through the covenant.

8

A dialectical process is at work constantly. On the one hand, humans are totally dependent on God. On the other hand, they can appeal to certain promises made by God because of the election and the covenant. They can sin by failing to show confidence in God or by haughtily declaring their independence from him.

In any case grace is lived out and pondered in historical terms and in our awareness of the gracious deeds God performed, deeds which became history in the memory of his people and which paved the way for some cosmic fulfillment in eschatology. There is a yesterday, a today, and a tomorrow. Grace creates opportune moments and situations that serve as basic reference points for the historical memory of his people. In them they recognize the concrete goodness of God. Such were the exodus from Egypt, the Babylonian exile, cultic worship, and the tranquility of a society at peace.

The New Testament

For the New Testament grace is a saving way of acting in particular. The goodness and sympathy of the one God is personally embodied in Jesus Christ as goodness and kindness. The christological facts and events are remembered. In memory they become operative and effective for the here and now, paving the way for definitive fulfillment.

Grace is a new salvific atmosphere, an eschatological happening that makes us participants in the definitive reality of the kingdom and the life of God himself. In Jesus Christ grace was the presence of God's salvation embodied in history. As such it aroused eschatological hopes for the imminent arrival of God's loving communication in all its fullness. As the Parousia was postponed, stress came to be placed more and more on the grace already present. The later books of the New Testament, in particular, stress this in terms of Christ already present in the sacraments, the divine Word, the Spirit, the new life of faith, and the church.

Greek Theology

Greek theology framed these *here-and-now* aspects of saving, liberative grace in terms of its own cultural categories. Grace is the glory that radiates from the deity and transforms humanity. It comes to human beings ontologically through the sacraments, ethically through a life based on the divine virtues and the imitation of God and Christ, and mystically through ecstatic union with the deity. The hypostatic union is the model for this view of grace and its effects, for its spells out the divinization of the human being who was Jesus of Nazareth.

In short, the great theme of Greek theology is the deification of human beings.

Latin Theology

Latin theology described the presence of grace in Jesus Christ and the church in terms of liberation from sin and the corruption of human nature. Grace is primarily the justification of sinful human beings, which leads to their divinization. In Latin theology grace is viewed primarily as an alteration of human beings (created grace) effected by the loving, purifying presence of God (uncreated grace). Thanks to grace, humanity can turn from not being human to being truly human once again. It can then be made fully human in deification.

Prescholastic Theology

In the period prior to scholasticism, theology concentrated on the ethical aspect of grace. The influence of Augustine was strong here. Grace is a force enabling humans to live in accordance with the virtues. Thus grace was viewed in a historico-individual dimension as something dynamic and open to the future. Grace is the basis for merit, which in turn leads to a future reward in the afterlife. Grace can also be experienced because we can experience and live out the virtues which are identified with grace.

However, this does raise a question that could not be resolved in terms of the virtues. There are errors and false virtues. How can we distinguish them if they present themselves psychologically with the same features as those of the real virtues? Is the Holy Spirit identical to grace as virtue? Is grace something created in human beings as the virtues are?

Scholastic Theology

This line of questioning paved the way for the flowering of scholastic theology. Prescholastic theology had said that grace is *illuminatio* and *delectatio* that are lived out in a virtuous life. When the great medieval masters of theology adopted metaphysical categories, there was a great turning point in our understanding of grace. Thomas Aquinas and Duns Scotus followed Aristotle in saying that action follows from being: *Agere sequitur esse.* Behind each action lies a principle that generates it. Grace as virtue presupposes some prior principle that generates the virtue. Before it is a virtue or an action, grace is a new ontological quality of the soul that originates action. It cannot be a substance however. If it were a new substance, it itself would be a subject different from the human being involved. Since grace presupposes the human subject, it must be an accident that affects human beings ontologically and produces virtues in them. Humans are graced ontologically and thus prepared for consummate fulfillment in the glory of heaven. This created grace in humans is what makes them pleasing to God and justifies them. It paves the way for uncreated grace, that is, the divine indwelling in the soul of the just person.

Criticism was directed against this view by the Franciscan school, and its underlying inspiration was Augustinian. Its attack on the ontological interpretation of grace was framed in terms of the concept of nature. Nothing created (i.e., nature) can make us pleasing to God. Gratuitousness is on a very different level than nature. Grace basically is a new relationship between humanity and God, which was made feasible and real through Jesus Christ and his mediating efforts. Thus grace is not primarily some new entity created in humans, for that entity is itself the consequence of something prior, i.e., the justification effected by Jesus Christ into whom we are incorporated. We become new creatures insofar as we are incorporated into him.

Postscholastic Theology

After its high-water mark had passed, later scholastic theology produced endlessly detailed tracts on the metaphysical dimension of grace. It considered it in terms of relationships between various elements, e.g., nature and grace, the natural and supernatural, freedom and grace, created grace and uncreated grace, habitual grace and actual grace.

There arose a famous debate between the Thomist school of Bañez and the Jesuit school of Molina about predestination to glory and the problem of sufficient and efficacious grace. This whole line of reflection concentrated almost exclusively on created grace until the advent of the nineteenth century. Only then would there be a reformulation of the basic theological frames of reference in terms that were free of neoscholastic rigidity.

The Protestant Reformers

Alongside the reflections of late scholasticism we find the views of the Protestant Reformers. For them grace was basically the benevolent and merciful attitude of God. It is that attitude that saves sinful humans. There was no systematic reflection on the ontological alteration in human beings which results from God's attitude. But Reformation thinking did elaborate a new horizon for grace that would have a profound impact on the further development of the tract on grace in both Catholic and Protestant circles. This was the horizon of personalism, with its concomitant categories of dialogue, mutual openness, confidence, and so forth.

Nineteenth-Century Theology

In the nineteenth century a trinitarian view of grace began to take over in Catholic circles. It was especially evident in the work of Scheeben. Under the influence of Romanticism, greater stress was placed on the experiential aspect of faith that had been neglected in the classic theology of grace favored in official circles. People began to go back to the Greek fathers and to rediscover the mystical dimension and the inner life.

Contemporary thought stressed life over being. Philosophies of existence and philosophies of history were on the rise. Grace was seen as the symbol for the life of the triune God which is communicated to humans in their inner depths. Humans thereby share in the life of the Trinity. God does not just offer humans the gift of grace. He himself comes to dwell in humans, sharing his personal, trinitarian reality (John 14:23). It is a new presence of God in human beings.

The category of "presence," which would be explored deeply by Gabriel Marcel later on, took on special relevance. Neo-scholastic theology maintained that created grace transforms humans from sinners into just people. It prepares human beings to share in the divine nature, in uncreated grace. Scheeben maintained that this view did not dovetail with the witness of the Bible. Instead God comes to human beings, and his entry into humanity produces an alteration in the latter. This alteration is what is known as created grace, and it is the result of uncreated grace. Uncreated grace comes first. Thus grace is an indwelling that leads to the adoption of human beings as the children of God.

Twentieth-Century Theology

In this century theology has contributed greatly to revitalized meditation on grace. To be sure, it was greatly helped by the historico-cultural influence of personalism, existential categories, a higher regard for real-life experience, sounder views of humanity, and the renewed interest in biblical and patristic sources. It is also true that discussion was forced to concentrate on the issue of nature versus grace because the church's magisterium intervened in the person of Pius XII. Despite the restrictions imposed by him, however, much was done to explore the ecclesial, christological, and eschatological implications of grace. Grace was integrated into an approach centered around salvation history. Though the latter had not been dealt with explicitly as a theological theme, it had always been present in the thinking of tradition insofar as the latter talked about the universality of salvation and the one saving history for all human beings.

Three names are of major importance in twentieth-century Catholic thinking about grace. The first is Henri de Lubac, whose books on the supernatural provoked much controversy. *Surnaturel: Etudes historiques* was published in Paris in 1946. *Le mystère du surnaturel* was published in 1965. He convincingly tried to point up two points in the mainstream of Christian tradition. First, grace is a favor given gratis. Second, it is also the object of a desire rooted deeply in the personal nature of human beings. What humanity yearns for is a free gift. It is because it is free and gratuitous that this gift sates human desire. De Lubac showed convincingly that these two points were present in the thinking of Augustine and Thomas Aquinas. But later they were overlooked in the heat of polemics, particularly in the ongoing dispute between Dominicans and Jesuits during the sixteenth and seventeenth centuries.

Another important name in this century is Karl Rahner. Operating on the level of a basic religious ontology, he tried to show that there exists in humans a *supernatural existential.* It is an ontological openness to the Absolute. Thanks to it, in every action and at all times human beings are in contact with God and his grace; or else it is possible for them to close up in themselves and sinfulness.

The third important name in this century is surely Romano Guardini. He was one of the first to describe the horizon of grace as a dialogue between God and humans. With keen phenomenological analyses he pointed up the experience of gratuitousness that characterizes many dimensions of human life.

In Latin America the name of Juan Luis Segundo, a Uruguayan Jesuit, stands out. His book *Grace and the Human Condition* brings out clearly the social dimension of grace as well as its historical and liberative cast. It is a valuable work that breaks with the common scheme of theological manuals and articulates a critical, liberative view along the lines of Latin American liberation theology.

Four Approaches to Grace in the Western Theological Tradition

Since we find ourselves within the western theological tradition, we might do well to consider briefly the principal approaches that have been taken to the theme of grace. I do this here because my effort departs from the hallowed approach of theological manuals. I consciously choose to adopt an approach that seems to be demanded by concrete experience and faith-inspired reflection in the context of Latin America.

Psychological experience as the starting point. This approach starts off from the psychic life of human beings enlightened, attracted, and re-created by grace. Insofar as its psychological repercussions are concerned, the experience of grace is described in terms of the integration of concupiscence, charity, and lost freedom that is recovered in Christ. Experience of alienation in life opens human beings up to their true identity through justification; then they are gradually led to eternal glory through participation in the life of God.

The starting point is always the existential experience of sinfulness and the novel reality of gratuitous redemption, as it was for Paul and Augustine. The Franciscan school adopted this approach, under the influence of Bonaventure in particular. In modern times it has been explored by the phenomenologists. Here the experiential element is vividly alive, but one cannot get too far if one stays on the level of psychology. There is an ontological dimension that underlies the psychological dimension and makes the latter possible. The former touches the totality of human beings and not just the realm of psychology. But the ontological dimension is not pondered sufficiently by this approach.

Classical metaphysics as the starting point. In this approach grace is considered in relationship to human nature, and the latter is viewed in well-defined terms. Starting off from classical Aristotelian metaphysics, this approach makes use of such abstract terms and notions as "substance," "quality," "habit," "action," "passion," and "accident." This approach prevailed in the era of high scholasticism and in post-Tridentine theology. It begins with general notions and then proceeds to their subdivisions, so that we end up with all the familiar divisions of grace in the textbooks. Grace is always contrasted with nature, though the point is made that grace also perfects nature.

This approach does not do a good job of relating grace as a gift to the human person. The latter does not enter the picture as a category. Humanity is considered on the level of nature where necessity, mechanism, and iron logic prevail. A human being is that, too, but a human being is specifically a person. This implies freedom, dialogue, gratuitousness, vital transcendence, and so forth. Grace does not come from outside as an extrinsic gift to a nature that is closed up in itself. Grace is not a thing; it is God giving himself as a gift.

Personhood and dialogue as the starting point. This approach starts off from the reality of human beings as persons who establish a relationship with the Trinity in Jesus Christ. Sin is the breakdown of that dialogue. Redemption is the restoration of dialogue and encounter, and it finds its definitive form in Jesus Christ. Grace is essentially an encounter between the divine persons and human persons. Here grace shows up in all its gratuitous character, an aspect that is hidden for the most part in the metaphysical language of the classic treatises.

Modern-day treatises of a more systematic and classical stamp tend to combine these three moments, tracing the course of salvation history. They start off with fallen humanity, move on to humanity justified, and then consider humanity elevated to glory. An example is *Il Vangelo della Grazia* (1964) by M. Flick and Z. Alszeghy.

Social and structural realities as the starting point. Latin American experience of structural injustices and social sinfulness, when viewed in the light of faith, inaugurated a new and different approach to the theme of grace. It starts off from the realization that the social, political, and economic structure is not external to human beings. It pervades them to the very core, generating a situation of dependence on our continent in which the vast majority of our fellow human beings are oppressed and held in bondage. Since classical reflection on grace did not pay sufficient attention to the social aspect of sin, it did not discuss justification in social and structural terms. It discussed justification in terms of the private individual and the inner life, thus serving as an ideological support for those in power and those responsible for oppression.

Now grace is being discussed in terms of the liberation of humanity from every sort of oppression. People are unmasking the situations embodying dis-grace and calling for the creation of situations where God's grace can be fleshed out in history in more fraternal and more just mediations.

This kind of reflection is still in its infancy. But it is taking concrete shape as a distinctive and independent way of doing theology. In the light of faith it examines societal situations with a critical eye, trying to discern the dimensions of grace and of sinfulness therein.

Summary Overview of Doctrines About Grace

The chief problem in discussions about grace lies in the effort to maintain the proper balance between the two poles involved: God and human beings. Grace is essentially encounter and relationship. It is God communicating himself and human beings opening themselves up. When we maintain this polarity then we can properly ponder and talk about grace.

Under the conditioning of cultural factors, the history of theological reflection has oscillated between one pole and the other. Greek Christian tradition put the emphasis on God and on deification. Latin Christian tradition put the emphasis on the human experience of sinfulness and on grace as the justification of human beings. Both traditions ran the risk of overlooking the specific feature of grace as encounter. As a result they reified grace. On the one side grace was God in himself (uncreated grace) who took in humans and divinized them. On the other side, grace was the effect of God's love in humans (created grace), an ontological effect that alters humans.

The latter view led people to develop their views of created grace. What was its nature? It is an accident, said the medieval theologians and the neo-scholastics, because it is something added to the substance of human beings. It itself cannot be a substance because then it would be another thing alongside the human being and could not modify the human substance. Yet in this case the accident, grace, is more noble than the substance, the human being. Isn't that very odd?

Such problems arose because of the inadequacy of the theoretical tools used to comprehend the reality in question. A more satisfactory approach had to be found. The theoretical armory of the medieval scholastics did not allow them to deal with the dimensions of encounter and dialogue that are part and parcel of the reality of grace. Grace implies the alteration of both God and humans. It establishes an encounter, a dialogue, and a flow of mutual love. Both are vulnerable because grace operates in the framework of freedom, where there can be a flowering of the unexpected or degeneration on the part of human beings. Humans can close up in themselves and reject love. Thus grace reveals the authentic structure of human beings. On the one

DOCTRINES ON GRACE

GOD ─────────────→ GRACE ←───────────── HUMANS

OT: covenant
NT: Christ;
    the appearance of grace

GREEK THEOLOGY:
divinization; John-Origen; un-created grace

Baius (1513–89): "All the works of infidels are sins, and the virtues of their philosophers are vices."

Jansen (d. 1638): "Everything is sin that does not derive from supernatural Christian faith, which works through charity."

Bañez (d. 1604): predestination. Grace is sufficient for all. It becomes efficacious on its own because God foresees its acceptance by human beings.

Scheeben (*The Wonders of Divine Grace*, 1862): indwelling.

LATIN THEOLOGY:
justification; Paul-Augustine-Luther; created grace

Scholastic theology: ontology of grace (varieties of grace; nature and grace; *de auxiliis*).

Pelagius (5th century): We can carry out all the divine precepts without grace. It is merely a supplemental tool.

Semipelagianism: Humans need grace for salvation, but not to initiate the salvation process or to persevere. Their own strength and freedom suffice for that.

Molina (d. 1600): synergism. Sufficient grace becomes efficacious grace with the collaboration of the human being.

GOD ──→ **H. De Lubac:** humanity's natural longing for God and ←HUMANS
    gratuitous encounter: *Le surnaturel*

    K. Rahner: supernatural existential.

    R. Guardini: grace as encounter.

    J. L. Segundo: grace as a force for personal and social liberation in history.

hand, they embody a native desire for God; on the other hand, they can also reject this God.

In the reality known as grace we find an opposition, in the original sense of that word (ob-pono). Two things are placed before each other, and so there is a relationship involved in grace. In the history of theological reflection on the experience of grace, people mistakenly came to express this opposition in terms of a straight clash between the two poles. That is what happened in the interminable discussions about nature and grace. Theologians stressed the part of God sometimes and the part of human beings at other times.

But grace does not refer to God solely as an infinite nature closed up in its own omnipotent autonomy. Nor does it refer solely to human beings as natures closed up in their own natural self-sufficiency. Described in terms of nature, these two images of God and the human being do not succeed in communicating the dialogical reality of God and humans, which is characterized by freedom, gratuitousness, and an openness to the other. Grace is not just God, not just the human being. It is the encounter of the two, each giving of self and opening up to the other.

Thus grace presupposes and implies an adequate ontology of the human being and society as transcendental subjectivity on both the personal and the collective level. It must take due account of human openness, ex-istence, history, and freedom. Grace also presupposes an adequate image of the mystery of God, which is an intimate part of the person and communicates itself in history. God makes a proposal to each human individual and to the human community as a whole, offering himself as love and salvation. This mutual openness is the precondition for the grace happening, and grace itself is this interrelationship. It is the story of two loves written in the very arena of history.

To sum up, then, the aim of this chapter was to examine some of the dominant elements underlying theological reflection on grace. They bring out some of the authentic issues that we will have to reconsider and tackle from our particular standpoint in the following pages.

It should be clear by now that we must be particularly vigilant about our use of language when we are talking about grace. Whether I succeed or not, I shall try to live up to the challenge that Simone Weil posed regarding any attempt to deal with mysteries:

The mind can never penetrate mysteries. But it can be . . . responsible for the suitability of the words which give expression to these mysteries. In its use of words here it should be more acute, more penetrating, more rigorous, and more demanding than anywhere else.[1]

CHAPTER 3

Critique of Factors Conditioning the Traditional Elaboration of the Tract on Grace

Theology as a Closed System

The elaboration of the tract on grace as presented in our theological manuals owes a great deal to the great scholastic theologians and later academic systematizers. It is characterized by conceptual formalization and cold abstraction. There is no doubt that medieval reflection, borrowing the conceptual tools of Greek speculation on being and nature, did convey an authentic experience of grace. What is more, this experience was lived on all the varied dimensions of life.

This fact is proved by the division of grace—the one grace of God and Jesus Christ—into many subvarieties and species. Viewed in a favorable light, this division is simply a way of expressing in words the differences that are concretely experienced in life. Thus we get natural grace and supernatural grace, grace that precedes and initiates human proposals (prevenient grace), grace that occurs in the execution of human projects (concomitant grace, healing grace, elevating grace, consequent grace), grace as God's permanent presence in human life manifested in continuing openness to his will (habitual grace), and grace that is present in all the concrete actions which give concrete reality to the fundamental human project (actual grace).

The problem with this manual kind of theology used by preachers was that it simply proffered these concepts without making any attempt to recover the experience underlying them. It simply combined the various concepts and graces in various logical ways, dissociating them completely from the concrete life of faith. It created a closed system operating with concepts drawn from its own arsenal and with orthodox propositions that were endorsed by authoritative pronouncements. Such pronouncements occurred frequently in this realm since theology was regarded as a special kind of knowledge. The system in the manuals was no longer open. It did not relate to the concrete experience of grace or try to shed light on the course of human life itself. People forgot that it had originally been fashioned within the framework of ongoing experience. In reality such a system makes sense only insofar as it reproduces concrete experience and forces its adherents to retrace the course of that experience. It is in retracing the course of real-life experience that human beings, helped on by reflection, discover grace at work in their own lives.

The tract on grace was meant to help us discover the goodness, kindness, and gratuitousness of God at work in the history of humanity. Instead it became a storehouse of esoteric propositions that had been formulated more to condemn errors than to embody and vivify the experience of Christians. When we examine a manual on grace, even the one published in 1974 in the *Mysterium Salutis* series, we feel that somehow God's grace cannot be the cold abstraction embodied in its technical terms. We learn a great deal about what others thought and said about grace, from biblical times to today, but we learn almost nothing about grace itself and the concrete experience of grace.

Theology has become an affair of theologians only. It no longer helps us to understand something that has to do with all of us in the area of human and religious experience. Experience is the primary reality. Its translation into concepts is secondary. The manuals reverse this order of priority. The tract on grace has become an ideology legitimating the official conceptions of councils and papal teaching, instead of being a mystagogical initiation of the faithful into the experience of discovering, savoring, and talking about divine grace.

The manuals begin with the biblical data and the doctrines of tradition. They discuss the various theological disputes, particularly those with heretics. Then they present a systematic treatment of grace, taking the elements of tradition and putting them together in a logical, systematic, and coherent form. There is no prior mediation, no real advertence to the epistemological status of doctrines. The fact is that doctrines are meant to be in the service of experience. They are comments on experience, not substantive realities in themselves. The important task is to analyze and articulate the experience of grace as it took place in a given era and a given cultural context. Yet the theological manuals make almost no reference to this fundamental aspect. They prefer to point up the dangers and ambiguities of experience rather than to make it the core of systematic reflection.

So we must open up the system, and that cannot be done simply by revising or modernizing terms and concepts. We must go back to the core reality, the experience of grace. Then we can retrace our steps and have some hope of talking meaningfully of grace. Then we can speak in a way that lets grace itself speak.

Limitations Imposed by the Experiential World of the Past

Behind the classical elaboration of the grace tract lay a world that was inhabited by people of faith. It was in this sociocultural world that they had their experience of grace, and it is very different from ours today. There were highly stratified social estates which allowed little room for mobility. It was a medieval world with a clear hierarchical order and a harmonious outlook that supposedly mirrored the harmony of heaven. The social pyramid—pope, king, nobility, common people—reflected the heavenly scheme. Little thought was given to the problems of social conflict, to history as a producer of new values and meanings, to transformations wrought intentionally by human beings rather than nature. It was a natural, metaphysical image of the world rather than a historical, process-oriented view.

Grounded on this image, contemporary theological reflection talked about humanity in terms of nature. In its view nature signified constancy, permanence, ahistoricity, a world closed within the mechanics of its own functioning and containing its own meaning apart from the project of Christ. Human beings were not regarded as historical beings or as persons open to outside realities. It is certainly true that a human being is nature. Even more importantly, however, a human being is also a historical and cultural being. Human beings are the result of their own history and their own decisions as to what they shall be. They create meaning for themselves rather than just receiving their meaning from nature.

This historical dimension was present in humanity at all times because it is an enduring structure of human existence. But it did not become an object of clear awareness and thematic reflection until the modern age. It was in human beings but they did not have two eyes to see it clearly and act accordingly. They reified grace linguistically because they used categories based on nature. Grace was always regarded as something added to nature in the light of the latter's insufficiency. It was "the strength of God in the weakness of humanity."

Classical theology, then, did not use the categories that seem more suitable to us today in talking about the experience of grace, e.g., encounter, relationship, mutual openness, self-giving, crisis, progress, and so forth. In the latter, grace no longer is depicted as the duplication and growth of God's presence in the world. It is viewed as an expression of the creature's latent capability to let God appear as something new and novel in ever new concrete historical embodiments. Grace is no longer seen as the disfiguration or denaturalization of the world but as its maximum realization. Instead of stressing the weakness and insufficiency of nature, we stress the new capability that it has acquired and can exercise.

Today a theology of grace must take conscious note of these differences in perspective and try to rework its treatment in terms of this new way of experiencing reality. Otherwise it will not be able to meet out present-day demands and hope. For we want a theoretical explanation and a way of talking which deals more intelligently with the crowning aspect of Christian faith that is divine grace.

Cultural Conditioning Factors

The culture pervades every theological discourse. Every theological discourse is a cultural discourse. In giving expression to the experience of grace, theologians and other believers use the set of communicative tools made available to them by their culture. Only in that way can experience be meaningful. Only in that way can it be articulated in intelligible terms for the community of faith.

However, the culture does not just provide a set of tools. It embodies a particular view of life and being which humans have adopted for themselves. In one sense it is concrete, historical human beings. Thus a culture makes possible a particular way of experiencing grace on the one hand, and provides the tools for communicating this particular experience on the other. It is both a meaningful totality and a medium of expression.

Insofar as Christianity is concerned, grace was basically experienced in two cultural worlds: the world of Greek metaphysical thought and the world of Roman political and juridical experience. Our theological manuals reflect the influence of these two cultural worlds without usually taking conscious note of that fact. Instead of articulating our experience of grace in the context of the modern world, most recent manuals remain confined within the modes of expression peculiar to the Greek and Roman worlds. The system remains closed up in itself and in the language it found in those two vanished worlds.

That language, which once could communicate something, has now lost its communicative power. It must go back and find its roots in the experience of grace as we know it today. Theologians cannot be merely administrators of a doctrinal system from the past, nor can they simply serve as watchdogs of intrasystem orthodoxy alongside the official magisterium. Of course, it is easier to conserve than to produce; but tradition can be conserved only by producing something. Otherwise it will degenerate into traditionalism—not some new and original action but rather a reaction against any such new action.

The Greek expression of grace. In the Greek cultural world grace found one major expression in terms of divinization. Grace was God's sympathy elevating human beings and introducing them into the realm of the divine. It is not so much that God stoops to incarnate himself and enter the realm of human beings. Instead human beings are raised up by God; they give up their old situation and enter the divine realm through deification.

Divinization implied the transformation of humanity and its moving beyond the human state. This way of articulating the experience of grace was a good reflection of the structural thrust of Hellenic culture. Its main point of reference was not the historicity of the world but the absolute and permanent reality that is hinted at in the world (i.e., Being or God). This absolute and permanent reality is expressed in metaphysical terms and contrasted with the present world. The beyond is set over against the here and now. The basic frame of reference is God, eternity, the soul, and the ideal. By contrast, becoming, history, transformation, and time are regarded as decadent. Within such a theoretical framework divinization would naturally represent the high point of redemption, personalization, and God's grace-filled communication. To reach their human fulfillment, human beings must cease being human and become God.

Little attention was paid to the ambiguity inherent in the historical process, to the conflicts it entails, or to the future that must be prepared and created with sweat and blood. These factors were not seen as solid, consistent realities that served as vehicles for grace. Everything centers around God, and human beings in their concrete world almost disappear from view completely. Humans are of interest only in terms of their universal essence as rational animals.

This way of comprehending grace is incapable of grasping the historical mediations through which divinization is fashioned and verified. For it, divinization is not the outcome of a historical process in which God's activity joins forces with that of human beings (synergism). Instead it results from our participation in the central reality and in privileged moments that produce divinization, e.g., Jesus Christ, the church, the sacraments, ecstasy, and mystical union. The profane and humdrum daily aspects of the world are devoid of grace, hence of no religious interest.

The Roman expression of grace. The Romans were in a different cultural camp. They were concerned with the political order of the world, with military and legal dominance. Their point of reference was historical reality at first sight, with its ruptures, its various forms of bondage, and human efforts to liberate themselves and create a new order. In this context theology would not view grace primarily as divinization but rather as justification and human recuperation. Grace was seen as a process of making humanity human and then enabling it to reach total fulfillment.

The humanity it found in history was subhuman. It had fallen from its human status. The presence of grace raised human beings up, not so much to the divine realm as to the status of revivified and complete human beings. Grace is viewed as the restoration of human nature. Here we get a theology of created grace: its preparatory stages, its presence, and its effects. It goes into detailed study of the process of conversion and justification, as Trent would do later on. Every step in human life is accompanied by grace: prevenient grace, concurrent grace, and consequent grace.

In this framework theologians had a chance to elaborate grace in terms of historical liberation amid social and political conflicts. This did not happen because Roman culture became the captive of Greek culture, as Cicero put it. Even though juridical expressions were used, Greek metaphysical categories prevailed in the attempt to translate the realities of salvation history. Grace was not viewed in universal terms. No note was taken of the presence of God in the realm of politics, human interests, and the process of human development. Reflection was restricted to the church, the sacraments, and the process of religious conversion. Justification was considered in terms of the private individual: How am *I* saved? No thought was given to other human mediations, the profane sacraments as it were, which also communicate divine grace.

Thus justification became a matter of religion and the church. Contrary to what we might have hoped for, it is not a process of humanization that finds many mediating factors besides the specifically religious ones, e.g., in the realm of politics, economics, society, and culture in general. This theology reflected deeply on the ecclesial mediation of grace, to the point where it got closed up in itself. The theology of grace became a private matter, and this had disastrous pastoral consequences. The secular world, which would be the scene for the course of later history, was stripped of grace and salvific relevance.

Biographical Conditioning Factors

More than other theological tracts, the tract on grace has been profoundly influenced by the biographical situation of its chief elaborators. Paul, Augustine, and Martin Luther were the theologians who set the course for western reflection on grace. All of them had profoundly personal problems. Their reflection reflects this personal aspect and influence.

The three of them lived in what we might well call an atmosphere of pharisaism, where salvation was grounded on virtuous works and human efforts to ascend to perfection and God. They suffered the painful experience of alienation and a deep inability to carry out the human project of holiness. They experienced the paradoxical nature of the human condition: while human beings may know and will to do what they should, they find they cannot realize this in their concrete, historical course. This produces an experienced sense of failure, of concrete incapacity. For Paul, Augustine, and Martin Luther, the solution to this problem lay in God's intervention making up for the lack on the part of humanity.

Here grace is experienced in life as a gift from God that aids and sanctifies human beings and enables them to rediscover their lost identity. By virtue of the whole underlying experience, this sort of theology is rooted in a profound existential pessimism. The latter is clearly reflected in the formulations of Paul, Augustine, and Martin Luther, which have been badly misinterpreted in later history. Quandaries of a personal nature were transformed into objective quandaries, and they found their way into theological manuals in that form.

Another point deserves to be mentioned here. All the great theologians of grace were monks: Aquinas, Bonaventure, Jansen, Bañez, Molina, etc. This status places people in a very definite position vis-à-vis the world. To be specific, it puts them outside the world to a large extent and hence above and beyond its great conflicts. All of Latin theology, greatly indebted to such theologians as these, shows a markedly monkish tenor. The great problems that disturb people are filtered through the pure and rarefied atmosphere of the monastic world with its sacred, mystical aura.

By virtue of their religious vocation, the aforementioned people experienced a summons to raise their hearts on high; at the same time they experienced the abysmal depths of human frailty. For them grace is always set over against something else; it is the contrast between light and darkness. Their theology and piety never took conscious note of the historical mediations of grace, of the gratuitousness in their own day-to-day lives, of the presence of grace in countless profane dimensions. The result was an exaggerated theoretical formalism and the setting up of a sharp contrast between nature (the human person) and grace, the world and God, history and the kingdom.

Societal and Class Factors Conditioning the Grace Tract

As religious or priests, theologians were part of the class holding power within the church and favorably situated in the mainstream of society. They did not experience social marginalization, nor did they live out their lives in close contact with groups of believers at the grass-roots level. All this helped to narrow the horizons of their reflection on grace. Their talk is almost never about human beings; it is about the soul. It is the soul that is graced, justified, and inhabited by the holy Trinity. This led to a spiritualization of grace and a loss of historical substance.

Bodily human beings possess a historical dimension. They must eat, relate to one another, organize, and be humanly present in the world. This fact is not reflected upon in the classic tracts on grace. Real-life situations are not seen as possible sacraments of the communication of divine grace or of human dis-grace.

Certain themes simply could not make their way into the conscious horizon of traditional theology, or even of works written in relatively recent times. I refer to such themes as grace and political freedom, grace and social oppression, grace and the process of liberation, grace and social systems, and so forth. Traditional theology had much to say about grace in intramural terms, e.g., grace and the ecclesial community, grace and the sacraments, grace in its christological and eschatological dimensions. But it hardly realized that there could be any discourse at all about grace in relation to the pathways of a technological, secularized, non-Christian world.

One point should be noted right here. The tack of theology does not at all mean that grace did not have all the dimensions just alluded to. It did. Grace is at work socially and liberatively in all the dimensions of human reality. It has a dimension that is essentially public and political. But since this dimension was not reflected upon, it was not lived reflectively by the Christian community.

Suppose we ask ourselves this question: why didn't theology get around to reflecting these objective dimensions of grace? The answer must surely be that the position of theological reflection within the social order, where it has close ties with the wielders of societal and religious power, helped filter the themes of grace in a way that suited the best interests of the class in question. In the last analysis it unconsciously reflected what interested and supported the existing system. It did not reflect the real-life problems of the people of God, who were ravaged by conflict, caught up in the task of surviving in a human way, and struggling to salvage some religious meaningfulness from their downtrodden lives. The prevailing theology could count on the protection of official orthodoxy and on the scholarly cast of its elaboration. But such a theology is ideologically naive because it does not realize that it is reflecting the religious interests of the class it represents. Many of its problems are not objective problems; or they are objective only in the sense that they relate to that particular social class. Instead of reflecting an experience, they reflect ideological differences between schools of thought; they have no repercussions on the real praxis of the faith.

With this critique in mind, we can try to elaborate our discourse on grace from the standpoint of our own cultural context. Our discourse should leave room for the experience of grace to speak to us as it is taking place here and now in a very different time and place, in a world where the divine mystery is still the source of our own lives.

First, however, we must briefly examine the horizon of our own time and the factors that now condition our own reflection. Once aware of them, we can descry their scope and their limits, and we can guard against their ideological manipulation.

CHAPTER 4

Present-Day Horizons and Grace

Today we are living in a different age, and our cultural ethos is not the one in which the tract of grace was systematically elaborated. Let us consider some of the elements that are part of the human experience in the present age.

Secular Character of the World

For biblical and medieval humanity God was a socially established reality. He did not cause any concrete problems. The problems were theoretical and epistemological in the areas of philosophical and theological speculation. It was easy to see God's action in the world and to view important dimensions of life as grace.

Today we do not find this clear-cut evidence. In our culture God has become an empty word. Practical atheism is an undisturbing cultural phenomenon, even within Christianity itself. How are we to speak of grace in such a world?

Even a vital and liberating faith now sees mediations between God and human beings. An epiphanic conception of God no longer holds sway. Human beings have a history. There is a world of technological artifacts created by us. There is a world which is no longer the natural world that speaks of God but rather a second-hand world that speaks of human beings. Viewed historically, almost everything is not the work of God but the result of human effort. Humanity has altered and adapted nature to suit its historical project. Thus we can no longer take God as a universally accepted starting point in the tract on grace. We are secularized. The world—the *saeculum*—is the focal point that orientates our understanding. It has a consistency of its own. It is within this world that we must articulate the meaning of grace and see the experience of grace emerge.

Historicity of Humanity

Our conception of the world is historical, not natural. In other words, human life is subject to transformations that result from human intervention

26

rather than the mechanical operation of nature. Humanity alters the laws of nature, subjugates the world, looks ahead and plans for the future. The future of human beings cannot be deduced from their abstract, metaphysical essence; it is open-ended. They are no longer defined in terms of what they are and have already done. Instead they are seen in terms of what they can be, what they have not yet done or experienced but might possibly in the future.

Of course, this does not deny that humanity is a creature of God, ever dependent on him. On the level of history there is no opposition between Creator and creature because humanity itself is a creator and was made such. How are we to distinguish between what is due to nature and what is due to grace of the effort of humans aided by grace? Grace should be viewed as the actualization of what has not yet been tried but is possible for humans. And they themselves should be viewed not as some finished nature closed up in itself but as a nature that is totally open, its ultimate point of reference ever remaining the Absolute who gives himself gratuitously.

Furthermore, anthropologists tell us that humans are not natural beings but cultural beings. They are constantly interpreting and transforming the world. Now suppose we grant that grace pervades the whole of human beings and is therefore intermixed with all human action. How are we to distinguish between nature and grace? Obviously we cannot do so *a priori;* we can only do so *a posteriori*.

Sacredness of the Human Person

Another dominant trait of our time is the high valuation of the person as such. Today we recognize the ultimate grandeur of the person, which cannot be reduced to something else, even though the human person has never before been so demeaned either. We see the person as openness, hence as the possibility for encounter and enrichment. Encounter is not a matter of pure chance. It may be casual but it is experienced as a gift and a gratuitous happening. Encounter means the meeting of one personal openness with another. It has to be gratuitous and free. Otherwise it would not really be an encounter; it would simply be a mechanical act governed by fixed criteria. Encounter alters both parties. It is mutual recognition, confidence, gratefulness, sincerity, and fidelity. It brings a plenitude of meaningfulness that was not foreseen. It is not obligatory, and it cannot be deduced ahead of time; and yet it happens. Born of two freedoms, encounter signifies a growth in being and living; it fleshes out the gratuitous possibilities of human beings.

Within this context talk about the experience of grace becomes truly meaningful, and I shall return to this theme when I broach the experience of grace specifically.

Awareness of the Cosmological Dimension of the Personal

Encounter always takes place within a context. It involves two histories opening up to each other. It takes place in the world, in space, and in time. Thus encounter involves the world view or cosmic vision of both and the way they look at the totality.

The basic cosmic vision of today is no longer the monopoly of one caste. It is the shared way in which we all approach the world, and it is determined by the experimental sciences. If our awareness takes due account of hermeneutic implications, we can no longer separate the dimensions of interiority and exteriority in the person. The latter is a meeting point for all the strands of the world. We cannot divide things up as if there were two worlds: one an interior, private, personal world and the other an exterior, social, historical world.

This means that we must never separate reflection on grace from reflection on the world. Grace is always given in mediations, negotiations, relations, and social structures. We can never talk about grace in itself because it shows up in this particular thing or that particular thing. It has a sacramental structure, if we do not restrict the term "sacrament" to the seven chief signs of faith usually considered under that term. Here that term refers to all the mediations through which we arrive at God and his love. In other words, there are things, situations, persons, cultural data, and relationships that may be grace-filled or not, that may carry grace or not, that may be sacraments of grace or not.

Grace is not something isolated in itself that stands apart from other things. Grace is a mode of being that things take on when they come into contact with the love of God and are suffused with his mystery. In that sense the whole world is related to grace.

The Felt Weight of the Social Dimension

Modern thinking is vividly aware of the social dimension present in the personal dimension, and also of its peculiar weight and impact. The social dimension is not something added later to the human person. It pervades the human person and is a constituent element of the latter. In the form of institutions, values, forms of organization and power, it has its own independent density.

What does grace mean within the context of a particular cultural option and a particular kind of societal life? What does it mean within the context of capitalist society, for example? What does it mean and how is it mediated in the experience of human beings living in huge cities, working in large factories, and organizing in labor unions and class-interest groups? What experience of grace is articulated in the struggle of class interests and the quest for greater justice and participation?

Traditional reflection on grace did not reflect this dimension. Today there is an urgent need to take it into account.

Mechanisms of Social Oppression

Our society is deeply marked by mechanisms of alienation and oppression. There is poverty, dependence, exploitation of human beings by other human beings, and wars in which political interests are closely tied up with the economic interests of the arms industry. Today we feel that all these things are inhuman and immoral. The affluence and advanced scientific and technological development of the Northern Hemisphere are viewed as indecent because they have come at a high social cost. They have meant the impoverishment and marginalization of the dependent, underdeveloped nations. Internally the latter are torn by contradictions as the gap between the rich and the poor widens.

In opposition to all this, some people are now articulating thoughts of liberation, solidarity, and cultural revolution. They want to banish human exploitation of human beings once and for all. If a theology is to be meaningful to people today, particularly in Latin America, then it must indicate how grace is revealed in its social, liberative dimension and how it criticizes and unmasks those in power. What does grace signify in the context of Latin America, where the yearning for development and liberation is turned against the social interests of the majority and used to abet the interests of a small minority?

Awareness of the Critical Function of Grace Within the Church

Reflection on grace must also take conscious note of the painful fact that for centuries the institutional church on the Latin American continent worked hand-in-glove with those who were fostering humanity's exploitation of humanity. It supported and upheld a society based on arbitrariness and discrimination. It did not keep alive the memory of Christ's freedom in all its subversive and dangerous aspects. Instead it turned the figure of Jesus into an icon and restricted it to the intraecclesiastical sphere. The common people were not made aware that the preaching of Jesus and his gospel message is a force for present-day liberation, protest, and transformation. The sacraments were experienced solely in terms of the inner life and cultic worship. They did not lead to a transformation in one's way of living and in interpersonal relationships. They did not inspire people to overcome the structural injustices that sinfully separate brethren sharing the same faith. Such Christian values as humility, submissiveness, and the shouldering of Christ's cross were presented in ideological terms so that they ended up underpinning the status quo and castrating the people's potential for liberative reaction.

To what extent was the church institution a countersign of grace? To what extent did it participate in an anti-Christian system? What is the import of theological talk about the ecclesial dimension of grace? What should that import be? Should it not be critical and liberative in its thrust so that the church may be the sacrament of love and divine grace in the world, not just in its official pronouncements but also in its deeds?

The Problem of Meaning as a Universal One

Our understanding of the world is framed in terms of scientific and technological experience. On the one hand, we are taking more and more cognizance of the long course run by evolution to produce the world we see today. On the other hand, we are ever more aware of the factors that condition human beings and the cosmos, of the structures that underlie cosmological, psychological, and social phenomena. Does humanity control and guide the course of evolution, or is humanity itself guided by mechanisms whose determining influence goes unnoticed for the most part? Does the whole of reality possess some real meaning, or is it the result of chance and necessity?

Some people, like Teilhard de Chardin, see a meaningful course that eventually arrives at human beings. Others, seeing the twists and turns of past evolution, plump for nothing more than intrasystemic meaning and are sceptical about the meaningfulness of the whole. J. Monod, for example, has tried to show that there is no meaning; everything is the accidental result of forces that have combined to produce the necessity of a mechanically functioning system.

What is the reason for this diversity of opinion? Both interpretations are based on experiential data. It seems that experiences on the personal level have something to do with these opinions. Situations filled with meaning give people the impression that everything possesses meaning; situations devoid of meaning give them the idea that nothing has meaning. The scientific manipulation of the world to deal with domestic needs arouses the conviction that human beings can chart the course of evolution toward a meaningful goal. The slip toward ecological disaster leads them to question the prevailing model of progress. Humanity seems to be more like a cancer bringing destruction in its wake. It upsets the rhythms of nature and egotistically ravages the earth's resources, giving no thought to the plight of future generations.

The Latin American experience is that science and technology are in the service of the few who dominate the many. The few hold the reins of scientific research. Instead of helping to overcome the age-old problems of humanity, this research is used to increase the humiliating gap between the few privileged rich and the many marginalized poor.

We cannot talk meaningfully of God's grace as the presence of his love in the world to people who lack the bare means of subsistence in food, clothing, shelter, human dignity, and basic rights.

The Eroded Use of the Word "Grace"

In today's world the word "grace" does not possess any special or distinctive heuristic meaning. The word is still used, but it is not a key term or a major point of societal reference.

By the grace of God we no longer have kings and rulers who have been appointed by divine right. We no longer have professions or states in life that are interpreted as exclusive manifestations of divine grace, though some still talk about the religious or priestly vocation in such terms.

Today no one wants to get something gratis, or to depend on the good graces of another. Society is organized in terms of security, social welfare, and legal guarantees that cover the whole of life and leave nothing to chance. There is social security, unemployment insurance, and the retirement pension. Even Christmas is now seen in terms of some sort of guaranteed Christmas bonus.

The secularized idiom of our day talks equally about grace, fate, and chance. This does not necessarily imply any reference to some higher, transcendent court. It may simply refer to a happy or unhappy conjunction of certain natural and historical factors. The biological dimension of human life itself is explained in terms of controllable factors: the loving union of father and mother that results in the fertilization of her egg by the first sperm that manages to penetrate.

This scientific understanding does not inevitably lead to a mechanistic conception of the world. It does invite us to a closer study of the laws of the genetic code in order to improve the possibilities of life and to provide for more wholesome issue. Thus it is no longer a matter of simply assuming what comes down to us from the past. Nothing is worthwhile until it is tried and criticized. In principle, nothing is immutable. Everything is open-ended. By another route, then, we find a new way of looking at grace as it emerges from the still unrealized possibilities of creation.

These are some of the features that characterize the present day. Along with many others, they affect the way we experience grace today and the way we might express that experience in conceptual and linguistic terms. Any effort at expression will inevitably entail risks and limitations. But even the courage to take risks itself is divine grace. It is with this conviction that I shall proceed to present my reflections on grace in the following chapters.

PART TWO

EXPERIENCING GRACE

CHAPTER 5

Can Grace Be Experienced?

Getting Back to the Original Sense of Grace

When we talk about grace, we inevitably offer some image of it. We say that it is the loving attitude of God; or that it is God's liberative transformation of human beings which justifies them; or that it is some grand and incommensurable reality which surpasses our natural thinking and everything that exists in the order of creation. In speaking thus, we reify grace and turn it into an entity. It is *something* different from nature and humanity, some gratuitous *thing* that comes to humanity as a favor.

But what is that *something?* If we say it is supernatural, what does "supernatural" mean? If we say the supernatural is *something,* then we are reifying it too. By reifying the supernatural we are undermining what we mean to say with that term, because we are then operating in terms of beings or entities. All beings are created and natural. By very definition the supernatural (and hence grace) is not on the same level as the natural. It is a contradiction to say that there is a supernatural "being" or "entity," as Ripalda (1594–1648) wanted to do. If some supernatural substance exists, it can only be God: the uncreated, the ineffable, the mysterious. A nature can be elevated to that level; but the supernatural does not belong to nature because then it would be a created being, and that would be a contradiction.

When we talk about grace and the supernatural, we are trying to express an experience. "Supernatural" and "grace" are semantic signs in the service of an experience where grace and the supernatural appear. In reality the terms are meant to translate an experience.

What kind of human experience enables us to speak meaningfully of grace and the supernatural? That is the point here. Since grace and the supernatural are not realities closed up in themselves and alien to life, they cannot exist in disembodied form outside the world. They are related to human beings. Language inevitably dissociates the two, but language is not the original reality. It is a translation, an interpretation, a second stage. Before grace is spoken about, however, an experience has been lived through.

To comprehend the original sense of grace, we must call into question any schema that sets up an opposition between grace and nature, grace and human beings, or grace and creation. We must reject any schema which suggests that grace is a reality in itself, though somehow related to the world. Classical metaphysics, for example, hypostatized transcendence, presenting it as a realm or reality set over against immanence. Transcendence came to signify the realm of the supernatural while immanence came to signify the natural realm. But such notions are really objectifications of a human experience.

Modern thought has taken cognizance of this fact. Realizing that such objectifications do not constitute the original reality, it talks about the death of metaphysics. This is not necessarily a denial or rejection of metaphysics. It merely means that the classical metaphysics of the Greeks and the medieval age was one stage in human thought, a stage when Being was conceived in terms of an entity *(ens)*.

Modern thought from Kant onward seeks to do its reflection from a more original starting point than that of classical metaphysics. It regards the latter as a mistake for neglecting being as being and identifying its representative images—e.g., transcendence and immanence as two opposed realities—with reality itself. But in language we always create two worlds, so modern thought is semantically as dualistic as was classical thought. Within the context of this semantic dualism, however, it attempts to ponder the original reality that is one and identical.

What is this original reality? It is history.[1] History is not just a logical narration of events and happenings. It is really the human situation or humanity itself as ex-istence, situation, decision making, and commitment. It is human beings defining themselves by living in the world with others in society and thus fashioning their identity. It is when human beings thoroughly live their historicity, open out to the world and others, and commit themselves to the process of liberation, that they begin to glimpse what they really are. Human beings are beings who are there with others, who can manipulate their world and their relationships when allowed to do so. This is the experience of what is called immanence. On the other side of the coin, they see people who can rise infinitely above the situation in which they are confined. Human beings can accept, reject, or protest against the given situation, opening up to a future that has not yet been experienced or defined. This is their experience of what is called transcendence.

Thus immanence and transcendence are not two separate entities. They are two dimensions of one and the same life. They come joined together in the historicity of human beings as two facets of their radical reality. Human beings appear as beings who are immanent and transcendent, already fashioned and still in the making, established in the present and open toward a yet unknown future. That is the pristine reality. In giving expression to it, we objectify and reify both immanence and transcendence as if they were two separate worlds. Language and thought can find expression only in such terms, so we must be careful not to identify our representations and objectifications with the pristine reality. We must continually dismantle the metaphysics imbedded in our linguistic structures. We must keep relating our images to the underlying reality, i.e., the history or ex-istence of humans. That is the task for all thinking that seeks to be real thinking.

Aware of what has just been said, we can then make such statements as the following. We can say that God possesses real meaning only if he emerges from within human history. In the real-life struggles, decisions, and yearnings of human beings, there appears something that always escapes them, that always remains open-ended no matter how much they try to close it up. This something is someone greater than human beings, a Mystery, and we call it God. As Vatican II puts it, God is "that hidden power which hovers over the course of things and over the events of human life" (NA 2).

We can only speak meaningfully of God if God emerges from within the experience of humans and their way of life with others and the world. Hence God cannot be viewed as being above the world or, much worse, outside the world. God makes his appearance within human experience and the world as someone who remains further on, who cannot be laid hold of, who stands where human effort opens out to the future. When we talk about God, however, it comes across differently. In our vocabulary and our doctrines it seems as if God were closed up in himself outside the world as some sort of absolutely transcendent mystery. The impression seems to be that God then enters the world and dwells inside humans. The fact is that it is they who are inside God. And this is simply a way of translating their experience in history.

We can thus reread the Old Testament and the New Testament in the light of the pristine, original reality mentioned above. Those books do not talk about God as a metaphysical entity but as a historical force. God appears in the historical journey of his people, accompanying them in good times and bad. He is the real meaning of life, which must ever be spelled out in terms of historical vicissitudes.

We must proceed the same way in talking about grace. The experience of grace means the experience of human historicity. Within the latter human beings experience what the term "grace" signifies: gift giving, gratuitousness, benevolence, favor, beauty, and so forth. These things do not exist abstractly in themselves. They occur in the ongoing life of humans and the world. Grace always appears in conjunction with something else. It is this particular thing (immanence) and yet it is not at the same time (transcendence). It is a mode of being for human beings and all things insofar as they are viewed in relationship to God and their lives are experienced as gratuitousness, beauty, and so forth. It is their life viewed as the presence and activity of God in the world. As the medieval theologians said so well, grace supposes and perfects nature: (Gratia supponit et perfecit naturam).

The "Experiencing" of Grace

Speaking in general, we can say that some experience of grace lies hidden or buried behind all our theological talk about grace. It is quite possible, given the cultural framework in which we live today, that the language employed no longer evokes the original experience of grace for us. We end up spouting and combining propositions that no longer say anything concrete to us. We must dismantle our ready-made propositions in order to arrive at the authentic, original experience of grace. The latter comes first. At a later stage it finds expression in doctrines or metaphysical objectifications.

What do we mean by "experience" here?[2] The term does not refer solely to the inner life or purely psychic happenings. It is not just inner motions, divine visions, or intimate feelings. Such phenomena are real enough, and they can be verified in the lives of the saints. The inner life is a real component of "experience." But if the experience of grace were restricted to that, then it would be the privilege of a few select initiates. Such is not the case.

By "experience" here I mean something much more profound and complex. Experience is the way in which we relate ourselves to the world: the way in which we make the world present inside ourselves and the way in which we render ourselves present in the world. Experience is our particular way, within a given culture, of interpreting all the reality we find around us, e.g., the self, others, society, nature, God, the past, the present, and the future. The mode of interpretation varies throughout the course of history, and each variation is present in subsequent ones. Once upon a time humanity experienced the world as a numinous and sacred reality that was linked up with the divine through myths. Later it viewed the world as a self-subsistent reality, thanks to metaphysics. Today people tend to view the world as self-subsistent also, but now they also regard it as something that can be laid hold of and changed with the help of science and technology. Each of these different experiences of the world has led human beings to redefine the meaning of nature, humanity, God, the past, the present, the future, and so forth.

Viewed thus, experience is obviously quite complex. As Aristotle[3] and Thomas Aquinas[4] suggested, it seems to be a synthesis of many perceptions and approaches in which human beings managed to overcome obstacles, dangers, and temptations, confirm prior suppositions, and learn through joys and sufferings.

A brief semantic overview of the term "experience" may help us grasp its overall existential meaning. So let us do that now. "Experience" is made up of the preposition "ex" and ancient verb "periri." The Latin *periri* means to "try," to "attempt" *(conari),* to "run a risk" *(periculum facere).* It is connected with the Greek verb *peirao* or *peiraomai,* which may mean putting oneself or another to the test.[5] "Experience" (Latin *experientia* and Greek *emperia*) is thus associated with the notions of "danger," "test," and "attempt" or "temptation."[6] It is also associated with the Latin word *peritia,* which means both "knowledge derived from experience" and "skill." A *peritus* is a person who has been tested by trial and who has thus become "expert" in something. The Latin *ex-periri* also means to "endure difficulties." In a broader, more extended sense it means to "know," "comprehend," "sense," and "see."[7]

In short, then, the term "experience" is associated with two basic areas of human "experience." On the one hand, it has to do with danger and trials (*periculum* and *periclitatio*). On the other hand it has to do with knowledge acquired (*peritia, scientia, notitia*). Let us consider the semantic makeup of the terms *periculum* and *peritia*.

Both share the semantic nucleus *per* ("through," "by means of"). It can be found in the Latin word *ex-per-ientia*, the Greek word *em-peiria*, and in the Germanic cognate *fahr*. German *fahren* means "to journey" and *erfahren* means "to experience." We find the same *per*, interestingly enough, in the Latin word *portus* ("port") and the Greek word *poros* (a "way through" a body of water or the mountains). Any pathway that provides such a "way through" is *opportunus*.[8]

The word "per," then, has both abstract and concrete connotations. It may connote an "attempt" or more concretely, a "perilous journey." The notion of journeying in the midst of dangers and experiencing things seems to lie at the root of it. Both Ortega y Gasset[9] and G. de Mello Kujawski,[10] a Brazilian philosopher, stress this point.

The word "experience" also contains the Latin preposition *ex,* which connotes "out of, away from." This reinforces the meaning of *per* as indicated above.

Let us now try to bring together the meanings of *periculum* and *peritia* in the term "experience." Obviously we must deal with the level of concrete human life. Human beings gain "experience" insofar as they go out of themselves, confront inner and outer realities, meet others, endure dangers and trials, set out on a journey, and find their way to get through. This is the drama of human life itself since it is never given ready-made. Life must be put together, a road must be found, some meaningful way through must be discovered. In so doing, human beings will have to make attempts and overcome trials. Experienced human beings are people who have passed through trials and sufferings, who have plunged into life and its dangers, and who have learned from all that. Their knowledge is not book knowledge; it is knowledge they earned with their own sweat and blood.

Experience, then, is knowledge that has a taste and flavor all its own because it was earned the hard way. It is critical because it is the result of many trials and direct encounters. Taking an ocean voyage is quite different from simply hearing someone talk about such a voyage. Direct experience provides us with a kind of evidence that cannot be mediated through rational argumentation.

Human existence is grounded on radical experiences that each individual goes through. So it is with the Christian faith as well. On the one hand, it entails the experiences that the first apostles went through in daily contact with the Word of life: "What we have heard, what we have seen with our eyes, what we have looked upon and our hands have touched . . . " (1 John 1:1).

On the other hand, it also entails our own personal experiences with God and his grace which enable us to bear witness to his wondrous deeds.

From what has been said above, it should be evident that experience is not restricted to the senses. It embraces all of life with its dangers and escapes, its challenges and its perplexities. It is not surprising that narration is the best way of communicating the fullness of experience. The closer faith and theology are to experience, the more they turn to narration in their form of expression.

However, experience is not just a *scientia,* a kind of knowledge. It is also an authentic *conscientia,* a kind of awareness. In going out of self and approaching the world, human beings bring all that they are with them: their *a priori* categories, their own experiences, and their historico-cultural heritage. The world reveals itself to human awareness in accordance with the structural norms governing that awareness. Experience is never without certain presuppositions. It is always given direction by some prior model, which is then tested in the critical confrontation with reality in order to be confirmed, corrected, improved, or rejected. Experience arises in the encounter between the world and consciousness. It is structured as history, as the journey of a given individual or a given human group.

Today we do not experience the world as a numinous, mythical reality nor as a self-subsisting metaphysical reality. Instead we experience it as a historical reality that has grown out of the past and is still moving toward some open-ended future. We approach the world in scientific and technological terms and study its inner laws, which can be grasped phenomenologically and explained in rational terms. That is our age's way of experiencing the world, and it stands alongside older ways that still persist in society or on the level of the individual and collective unconscious.

Grace can be grace for us today only if it emerges from within the world in which we ourselves are immersed. Only then can it signify what it is meant to signify in Christian terms: the reality of God's free love and his liberating presence in the world. Grace appears within our concrete world, liberating us *from* a decadent human situation and *for* a fuller, divinized one. We must detect its presence, though it may be concealed by our prevailing mental outlook and the concrete situation. Only by immersing ourselves in the reality around us can we experience its aspects of gratuitousness and grace.

The Necessity of Correctly Understanding
the Relationship Between Natural and Supernatural

To move toward an authentic experience of grace as such, we must get beyond an erroneous view of grace. This view sees grace as an order or realm apart from the one in which we must live here and now. It is what is called the supernatural order. Talk about the supernatural order and its relationship to the natural order is based on a particular metaphysics of grace and creation.

We know that the term "supernatural" came relatively late in the history of theology. It began to operate as a technical theological term only in the thirteenth century, when it was used by Thomas Aquinas in his *Quaestiones Disputatae de Veritate* (1256–1259). Early indications of its use are to be found in the Greek fathers. Operating out of a neoplatonic world view, which depicted reality as a series of hierarchical levels, they talked about a reality that was supercosmic *(hyperkosmikos)*, superphysical *(hyperfues)*, and supercelestial *(hyperouranios)*. The first literary use of the Latin term *supernaturale* dates back to the sixth century. Its use grew in the eighth and ninth century when the works of the Pseudo-Dionysius were translated, and it continued to gain ground in the following centuries.[11]

However, neither the Bible nor early Christian literature was familiar with the term "supernatural." The happening embodied in God's gratuitous, salvific love was expressed in terms of relationship, encounter, covenant, and so forth. Grace is something that is to be concretely experienced and sung about. Thus the whole notion of the experience of grace was profoundly altered when the biblical experience was translated into alien categories.[12] Personalist and historical categories were traded in for the Greek category of nature *(physis)*. A happening of freedom was now framed in the categories of necessity, and grace came under the wings of nature. Nature became the basic category governing all the rest. Grace would be examined in terms of nature rather than in terms of itself. Hence grace could only be something supernatural, lying beyond the bounds of normal, natural human experience.

Theological thought continued to develop during the Renaissance, when nature and human beings became objects of science. This development, which culminated in the Council of Trent, presented the natural and the supernatural as two complete realities in themselves, each with its own order and perfection. They were like two separate floors in a house. This point of view was never accepted by all schools of theology. Those in the Augustinian tradition, for example, tended to reject it; and the Augustinian tradition continued to exert an impact on Christian thought. According to that tradition, nature and grace were not separate from each other. But the prevailing scholastic view was otherwise. As F. Diekamp expresses it: "A nature which is complete in itself and has everything necessary for itself receives the supernatural as something added on to it."[13]

On the *theoretical* level this view has obvious advantages. Nature seems to enjoy independence and reason seems to enjoy autonomy. God and his grace do not have to be used to plug up missing gaps. By the same token grace appears in what seems to be its own distinctive form, i.e., as something gratuitous and wholly unowed to nature. Yet there is also a grave inconvenience here which does not allow the mind to rest content with this solution. For the fact remains that grace seems to be something added, something external, something wholly superfluous.

We need only examine some of the definitions of the natural and the supernatural offered by this view to see the predominance of the category "nature" and the externalist viewpoint. *"Naturale est, quod vel constitutive, vel consecutive vel exegitive ad naturam pertinet"* [Natural is what belongs to nature by virtue of its constitution, its consequences, or its exigencies]. Here we have a clearly dynamic concept of nature and natural. "Nature" (from Latin *nasci,* "to be born") is an essence in action within a certain area that belongs to it by right. Thus, for example, the power of seeing is part of the *constitution* of the eye. As a *consequence,* it does in fact see everything that is illuminated and that falls within its capability. And if this capacity for seeing is to be effectively used, it also *needs* light.

Now what about the supernatural? Here the definition is a negative one. *"Supernaturale est id, quod neque constitutive, neque consecutive, neque exegitive ad naturam pertinet"* [Supernatural is that which does not belong to nature by virtue of its constitution, its consequences, or its exigencies]. To put the same thing in more positive terms, we can say that the supernatural is "an added gift given to nature which it does not deserve as such." This gift need not be a fleeting thing. It can endure as an elevation of human nature to a share in the divine nature (see 2 Pet. 1:4) so that the former becomes a new reality.

All possibility of experiencing grace is ruled out in the framework of such an interpretation. For grace belongs to the supernatural realm, which infinitely exceeds the natural realm. Any possible human experience must fall within the horizon of nature; hence it cannot be an experience of grace.

Yet this nature possesses a curious quality. Despite original sin at the very start, it was spared and left intact. The theological manuals tell us that original sin stripped humans of the supernatural and wounded their preternatural gifts (e.g., immortality and full integrity).[14] But such a preserved nature is no longer historical nature at all; it is a metaphysical construct. No wonder, then, that this view should give rise to excessive naturalism and rationalism within the church. On the one side, we get a reason and a nature that are wholly self-sufficient. And in reaction to this view, we get an image of nature as something totally corrupt and depraved which can even reject and crucify the Son of God (Baius, Jansen, and Luther).

This theological view of grace and human nature as two separate realms began to crumble in the twentieth century. Theologians came around to the view that, in the concrete, nature is ever suffused with the supernatural. There were several reasons for this change of view. Some were pastoral in character. The older construct seemed to dig an ever widening gap between the real problems of society and the answers Christianity might provide. In the last analysis human beings do not find themselves to be ontologically divided into natural on the one hand and supernatural on the other. Christ's work was not restricted to the supernatural. He wanted to save human beings in their totality, and his work touched upon every one of their dimensions, i.e., nature, grace, sin, and their capability of being divinized.

A second reason for the change in view was the careful work of theological reflection itself. Amid heated discussions and wrong turnings it began to explore some of the data of tradition more thoroughly, e.g., love of God as a natural desire of humans, the human person as a transcendental subjectivity, the dialogal structure of grace and salvation, and the historico-salvific character of God's redemptive and divinizing work.

Consider the definition of grace, for example. Using the philosophical category of nature, the medieval theologians had defined grace as an accident, as something added on to nature. How was this accident to be understood? The neo-scholastic manuals all too quickly lumped it with all the other accidents because grace could be lost, recovered, increased, and diminished. Exploring the question more deeply, however, some came to understand grace along the lines of Saint Bonaventure. Grace meant being in relationship with God. When a natural reality is placed in relationship with God, then the supernatural surfaces. It is not a substantive creating some new reality alongside nature; instead it is an adjective qualifying one and the same reality. While this new qualification obviously possesses an ontological character, it itself is not some portion or part of the reality. It is a new form of being and acting that is assumed by the latter. And if grace does signify being in relationship with God, then the way is open to experiencing this relationship.

By the same token this view of grace also brings us to the theme of the human being as a person, as a being who is supremely relational. A human being is in reality a web of living, operative relationships. Human beings were created for an absolute relationship with God so that in present history there is really no relationship that is not supernatural.

Consider the human being as spirit. What exactly is it? Is human nature as closed up in itself as neo-scholastic theology suggested? In this century Christian theologians have delved into the phenomenology of humanity as spirit and gone back to the roots of their Christian tradition. The results have been very fruitful for the topic in question here. A host of names deserve mention in this connection: Henri de Lubac, Romano Guardini, Hans Urs von Balthasar, and J. Marechal. They have done much to spotlight some of the typical intuitions and perspectives of theological anthropology that tradition has always considered in discussing grace and the elevation of humanity to a share in the divine nature.

For example, in humans spirit is not a reality standing alongside matter (the body) and circumscribed by the latter. The spirit is the whole human being, its mode of being insofar as it is living transcendence, total openness, and all-around relationship. Humanity as spirit signifies a yearning for the Infinite, a longing for God.[15] Nothing in this world and no one by his or her humanity alone can claim to offer fulfillment. Human beings do not want just this or that. They do not ponder just this or that reality. They want everything and they contemplate totality. Only God seems to be the satisfactory pole toward which their interior compass points. Only in God will they find rest. Their natural desire to love God is rooted in the very depths of their being.

Without it we could not possibly understand historical human beings, the only human beings who are of interest to us here. And yet, without grace (or the supernatural) they cannot attain their full humanity.

This phenomenology of humanity as spirit reaches the conclusion that the natural desire to love God establishes a need or exigency in human beings. It is at this point that a question arises and that the debate grows more heated. If this desire is in fact an exigency of nature, then it is no longer supernatural; it is a part of nature itself. Does this mean that grace loses its quality of gratuitousness, and hence is no longer grace at all?

We must proceed calmly here, avoiding oversimplification. We are dealing with theology here, not with physics. Theology is not just a phenomenology articulated from below. It is primarily a way of understanding things that derive from above, from God and his transcendent design. Theo-logy is a discourse about God that derives from God. When we view humanity's natural desire for God in theological terms, we see a glimmer of light. The natural desire to love God is not a symptom of humanity's unbridled egotism or its desire to expropriate God; nor is it a merely human exigency. It was God himself who created human beings in such a way that they can be fully human and happy only in union with him. It was God himself who placed this desire in human hearts, so that they yearn to see and love him face to face.[16] It was God himself who structured human beings in such a way that they are permanently open to hearing the voice of God as it comes to them through things, their own conscience, other human mediations, and God himself. As Guardini put it: "Things arise through divine command, human beings through God's call."[17]

The natural desire to love God is not a merely human exigency. It is the call which God places within human beings. They hear that call and cry out for God. *The cry of human beings is merely an echo of God's voice calling them.* All this is gratuitous, and must be, because gratuitousness is an inevitable attribute of the deity. This same gratuitousness is present in the creation of human beings, who are called to gratuitousness. The case here is the same as that with respect to merit. In the latter God really rewards his own works. In the act of fulfilling the exigency that echoes in our nature, God is really responding to the voice which he causes to cry out within human beings.

The whole phenomenon must be considered in all its aspects. From below we must provide a correct existential analysis of the human being as spirit. From above we must consider the matter in the light of God's creative design; for it is he who summons humanity to the supernatural, to life with him. The fact that this phenomenon is framed in the context of gratuitousness rather than necessity can be seen from the very structure of the natural human desire to love God. Humans long for the absolute, but not as their own proper prey. They long for a God who gives himself freely as a gift. Humans feel the need to love, but they want only free, gratuitous love. If *per impossibile* they could lay hold of it violently, love would no longer be fulfillment because it would have ceased to be gratuitous. That is the way it is with the supernatural.

The above remarks should make it clear that there is no such thing as a pure nature that constitutes its own isolated order. The only purely natural element is the fact that a human being is a personal subject who is capable of receiving God's grace. Created being as such is a formal concept. It is the precondition that allows for the possibility of God's loving communication of himself.[18] In order to give himself *gratis,* God gratuitously creates a personal being (a subject). This minimum is what makes possible God's union with human beings and their union with him, both on earth and in heaven: yet this union is never mere fusion, absorption, or a divine emanation. The union between God and humanity in grace is analogous to the union of the two in the mystery of the Incarnation: it takes place without confusion, alteration, division, or separation. The distinction between the two makes their union possible; and the latter is a real union because there is no confusion between them.[19]

Going beyond this purely formal aspect, however, we can consider grace in concrete history and the day-to-day actions of human beings. Here we find that nature is always suffused with grace. For that reason we can never say what is "natural" in our actions and what is "supernatural." In any given concrete context it is impossible to isolate the two and look at each in its pure form. Once we consider creation within the framework of the christological project, as we shall do further on, it becomes clear that everything is bathed in the supernatural.

This view of the matter offers us vast possibilities for experiencing grace. As this whole book will bring out more clearly, the experience of grace is always a mediated experience. It comes to us through gestures, words, encounters, prayers, liturgical acts, and so forth. We can immerse ourselves in those realities and experience the dimension of grace which they contain.

This realization of the interpenetration of the natural and supernatural has had its impact on theology. More and more present-day theology is rejecting the contrast between a natural end and a supernatural end. Vatican II, for example, preferred to talk about the one vocation of humanity (GS 10, 11, 57, 59, 61, 63, 91; AG 8). Moreover, because the terms "natural" and "supernatural" have led to many false associations and misinterpretations, a lot of people are suggesting that we abandon these categories altogether. Here again Vatican II offers us a good example. It rarely used the term "nature" (GS 7, 8; AG 3), and it used the term "supernatural" only fourteen times. In *Gaudium et Spes,* which dealt directly with the mystery of human involvement in the universe and history, the term "supernatural" was never used at all. Flick and Alszeghy have this to say about the matter: "This reserve is certainly intentional, and it accords with a tendency in contemporary theology. In view of certain inconveniences, various efforts are made to explain the gift of Christ which will put greater stress on its positive aspect and its relationship to the whole of the Christian message without disregarding its transcendence vis-à-vis the creature."[20] Juan Alfaro has successfully tried to point up the transcendence and immanence of grace in the human person without ever having recourse to the categories of natural and supernatural.[21] My reflections in this book will follow the same line.

The Experience of Grace as Embodied in the Word "Grace"

The meaning and use of the word "grace" itself contains an experience of grace, though it may be latent and hardly adverted to. Let us consider this point.

Originally "grace" signified the benevolence of a superior toward an inferior. It was the attribute of a superior who "looked benevolently" or "*favor*ably" on his subordinates. Those are the connotations of the Hebrew word "*hen.*" Such a superior was open to others, wishing them well and treating them sympathetically. Though forbidden to do so, Esther approached Ahasuerus and "found favor" with him (Esther 8:5). In the New Testament we are told that Mary "found favor with God" (Luke 1:30; see Gen. 18:3; 19:19; 30:27).

A person displays grace and its import when he or she relates amicably to others. Such a person is not kind and benevolent because others are in turn, but simply because that is his or her basic attitude. It is an action that wells up from inside, not a reaction to the kindness of others. Grace signifies the basic inner attitude of people themselves, no matter what the attitude or conduct of others may be.

Obviously such grace must overcome the temptation it feels when it meets with the wickedness and ill will of other human beings and of malevolent situations. If human beings continue to be benevolent, open-hearted, and loving in their relationships, no matter how malevolent the circumstances may be, then the real import of grace as an action and a basic attitude shines through clearly. In this vein the New Testament talks about the kindness and mercy of God, who is not restricted or coerced by the maliciousness of others. God is love and ever remains so. He continues to love the ungrateful and the wicked (Luke 6:34), persevering in his attitude of grace toward human beings.

That brings us to a second meaning of "grace." As we just noted, people who have grace as a basic attitude are benevolent no matter what the reaction of others may be. They embody grace as *pure gratuitousness.* They are kind and benevolent to others in a wholly pristine and gratuitous way. They do not love others because the latter are good or beautiful; rather, the others are good and beautiful because they are loved by people endowed with grace.

Consider God, for example. He does not love human beings because of their merits or their goodness. He loves them simply because that is his own basic mode of being and existing. He is gratuitous love. His benevolence is extended gratis to all, even to the wicked and ungrateful (Luke 6:35).

"Grace" also signifies *the beauty, charm, and likeability of a person* (Prov. 1:9; 3:22; Luke 4:22; *Iliad* 14 183; *Odyssey* 6 237). We talk about a "graceful" person or a person who walks with real grace. Now if we consider this use of the word "grace," where it is associated with charm and beauty of some sort, we will find that it usually has something to do with spontaneity, vitality, and an absence of rigidity. We find little charm in anything that is wholly ensnared in laws and conventions. Beauty and charm presuppose a certain amount of spontaneous vitality and interior abundance that shines through automatically. Here we might do well to quote Péguy on the germ as the rudiments of any organism:

The germ is the minimum of residue, the minimum of ready-made, the minimum of habit and memory. Hence it is the minimum of decrepitude, rigidity, hardening, and lifelessness. And, on the other hand, it is the maximum of liberty, playfulness, agility, and grace. The germ is the least habituated thing that exists. It contains the least possible amount of hoarded material already fixed by memory and habit. It contains the least possible amount of matter consecrated to memory. It contains the least amount of file papers, memories, paperwork, bureaucracy. Or, to put it better, it is that which is closest to creation and most recent in the sense of the Latin word *recens*. It is the most recent and fresh thing that has truly come from the hands of God.[22]

In the social arena of human relations we see most clearly what is meant by grace. Grace can mark the way a person talks and walks, the way a person looks and smiles, or the way a person is present on the scene. Luke says of Jesus:

All who were present spoke favorably of him; they marveled at the appealing discourse which came from his lips. They also asked, "Is not this Joseph's son?" (Luke 4:22).

In its theological dimension we can say that grace is the beauty and charm of creation as a manifestation of God and his benevolent love. This grace is concentrated in humanity. Human charm and beauty are the reflected presence of God in the world. The grace of God (as a basic attitude) produces grace in human beings (as beauty and charm). As Augustine put it: "Because you loved me, you made me lovable."

In the same vein "grace" can also signify "gift, favor, something received gratis." It is something not due to my efforts or my own creativity. Thus nature or God may freely endow people with the charm of their smile or their gait. If a person learns these things through some sort of training, we can usually spot that at once. We detect the lack of spontaneity and the artificiality; the charm evaporates quickly.

Aristotle *(Rhetoric* 2:7) rightly noted that grace *(charis)* connotes a present, because every present is synonymous with an abundance of liberty and generosity. Charm and beauty are things that people either have or don't have. We feel that they cannot be manufactured. This experience brings us right to the theological issue. Human beings feel that they have been visited by Someone, though they may not know the latter's name. They feel that they have been the recipient of gifts and presents that lie beyond the capacity of human creativity, e.g., life, consciousness, intelligence, will, love, and the power to reflect and make decisions. All that is a gift. To live in the awareness of that fact is to savor the gratuitousness of all things.

Aware of such gifts, human beings feel grateful and are stirred to *give thanks*. Grace is requited with grace, even as love is requited with love. To give thanks is to acknowledge a debt of gratitude and pay back the favor. When people feel that they are the recipients of God's favor and love, without any merit of their own, they can only put their hands together and give thanks.

Now we can sum up this overview of grace in theological terms. First, grace is the benevolent attitude and openness of God which unfolds in love for human beings. Second, in human beings it produces charm and beauty of all sorts. Third, these qualities are experienced as gratuitous gifts from God. Fourth, they prompt human beings to give thanks to the giver of all good gifts. This perspective is summed up succinctly in *Gaudium et Spes:* "Man, who is the only creature on earth which God willed for itself, cannot fully find himself except through a sincere gift of himself" (n. 24).

Grace as the Expression of the Original Christian Experience

Why did the New Testament use the term "grace" to express the basic, original experience of the whole Christian mystery?[23] Well, as a matter of fact, the term is rarely used in the gospels at all. Matthew and Mark use it only once. John uses it only three times, in the prologue of his gospel. Luke uses it eight times in his gospel (Luke 1:28–30; 2:40–52; 4:22; 6:32–34 three times) and seventeen times in the Acts of the Apostles.

In Luke 6:32–34 Jesus uses the term for "grace" *(charis)* three times in a mundane sense:

If you love those who love you, what *credit* is that to you? Even sinners love those who love them. If you do good to those who do good to you, how can you claim any *credit?* Sinners do as much. If you lend to those from whom you expect repayment, what *merit* is there in it for you? Even sinners lend to sinners, expecting to be repaid in full.

The point seems obvious. That sort of love is not gratuitous or spontaneous because there is always some sort of recompense involved. It is love for one's enemies that is grace-ful because one does not get back any love in return. Assuming that Jesus did actually use the term in these verses, we can see that it retains its basic sense of gratuitousness and superabundance that lends charm to life. In the other passages where Luke uses the term, he retains the basic sense implied in the Septuagint version of the Old Testament. There it refers to the favor or benevolence of God resting upon someone.

It was through Paul that the term "grace" entered the New Testament as the chief expression of the new reality embodied in Christianity. It occurs hundreds of times in his writings, connoting all the varied things we mentioned earlier: benevolence (2 Cor. 8:1); charm (Col. 4:6); gift (Rom. 12:6; Eph. 4:7); thanksgiving (1 Cor. 10:30). But Paul's main emphasis is on its basic meaning. Grace is the gift of the Father himself in Jesus Christ, the gratuitous and merciful love of the Father and Christ which penetrates human beings, liberating them, saving them from perdition, and turning them into new creatures (2 Cor. 5:17; Gal. 6:15).

Paul often talks about the grace of the Father (2 Thess. 1:12; 2:16; 1 Cor. 1:4; 15:10; Gal. 1:15; Rom. 3:24; Eph. 1:6; 2:4–8; 1 Tim. 1:14; Titus 2:11–14). He also talks about the grace of Christ (2 Cor. 8:9; 12:9; Rom. 5:15; 2 Tim. 2:1; Titus 3:7). As Paul sees it, God gave himself in Jesus Christ out of pure gratuitousness; it was not due to any merit on the part of us human beings because in fact we were God's enemies at the time. Paul's use of the word "grace" embodies a concrete experience: God loved me first, despite my sins, because he is good, benevolent, and merciful. Paul feels graced by a gift, the gift of God himself in Jesus Christ. Christ is grace: God present to us. This experience of being surprised by an unexpected gift is what Paul expresses with the word "grace."

Underlying that experience, of course, is Paul's experience on the road to Damascus. In his letter to the Galatians Paul points up two basic stages:

First stage: You have heard, I know, the story of my former way of life in Judaism. You know that I went to extremes in persecuting the church of God and tried to destroy it. I made progress in Jewish observance far beyond most of my contemporaries, in my excess of zeal to live out all the traditions of my ancestors (Gal. 1:13–14).

Second stage: But the time came when he who had set me apart before I was born and called me *by his favor* chose to reveal his Son to me, that I might spread among the Gentiles the good tidings concerning him (Gal. 1:15–16).

Here Paul makes reference to a *before* and *after*.[24] There was nothing to suggest that he would undergo any conversion. He was a convinced Jew and a dedicated Pharisee. Conversion came as a gift from God, as a grace. But God's love, or grace, did not begin on the road to Damascus. It was operative from all eternity, marking Paul out as a special object of God's concern even before he was born. It was the explosive experience of God's loving call that converted Paul into a new human being.

For Paul, grace is primarily God himself in his infinite benevolence and gratuitousness. God and Jesus Christ are seen to be overflowing with grace (John 1:15). They give themselves to human beings as a gift so that the latter feel profoundly favored and give thanks. Since the gift of grace is God himself, human beings will become a new creature, a new humanity. As the adopted children of God, they will enjoy eternal life and the Spirit will dwell in their hearts. Now we can live in the freedom of the children of God (Rom. 8:14–21; Gal. 4:6), as heirs and masters of the universe (Gal. 4:1–3). All this is implied in Paul's use of the term "grace," which embodies the determining experience of his own life.

I think that the above reflections offer us the possibility of identifying the potential grace in our own lives and concrete experience. But before I move on to consider the experience of grace in various dimensions of our life today, I wish to discuss two points of the utmost importance: the law of the Incarnation and the constant presence of the Holy Spirit.

The Incarnation is the way in which God chose to draw near to the world in his love. He did not choose to display his overwhelming majesty, power, and glory. Instead he came in lowliness and silent reserve. He did not spurn or despise the world that existed prior to the historical event of the Incarnation. Instead he assumed that world and buried himself in it, revealing himself gradually and respectfully. He was and is so closely united with the world he assumed that we can only know him if we are willing to accept that world first. So we must suffer the pangs of God's relative absence. We cannot see him face to face. The world must mediate his presence to us. Yet this is also cause for joy. For when we embrace the world, we know that we are also embracing God. He is distant and yet near, withdrawn and yet present, silent and yet vocal. He summons us to keep on looking for him because we will never know him fully or rightly until the barriers of this present world crumble. Until then theology will always be a process of deciphering the presence of God's love and learning from one experience to the next.

Like our previous remarks on the correct relationship between the natural and the supernatural, the law of the Incarnation tells us that the experience of grace is never pure grace; it is also the world. And our experience of the world is never mere world; it is also grace. It is important for us to hold on to this basic principle as we proceed to consider the experience of grace in various dimensions of human life. It is always a diaphany of grace rather than an epiphany: grace shines through some experience of the world and life. The realities of this world are mediations or sacraments of grace. Grace comes to us in them and through them.

Emphasis on the christological dimension (the Incarnation) should not prompt us to denigrate the dimension of the Spirit, however.[25] As the early church fathers pointed out, Christ and the Holy Spirit are the two hands of God reaching out to embrace and save us. But whereas the incarnational and christological aspect was elaborated in great detail in the course of Christian tradition, the pneumatological aspect has been neglected. This has led to serious gaps and misunderstandings in our understanding of grace and the whole experience of faith. As we shall see in Chapters 17 and 18, both the mission of the Son and that of the Spirit are critical for properly understanding Christianity. The New Testament understood this clearly. That is why it placed both the Son and the Spirit at the heart of the salvation happening, stressing both Easter and Pentecost.

Even more than the Son, the Spirit has hidden himself behind the movement of history and the world with which he is so closely associated. The Spirit was experienced as a nameless force, an imperceptible vitality, and an invisible wind that made his presence felt. After the event of Pentecost we know his name. He is the Spirit of God, the Spirit of Christ, the Holy Spirit. This presence is manifested in the human experience of faith, grace, and salvation. He lies buried in these experiences, not diminishing human personalities but arousing them to free activity. He nourishes their creative imagination, helping them to move forward in history or to change its direction. So when we talk about the experience of grace, we should always remember it is an experience of the Holy Spirit and his activity in the world. It is part of all life and experience that contains an element of surprise and breaks down existing limitations and barriers. To experience grace means to allow ourselves to be overtaken by the presence of the Spirit. And that can happen only if we join with the Spirit.

CHAPTER 6

Experiencing Grace in Our Scientific and Technological World

Present-day experience typically occurs within the context of science and technology. The function of science is to gain knowledge; and the function of knowledge is power, the know-how and ability to do things. Science (knowledge) and technology (power) typify the present age in contrast to earlier ages.

Science and Faith as Two Basically Different Attitudes

Even before it is a set of data or a systematized body of knowledge, science is a basic attitude of mind. And I mean attitude in an ontological rather than a psychological sense. It is a way of being, a unifying and all-embracing vision. Insofar as it is a systematic body of knowledge, science is a concrete embodiment and projection of this basic attitude. It is characterized by objectification. Humans move away from nature and themselves in order to make themselves and nature an object of knowledge. Objectification breaks humanity's direct relationship with the world and introduces the dualism of subject and object, mediating between them with the aid of language.[1]

First, let us consider *the nature of the scientific project*. Its primary function is to comprehend, explain, and justify everything in terms of necessity. It seeks to describe the laws governing reality and to eliminate our surprise in the face of events. Rain, for example, ceases to be a surprising phenomenon once we know the general laws governing cloud formation, warm and cold fronts, and so forth.

Science is interested in reasons, laws, causes. Facts are its point of departure, but it does not confine itself to them alone. Its aim is to grasp the intelligible system behind the facts. The latter are projections of the system. In science, then, understanding and explaining mean moving from the plane of facts to the realm of system. The former are viewed in the light of *theory*. The scientific logos has its own particular clarity, providing orientation amid the sensuous confusion and obscurity of the phenomenal world.

Because this attitude is unifying and all-embracing, it generates a world of its own. It is not just the sum of particular pieces of data; it is not just *a posteriori.* It is a form of existence and coexistence that enables the particular data to surface. It is thus a precondition for the emergence of that data. The scientific attitude or mind set is prior to the data.

In recent times epistemological exploration has shown us that science arises from the interaction of subject, object, and language. It articulates the logos (the rationale) of the world. Humans serve as the vehicle whereby the latter can reveal itself. The logos of the world awakens the human logos. Science (knowledge) is converted into conscience (conscious knowledge). The encounter of the two in a dialectical experience generates the scientific attitude, and the latter is then concretely embodied in science as a systematic body of knowledge. Without the action of the logos of the world on human beings, the latter would not awaken to consciousness. Without the conscious awakening of humans, the logos of the world would never emerge from its anonymity. Thus human beings are responsible for their world, and for making the intelligibility of the world transparent.

Though science is a particularly noteworthy feature of our present age, its roots go back to the obscure byways of mythology. The latter always showed some concern for the principles underlying all things. Today's science carries on and seeks to clarify the yearnings of ancient forms of magic, which sought to satisfy the secret human desire to dominate the mysteries of the earth through knowledge and power. Science has not obliterated the older realms of myth and metaphysics. It is an extension of them insofar as it moves beyond them through dialectical interplay. Though no longer dominant in our age, the older realms continue to hold a place. They are windows through which we can contemplate and construct reality. At bottom our thinking continues to be *savage* and *primitive* and *metaphysical;* and it probably will remain so. The full import of the emergence of scientific knowledge escapes us because it is still in the process of taking concrete shape in history. But it does reveal the ability of humanity to develop in history.

Second, there is *the nature of the technological project.* Technology seeks to transform knowledge into power, into the ability to alter the world. It is a truly collective project with its own approach and goals. Technology is not a set of inventions or alterations. It is an authentic enterprise that has its own import and unity. But as is the case with science, the full meaning of technology cannot be discerned because we are enmeshed within its ongoing process.

It is the potentiality of the world that serves as the basis for the technological project. In nature we find unstable elements that represent so many open-ended possibilities. Humans have access to them, and they can utilize them for their own benefit. Interest and utility are the objectives of the technological project. At the same time, however, these objectives trigger an ongoing spiral of new needs and interests. The rate of technological applications accelerates to a frantic pace.

Where will it all lead? That is an open question. The tendency of technological manipulation is to extrapolate, to take its applications that deal with nature and use them as mechanisms for social tinkering and control. Some of these uses are now reaching apocalyptic levels—genetic tinkering, for example.

The Epistemological Status of Science and Faith

To talk about faith in the context of a scientific and technological world is to cross over into a different epistemological camp, a different order of knowledge, as Pascal might put it. The category "faith" does not exist for science. On the scientific level it cannot be denied or affirmed. It simply does not enter the purview of science. Faith has meaning only within the context of a different basic attitude.

Faith embodies the basic attitude whereby humans feel oriented toward some transcendent reality of definitive importance. It is oriented toward a supreme mystery which the religions of the world call God. Christianity specifically calls it Jesus Christ and the Trinity. On the basis of this attitude, all the things of this world begin to show up as revelations of the transcendent mystery. Faith is joyous acceptance of one's dependence on that mystery. It means interpreting the realities of this world as manifestations of that mystery.

The basic attitude of the scientific mind is not grounded on any such mystery. It is grounded on the logos of rationality and power. For there is no mysterious reality which cannot be penetrated by reason and manipulation.

The epistemological difference between science and faith should now be clear. Each possesses its own legitimate autonomy and its own kind of intelligibility. Moving beyond centuries of polemics, Vatican II acknowledged that fact plainly:

This sacred Synod . . . recalling the teaching of the first Vatican Council, declares that there are "two orders of knowledge" which are distinct, namely, faith and reason. It declares that the Church does not indeed forbid that "when the human arts and sciences are practiced they use their own principles and their proper method, each in its own domain." Hence, "acknowledging this just liberty," this sacred Synod affirms the legitimate autonomy of human culture and especially of the sciences.[2]

This statement of Vatican II was not prompted by apologetic desperation. It was not a last resort when all other means of persuasion had failed. It marks an objective advance in posing the basic issue correctly. For the real issue is not a difference in content between science and faith but rather a difference in basic attitudes.

That raises another question: what unity, if any, exists between these various orders of knowledge which are legitimate and autonomous in themselves? Are human beings condemned to live in isolation on separate epistemological islands? In the last analysis it is concrete human beings who simultaneously live these different basic attitudes, engaging in the scientific project, the political project, or the project of faith. Is each such project an absolute closed up in itself with its own all-embracing mode of existence, or is there some interaction among them all? Are they open to each other and, if so, in what sense?

Here I will propose my thesis with regard to science and faith. When we get down to the ultimate roots and limits of each of these epistemological orders, we find a common denominator shared by them all. They always end up in not knowing, in impotence, in some obscure mystery that is the embodiment of the mystery of God (or God as mystery). This is the ontological foundation and the permanent openness of all the areas of human epistemology. In the next section I shall try to show how this is so in terms of the basic attitude of science and technology. I hope to show that when science and technology get down to their foundation, they run into certain limits. There emerges a reality which is no longer scientific but which is the basis of the scientific attitude.

The Potential Emergence of Faith and Grace at the Roots and Limits of Scientific Knowledge

The scientific attitude has largely carried out its initial project of acquiring knowledge and power vis-à-vis nature. Its implicit premises have been made explicit. It has found its own proper methods and verified its ambitions. It has become more rigorous. In its own eyes it is now a basic dimension of human awareness. Science can now be exported to the whole world because it satisfies the demands of human consciousness both in the Orient and the Occident. Though it was articulated in the Occident, it is no longer simply occidental. It is simply human.

However, science has not rested content with operational knowledge and technology. From the time of Kant on, it has also been concerned with the epistemological foundations of scientific knowledge and the ethical implications of power and its limits. These two aspects of the basic scientific mentality seem to prompt science and technology to move beyond their own proper dimension. In certain areas of activity at least, science and technology seem to be mature enough to reflect fruitfully on the foundations and limits of the epistemological horizon within which they operate. Science is now asking itself about the preconditions that make it possible and about the ambitions that start it off. It is trying to spell out the components of the process which it embodies. It is trying to get to the roots of its own concepts, and here philosophy serves as the model.[3]

Science has adopted the concern of philosophy. It has moved away far enough from itself to allow for the possibility of overcoming itself. It is in a position to recognize its own limits and how far its own discourse retains validity. Many scientists have shown a keenly critical awareness of the scope and validity of the scientific enterprise, e.g., Einstein, Born, Heisenberg, Von Weizsäcker, Jordan, Wittgenstein, and Monod.

The first obvious point is that a scientific fact is always the projection of a prior hermeneutic model. We find only what we have been looking for previously. The model itself is a projection of human questions and social interests. Once the model is laid down, then objectivity prevails. One seeks some correlation between the model and experience. But the model itself was produced by a human being. Despite its scientific objectivity, therefore, science always possesses some anthropological, political, and social ingredients. Today more than ever before in history, science is under the control of political power and authority. We can no longer picture the lone scientist working in his little cubicle. All major research requires a host of resources. Their acquisition and allocation are decided in terms of political interests. It is politics that conditions science, spelling out its tasks and setting its goals.

This phenomenological datum confirms the fact that science is a basic human attitude, a particular way of existing and living in the world. It is not only a tool but a basic human attitude that gives rise to the tool. The atomic bomb, for example, is first and foremost an attitude of the human mind and heart. It is a spiritual atmosphere that allows for the production of atomic bombs. The real danger and the real problem is not so much the atomic bomb but the human spirit that is capable of fashioning it.

Why did humans take the historical course of stepping back from nature and learning to manipulate both it and themselves? The answer clearly is that they saw some sense in doing so and were looking for some sort of human fulfillment. But what sort of human fulfillment specifically? Science and technology present human beings as perfectible, as transcending the world and capable of raising questions about it and themselves. The questioning knows no bounds; it is universal. It has already reached out to encompass everything, and every indication is that it will never be fully satisfied. The question remains open, and we might well wonder where we will find the response to give us full satisfaction. In his *Tractatus logico-philosophicus* Ludwig Wittgenstein subjected scientific discourse to the sieve of critical examination. Toward the end of that work he says:

Even when we will have found an answer to all possible scientific questions, we will see that our vital problems have not yet even been touched (6.52).[4]

Science can explain all the phenomena in the world, but the world itself remains a mystery.[5]

Knowing itself presupposes nonknowing. Research presupposes ignorance. What makes humans go on knowing and learning continually and trying to domesticate the world? They are dominated by a daimonic force that lures them on to scientific and technological conquests. By the same token, however, they cannot lock up this daimonic force in their scientific baggage because they need it in order to do science. Science never succeeds in encompassing its own foundation. It builds on that foundation but it does not know what it is. The foundation is presupposed in any attempt to express it in a formula. Science itself always comes afterwards.

For this reason we can say that the foundation of science itself is a non-knowing, a mystery that is not rational. Science looks for the reasons of everything but it cannot furnish the reasons for its own foundation. Reason itself, the very foundation of science, is nonrational. While reasons begin with reason, the latter itself has no reason. There is no rational motive that calls for the existence of reason. Reason itself is gratuitous. It exists as a bare fact, grounding rationality on a base which itself is not rational. The nonrational does exist, therefore, and it is seen as a limit by science itself. Science is confronted with a mystery. Here mystery is not the residue of what cannot be known; it is what precedes any knowing and what remains after all our knowledge has been processed. It is the foundation that makes knowledge and science possible at all.

The same experience can be verified in technology, the process in which we try to gain power over the world and human beings. What are its limits? At a certain point the technological project began to expand so rapidly that human beings began to notice its destructive potential and its terrible dangerousness. Now this destructive power is moving from the hands of a small elite to more and more people. Physical, chemical, and bacteriological weapons can jeopardize the whole planet. Natural resources are being used up so extensively that we can estimate when they will be exhausted completely. Humanity's break with nature and ecological imbalance have reached the point where entire populations may be endangered. This has brought up the whole problem of limiting and controlling the power of technology.

But what criteria are to be used?[6] Technology itself is more perfect, the more it attains its aim; and its aim is power. If we should manage to create some ultimate weapon that could destroy everything and render all other weapons useless, that would be regarded as a scientific and technological success. What is to set limits on power? It cannot be any scientific or technological criteria because they aim for ever greater efficacy. Here again the basic scientific attitude feels itself summoned by options that stem from a different basic attitude, i.e., some sort of humanism or faith. It senses its own limitations and must open up to a position that lies outside itself.

Thus in going down to the roots and limits of the scientific and technological project, we suddenly glimpse another dimension in which it becomes meaningful to talk about grace. Instead of continuing to talk about science and technology, we find another dimension that can serve as an aid and corrective for them. We have moved beyond explanations to the quest for meaning.

Science has to do with the *how* of this world: how it arose, how phenomena show up, and how its laws are structured. Science does not have anything to do with the more basic fact that the world exists. It presupposes an existing world, and there is no scientific explanation for the world's existence. There is no reason that calls for the existence of the world. The latter is there as a gratuitous datum for science too. Science can study the internal structures of the rose and its flowering process. But the rose itself buds and flowers without any reason, for the sheer sake of doing so. It does not flower to please some onlooker (A. Silesius). Our study of natural phenomena presupposes their existence, but there is no reason why they should exist. We confront the gratuitousness of creation.

For science itself the world is a mystery and the existence of the things it studies so carefully is a grace. Their existence is presupposed at the start. And when science attempts to step back and reflect on its own basic principles, it runs into something in the order of grace and faith. Remember that it is science itself, not theology, which has taken this step. In going down to the roots and limits of its own discipline, science begins to glimpse another order, the order of faith and grace. Thus there is a point where science goes beyond itself, where it is possible to share a meaningful discourse about God in the world, grace, sin, and damnation. In short, we can engage in dialogue about faith.

The Ultimate Foundation in the Order of Faith

The order of faith deals thematically with precisely that reality which begins to emerge at the limits of science, i.e., the nameless mystery that is the foundation of all things. For faith, God is the force that instills life into science, technology, and all the things of the world. He is not a phenomenon or an entity like those that are encountered in human experience. If that were the case, he would be a part of the world, a phenomenon. He could be analyzed and described as an object of scientific discourse. God does not exist as things exist. Instead he is the foundation of all existence, and his mode of being is that of a mystery: ineffable, beyond the reach of language, ever transcendent and ever present. God ever remains the foundation of all, even of the effort to say something about this foundation. God is the Absolute, not outside or above the world, but at the very core of the world.

The world is a manifestation of God. God is present in the world but not as a part of the world. We find something similar in the case of human beings, and it may help us to see what is meant here. Human beings can produce a book, a statue, or a speech. These things are not human beings, but they are manifestations of them. Human beings retain their transcendence. Their products come from them, reveal them, and owe their existence to the life-giving power of humans. The case with God is similar. God produces all things and is present as their foundation; but God himself remains transcendent.

The world as a whole and the phenomena that take place in it are revelations and manifestations of God. They are purely gratuitous manifestations of the supreme mystery projecting itself into history. Now the order of faith looks at everything from the standpoint of God. It sees all things as sacraments of God, as signs and images of the supreme mystery. For faith, the world is a symbol more than it is a thing. Its most fundamental reality is to serve as a sign revealing God, as a bridge leading to him.

In the order of faith, then, everything suddenly is grace. That is how Bernanos put it in *The Diary of a Country Priest,* borrowing from Saint Thérèse, the Little Flower. We must understand the remark correctly, however. It does not mean that everything in the dimension of history is grace; we find dis-grace there also. It means that everything is grace at the level of its ontological foundation because everything—both good and evil, grace and dis-grace—is sustained and supported by the supreme mystery. If there is only one foundation and one Absolute, then everything in existence must be sustained by it.

This does not mean that the supreme mystery is responsible for everything. To think that way would be to envision the ultimate mystery as a secondary cause *(causa segunda),* a something in the world which also produces evil. God, the foundation, does not produce evil; but he does give the vitality and force that enable evil people to do their evil. The evil comes from human beings, but it is God who gives them the *power* of freedom to commit evil or not.

It is on this ontological level that it makes sense to say that all is grace. It would be a mistake, however, to apply the same expression to the historical level. We cannot say that everything is grace even when it seems to be dis-graceful. We cannot use the expression to justify all the calamities of history. The only thing we can say is that human beings can be motivated by dis-grace to ascend to God because God is the ultimate ontological foundation of both. No dis-grace is so absolutely disgraceful that it does not contain some appeal to its ultimate ontological foundation, God. Dis-grace is always a relative thing. It is the dis-grace of a creature, not of God who is absolute. Bad as creatures may be, they can never establish their independence from God or break their ontological tie to him. Dis-grace itself does not produce grace, but it offers an occasion for human beings to look to the transcendent foundation which makes it possible in the first place.

It is undoubtedly on this basis that Jesus Christ and the New Testament teach us to love our enemies. This commandment is not a purely voluntaristic one. It is grounded on an ontological consideration. However bad our enemies may be, they can never obscure the reflection of God or stifle his mysterious presence. For that reason they remain lovable. God himself loves the evil and the ungrateful (Luke 6:35) because he can see the reflection of himself in them. Dis-grace ever remains a summons to the experience of grace. It never offers us any reason for remaining with it. We must try to combat and overcome it with all the means and energy at our disposal. Yet dis-grace confirms the supremacy of grace because it never succeeds in limiting grace or absorbing the latter within itself.

To repeat briefly: in the light of the ultimate foundation, God, everything is grace because everything is referred back to him, sustained and supported ontologically by him.

Science and Technology as Grace and Dis-grace in History

The above ontological consideration is important if we are to preserve the absolute character of God. He has no rivals and his grace is always victorious. Grace is not some substance existing alongside another thing; it cannot be detected or defined as such in the world. If it were such, then it would be a phenomenological reality and would come under the purview of science. As we noted earlier, grace is the presence and activity of God in the world. It shows up as the underlying foundation of all when we go to the roots and ultimate limits of every particular articulation in this world—in this case, of the scientific and technological order.

By the same token, however, this foundation is not a static reality living in hidden retirement. It enters history and appears in science and technology as the way in which we do them. It is the divine way or manner of worldly things. It is these things when they appear as graceful and benevolent. When and how does this divine mode appear? To ask that question is to ask for the concrete mediations of grace, of God's presence in the world.

This divine way is not mechanical or epiphanic. It appears as something offered to human freedom. It is loving dialogue, not imposed power. Thus it appears in the framework of history and encounter, of re-cognition and acceptance. Instead of crushing humans, it invites them to express themselves and to respond in turn. This encounter is the reflection of God in the world, the process of grace manifesting itself in all things.

If human beings refuse this encounter, then grace does not turn into history. It ever remains as the underlying foundation, but it can be rejected in reality. Thus grace is ever present; but in one case it remains solely as the underlying foundation while in the other case it is a foundation accepted in human life and spelled out in history. The concrete acceptance of grace initiates a style of life which we can call grace-ful and beautiful; the rejection of grace produces a self-sufficient style of life that is filled with overweening pride, falsehood, violence, and domineering impulses. The latter is the concrete manifestation of dis-grace; the former is the visible embodiment of grace in the world. So let us briefly consider dis-grace and grace as concretely embodied in science and technology.

Dis-grace appears in the attitude of science when that attitude poses as the one and only epistemological arena, as the only human order that is truly justified and fruitful. Here science claims that the meaning it gives to the world is the only possible and reasonable one. It reduces everything to one single sense, levels all differences, and does violence to all the other possible areas of experience in human life. Presenting itself as a totalitarian enterprise, it subjugates all other enterprises to itself or else rejects them as outdated history.

This danger is immanent in the scientific logos, which seeks the utmost in rationality and intelligibility. By its very nature it prescinds from any reference to the transcendent or to a higher destination. It analyzes and tries to understand what is presented to it, so it is always possible for science to get closed up in itself. When that happens, we get scientists who are bloated with their own self-sufficiency and haughtiness. They know no limits and refuse to recognize other ways of being and living. They see humanity as the measure of all things and may even go so far as to deify human beings.

In such a case the scientific method no longer has respect for anything. It destroys the balancing tensions of life and subjects everything to its own analytic and manipulative power. This closed scientific model creates a caricature of the kingdom of God. Grace remains merely as the underlying foundation of all. It is not allowed to flesh itself out in history or to foster encounter, beauty, and graciousness. And the absence of grace in history is attested to by the tedium of monotonous living, by insolence, and by impositions on human beings.

Dis-grace and its consequences are even worse on the level of technology. There is the accumulation of knowledge and technological power in the hands of a few nations. They impose their will on other nations, requiring submission or dependence. While some people enjoy the benefits of technology, other are exploited and marginalized. Whole continents are impoverished and deprived of access to freedom, health, and progress. Ecological balance is undermined, advanced discoveries are used for military purposes, and human beings are manipulated as if they were just another object in the natural world. The mass media and transportation facilities are utilized to keep people enslaved to the values of production and consumption systems. Subliminal advertising tries to introject the values of a small elite into the consciousness of the masses. These are but a few of the ways in which dis-grace shows up in a technological world.

This dehumanizing use of technology presupposes a certain attitude of mind and heart. It is the attitude of people closed up in themselves and impervious to any higher frame of reference. They would never ask what the purpose and aim of so much production and power is. Manipulative power is an end in itself. It becomes concentrated more and more in the hands of fewer and fewer people or nations; and they become more prone to violence as they sense the fragility of their power. We get a host of nameless, faceless people in a desert waste. The gods and all meaning disappear without a trace.

These phenomena are the concrete face of dis-grace. It does not exist alongside science and technology. It is science and technology insofar as they close up in themselves and become the sole norm of life and experience.

People become blind to any other court of appeal and lose their openness. One-dimensional human beings are the anticipation of what faith would call absolute frustration and damnation.

On the other hand *grace* appears in the realm of science when it overcomes its narrow-mindedness and senses its permanent openness to mystery. Rejecting haughty self-sufficiency, it humbly accepts its place within the broader horizon of the underlying foundation that is God. As an *attitude of faith,* then, science here sees itself as one order among many possible others. It is an order of knowledge and power that enables human beings to gain control over the world, unveil the rationale of nature, and thus become free, responsible masters of the world.

This accords with the view of faith. In its eyes science is the means whereby humans reveal the hidden logos of the world. Through them the intelligible structure of the world surfaces and the world itself is perfected by their activity. Through human beings the world is elevated to the divine realm. The scientific unveiling of the world is the work of grace which operates through the labor of human beings. Without them the original potentialities of the world would never be concretely spelled out in history. Here science is grace perfecting the world and concretely manifesting the loving wisdom of God.

As a collective enterprise science unveils the truth about the world even though its practitioners may have other intentions and be totally unaware of this dimension of science. It follows its grace-ful course toward perfect completion, but only faith is granted the gift of glimpsing and admiring the underlying meaning of the work being done by science.

It is important for science to explore its ultimate foundation and take cognizance of it. In accepting the limits and gratuitous nature of the world and reason, science and the scientist adopt a different mode of existence. They are no longer driven by the demon of arrogance or the dark power of omnipotent technology. They are free. Scientists know that science itself is only one way in which human beings approach and fashion reality. They take cognizance of the temptation to self-sufficiency, objectification, and the aggressive spirit underlying these tendencies. They can distance themselves from the danger inherent in any logos.

Grace signifies the ability to escape the evil that lurks as a possibility in the epistemological status of science. It means overcoming the temptation to self-enclosure. But grace is more than just liberation from immanent dangers. It is also a joyous spirit of scientific freedom that gives science a freshness and transparency all its own. Grace enables science to stick to its proper aim: the task of revealing the rationality of the real. Science will then pursue its investigations respectfully, aware that it is the recipient of a present. It will formulate and tackle a given problem in such a way that the world and human beings are humanized rather than manipulated for selfish interests or the quest for power.[7] Loyal to its proper exigencies and respectful toward other attitudes, it will produce not only scientists but wise men and sages. Involved in science, they will taste the ultimate Mystery in the process of unveiling the mystery of the world. They will realize that they have not created that Mystery, that instead they are its revealers and spokesmen. As the instrument God uses to manifest his presence in the world through order and latent possibilities, they will sense the contemplative and poetic dimension of humanity's confrontation with the world. The world remains world and science remains science, but at a deeper level both symbolize another reality that shines through them. It is the loving goodness and rationality of God and his work, his presence in the world that is called grace.

Technology, too, is a way in which grace can appear in the world. Despite the dangers it may contain, it is a powerful tool for the creation of more justice. It can liberate human beings from the bonds of hunger, illness, and natural forces. Technology can create a world that is really more just, more fraternal, and more wholesome. Technology is a tool that can promote the love of God and human beings, incarnating it in more suitable forms.

Technology also creates the basis for a new humanism. It enables us to transform the world around us and establish a different kind of relationship between human beings and nature. Far from being merely external, this has a critically influential impact on human beings. When the latter realize that the power of technology is something granted and upheld by God, they can alter the face of the earth in a more rational and humane way in accordance with the laws they discover. Technology can then be a humanizing force, generating sound relationships between human beings. Through the transformations it brings about, it can create an anticipatory image of the kingdom of God. Thus it, too, can incarnate the reality and import of grace in the world.

Summary: Grace and Science

To reiterate the matter briefly, we must remember that grace does not exist as other realities exist. Since it is God himself at work in the world, it possesses God's mode of being. God is real only if he emerges as the radical meaning of the world, as its foundation and open-ended future. So it is with grace. It emerges in the world insofar as it appears as the goodness, rightness, and gratuitous transparency of all things. These qualities possess value in themselves, and they can be detected and savored. Indeed it is all the more important that they should be because their opposites, which hardly seem possible at all, can also appear concretely in the world. And when we view these good qualities in the light of faith, they become so many symbols and manifestations of God's grace—of God communicating himself in the world.

Grace does not come upon the ruins of the world and humanity. It presupposes both. As the classic scholastic adage put it: *Gratia supponit naturam.*[8] Viewed in the light of faith, rightly ordered nature appears as the gratuitousness that embodies God's presence in the world. Grace, then, is not a thing. It is a mode of being for all things insofar as they are seen in the light of God, their ultimate foundation. Above and beyond their nature as creation, they reveal God present in creation and sharing himself with it. Their created nature falls within the realm of science and technology; the grace-fulness of this nature falls within the realm of faith.

Human beings must live and act on the basis of this fundamental attitude, which is grounded on faith and grace. Only then can they see the presence of grace in the world and its absence in dis-grace. Viewed in this light, the humanizing work of science and the responsible use of technology will prove to be something more than merely natural data. They will be seen as manifestations of God himself at work in the world.

God uses the mediation of human beings and their scientific and technological artifacts. Instead of annihilating human beings, he thereby exalts them and makes them sharers in his beauty, his goodness, and his love for all things. Human beings live in and through grace to the extent that they take cognizance of this dimension and concretely involve themselves in it. Living in and through grace, they elevate and sanctify the proper activity of science and technology. They make sure that the latter find and persevere in their true destiny: to help prepare the world for its ultimate transfiguration into the kingdom of God.

CHAPTER 7

Experiencing Grace in the Reality of Latin America: Challenges

The experience of grace and dis-grace in the realm of science and technology, which we discussed in general terms in the last chapter, finds a distinctive embodiment in Latin America. The framework or horizon that predominates here is one of dependence. Latin America stands on the periphery of the big-power centers and is dominated by them. In their concrete exercise science and technology are powerful instruments which the center uses to make Latin America its satellite.

This situation of domination and dependence "overdetermines" the main aspects of underdevelopment. If we do not take cognizance of it, we run the risk of being victimized by a false consciousness. Even with the light of faith and prophecy, we will not be able to discern the authentic manifestations of grace and dis-grace here. Instead we will completely confuse the two.

Starting Point for Our Reflection and Its Importance

In such an approach as this, the starting point for our theological reflection is of particular importance. Our hermeneutic locus is situated on the periphery of the prevailing system rather than imbedded within it. Our reflection derives from a locale which is regarded as critical and rebellious, which does not accept the prevailing regime and the kind of society implanted here. This nonacceptance is not due to any *a priori* position. It is due to a close analysis of reality on the most relevant terms possible.

Theological reflection does not just start off from itself and elaborate its thinking on the basis of its own sources in the Bible, tradition, the ecclesial magisterium, and past theology. It is also rooted in the cultural reality in which it is immersed, and it reads and interprets reality from that context. In that sense theology is always a second stage of thought. It is handed some reading of reality. It examines such readings critically and then accepts the interpretation that seems to dovetail best with reality and the faith. It rejects the interpretations that seem to come mainly from those who are concerned to uphold the existing establishment. Thus my theological reading here is mediated by a cultural reading grounded primarily on sociology, economics, and political science of a rebellious cast.

The pervasive phenomenon of underdevelopment in Latin America has challenged the best analysts to discover its underlying mechanism, the logic of its functioning, and possible ways out. Here I adopt the reading that has come to be known as the theory of dependence.[1] It is only a theory, not an established truth. It is one stage in an ongoing investigation and it has its own intrinsic limitations. It offers a good diagnosis of the structure of underdevelopment, but it does not do much to offer any viable way out. What interests us here, then, is primarily its analysis and explanation of underdevelopment.

Underdevelopment is defined as a global and dialectical social process resulting from the development of industrial capitalism. In order to sustain its scientific and technological progress as well as its growing affluence, industrial capitalism must create a central seat of power and a periphery around it. In the latter it fosters dependence, economic stagnation, social imbalances, and political tensions from which there is no internal way out. Thus development and underdevelopment are two sides of the same coin. They always come together, and there is an intimate relationship between them. Underdevelopment at bottom is not a matter of technical backwardness; it is not simply a phase preceding development. Underdevelopment is a political problem, a consequence of the development taking place in the capitalist system.

Economies are not independent. The central seats of power in the more advanced nations have absorbed the economies of the nations that are dependent on them for science and technology. An unequal system of exchange prevails, generating further imbalances. The periphery provides cheap raw materials while the center provides advanced science and technology. Instead of helping the periphery escape from underdevelopment, the overall process maintains the ongoing relationship of dependence. While much development may take place within the underdeveloped periphery, the structure of dependence is always maintained. The ruling center maintains satellite countries, introducing into them its own mode of production and consumption and its own cultural ethos. This structures all the manifestations of life, preventing the satellite countries from finding their own road to national autonomy and self-help. Dependence thereby reveals its underlying character, which comes down to domination of the center over the periphery.

Such an interpretation of the Latin American reality entails profound theological consequences. It denounces the existing model of societal interaction as one that is oppressive, as a manifest embodiment of sin and injustice on a worldwide level. It also announces the urgent need to break the ties of oppressive dependence and promote liberation, thus lending support to the forces that propose to do that.[2] No viable way out seems apparent right now, and there seems to be no viable strategy for breaking the ties of dependence. Yet this interpretation proposes liberation as an ideal, as a goal to be ultimately achieved after a long and painful process.

A different kind of theological reading, one designed to defend or even exalt the existing social system, would see grace where we see dis-grace. It would urge support where we would urge criticism and nonsupport. Thus one's hermeneutic starting point is a matter of some importance. In my opinion there is no possible third position. Either theology will adopt a critical attitude toward reality and thus be liberative or it will not. In the latter case it will cease to be a real theology, joining ranks with the ideological forces that seek to maintain the status quo and upholding the latter as more equitable and just.

By stating its position in these terms, theology recognizes and acknowledges its place in a world riddled with conflict. It takes sides rather than cloistering itself in some allegedly neutral position. Any such claim to neutrality is really an admission of support for the established order that benefits a small portion of the population and marginalizes the vast majority.[3]

Having made clear my own hermeneutic stance, in this chapter I shall try to offer a brief overview of the traces of grace and dis-grace on the Latin American continent.

Latin America as a Dependent Reality

Even before it was discovered by Europe, Latin America was made dependent on various centers of power. By the Treaty of Tordesillas in 1494, Pope Alexander VI handed us over to Spain and Portugal before the European consciousness had really taken serious note of us. The cultural atmosphere subsequently introduced here was a reflection of Europe, not an original image deriving from the native peoples. The production system, the division of labor, the forms of social and political life, the religion and customs, and the whole cultural ethos were not born here. They were implanted by the imperial centers of power. This meant that we have always been a Johnny-come-lately.[4]

As the outlook of science and technology inexorably made its way around the world, it was exported to our area also. We were introduced to the ideas of quantitative progress, mass production and mass consumption, and the private expropriation of natural resources and the means of production. This fostered the progressivist mentality, which has stressed fuller enjoyment of the world, an accelerated rate of historical change, and a frantic but hardly successful effort to close the gap between developed and underdeveloped nations. Our whole area now finds itself on the periphery of the technological, cultural, and religious world.

Political independence, which we won in the last century, represented merely one stage in a long process leading to authentic liberation. In almost every Latin American country it merely internalized the older system of dependence on European centers of power. Indeed the new system was more perfect because the national government was now used to maintain the whole structure of domination. National sovereignty was not the result of self-determination by the common people. It was and still is something used to advantage by national elites in conjunction with imperial elites.

The current system of dependence is a historical extension of the dependence imposed by imperialist western expansionism in the sixteenth century. Modern industrial capitalism is its most complete form. The latter process ensured that all the manifestations of life in our area would be shaped by decisions made in the centers of power. These centers would determine what we are to think, what we are to learn, what we are to produce, how we are to produce, what the social relations of production are to be, and how the international division of labor is to be organized. This infrastructure conditioned the ideological and cultural forms that would mesh with the system of domination and legitimate it. The people were to be convinced that socioeconomic progress could only come through submissive ties with the imperialist centers of power.

The pervasive system of dependence is a global process. For the sake of clarity I shall simply refer to three major axes of that system: economic dependence, sociocultural dependence, and political dependence. I see little point in debating which is the most basic of the three. There is a dialectical relationship among them, and the solution does not lie in transforming one of them first. What we must do now is create a new awareness on the grass-roots level so that the common people will be able to work up an alternative project and implement it through a new liberative praxis.

First, *economic dependence* must be viewed in structural terms. We must consider the makeup of the production structure. Historically it has been taking shape ever since the European discovery of Latin America. After the military defeat of the native inhabitants, the riches and resources of the colonies were carried off to the Iberian centers of power. These centers served as intermediaries for other centers, such as England and Holland, where industrial capitalism was born. First came a colonial process of growth determined by the external center of power. This center decided what would be produced for export to it. Then the internal market was consolidated. Capital and production forces within our countries replaced the older system of imports, but our national oligarchies solidified the ties with foreign power centers while gaining more and more control over our internal government. Finally, the present phase is characterized by what Darcy Ribeiro calls neocolonial industrialization or the internationalization of the market. Now huge multinational conglomerates, whose decision-making centers are to be found in the imperial nations, determine our production system and its priorities. The centers of power decide for both themselves and us what needs are to be satisfied and hence what goods are to be produced. Here is how Celso Furtado analyzes the matter:

The characteristic trait of capitalism in its present stage is that it prescinds entirely from the alleged claim of any national or multinational government to establish criteria that would regulate economic activity on the basis of general interests. This is not to suggest that governments are less concerned today with the general interest. Insofar as economies grow more stable, the activity of the government in the social arena can expand. But stability and economic expansion depend basically on international transactions. Since the latter are under the control of the huge conglomerates, relations between national governments and such conglomerates tend to be power relations.

To begin with, business enterprises have control over economic innovation within the national economy. They decide what new products and processes will be introduced, and international expansion is chiefly dependent on such innovations. Second, business enterprises are responsible for most international transactions. The initiative is theirs. Third, they operate internationally and are largely exempt from the control of any individual government in isolation. Fourth, their financial liquidity is largely beyond the control of central banks, and they have ready access to the international finance market.[5]

At the present stage capitalism puts the products of the whole world in one basket and standardizes consumption habits around the world. The countries at the center of economic power control scientific and technological output, exporting licensing arrangements to smaller countries and maintaining them in a state of dependence. Low wage scales and abundant manual labor entice big businesses to set up factories in the satellite countries and export finished products from there. This, even more than the imbalance of trade, accounts for the structural fact of economic dependence. A single cultural ethos of remarkable homogeneity is instilled throughout the range of the capitalist system.

The population living under the capitalist system is now about 2.5 billion people. About 800 million live at the center of the system, while 1.7 billion live on its periphery. The gross product of the center is about $1.6 trillion, while that of the periphery is about $340 billion. That comes down to a per-capita income of about $2,000 for those living in the center and an income of about $200 for those in the dependent countries.[6]

Behind these facts and figures lies a tragic human situation of hunger, poverty, marginalization, and exploitation.

This economic dependence, in turn, leads to *socio-cultural dependence*. It helps to configure social classes in a particular way. The privileged classes who benefit from economic dependence mimic the values and habits of the economic centers. Their culture is antipopulist, elitist, and imitative.[7] Generations of Brazilians were ashamed to admit their nationality or to speak the language of the country, and we find remnants of the type even today. Industrialization marginalized the majority of the population, luring them from the countryside to the big cities where they formed cordons of poverty. They were not given a role in the dynamic thrust of industrialization, and the ideologists of consumption ignored them because they lacked buying power.

The marginalization of the vast majority of Latin Americans was a direct result of the neocolonial industrialization promoted by the capitalist system. Rulers of the peripheral countries nurtured the illusion that we could achieve the well-being that had been achieved by the central countries. The accelerating pace of history meant that we were confronted with certain time limits for getting on the bandwagon. Fernando de Bastos de Ávila has compared our situation to that of a plane taking off from an airfield. We are reaching the end of the runway, and we must either take off or crash.[8] If certain schedules are not maintained, the distance between the affluent and the impoverished nations will only grow greater.

A price must be paid for all progress and all accelerated growth. Inevitably there will be conflicts. A country cannot maintain high rates of economic growth and make significant social investments at the same time. Opting for an accelerated rate of economic growth will entail a certain level of social inequity, and the latter may exceed the limits which justice and humaneness can tolerate.

The social cost of economic growth is not a fair one because it is producing an enormous amount of marginalization and poverty. In Brazil 75 percent of the population live a relatively marginal existence.[9] The Brazilian economic model does not directly benefit the vast majority of the population. All participate in the socio-economic buildup, but they do not share proportionally in the wealth produced, the freedom created, and the well-being so generated.

The weight of social inequity is not evenly distributed among all. It falls mostly on the social class that has been suffering privations for centuries: those who work for pay. Sacrifice is imposed on them willy-nilly. They cannot raise their voices against it, nor can they engage in consciousness-raising by indulging in class demonstrations.

The urgency of the economic time limits has led practically all the nations of Latin America to warp the original aims of their governments. The latter proposed to further social development through economic growth. Now all energy is concentrated on economic growth as an end in itself which will automatically produce social development as a byproduct. The perplexed remark of former president Médici (1970–74) sums up the situation: "The Brazilian economy is faring well, but the people are faring poorly!"

Certain sacrifices are entailed in any kind of real growth, be it economic, social, or spiritual. Other kinds of suffering, however, are the result of injustice: of an inhuman social order, an unfair distribution of wealth, and an unquenchable thirst for power. Significant numbers of thoughtful people in the affluent world have already taken note of the evils in the cultural system that has dominated the West for centuries. They oppose the excessive emphasis on quantitative measurements and the totalitarian exercise of economic, scientific, and technological power. Nausea, the social madness of

,the huge metropolises, and the anemic life-style of such a cultural ethos bear witness to its limitations. Frenetic possessiveness is not enough in itself. We must retain the spiritual dimension of human beings, a creative kind of asceticism, and a sense of social equity. In the capitalist system the social dis-grace of the modern world has revealed its diabolical and dehumanizing side.

In Latin America these same models have been imported without critical examination, even though they are now being contested by many people in the center countries. Here they are producing even greater contradictions than can be found in the central metropolises.

Third, we find *political dependence* resulting from the present system. The centers of economic power use elites within the satellite countries to impose their will. At an earlier stage in history the machinery of government was controlled by national oligarchies who had close ties with foreign sources of capital. Government was a prize to be fought over by different competing groups within the nation, but all of them had ties with foreign economic and political interests.

Of course, the whole process was not as simple as I have just described. There are many other twists and turns in it. Ideological and educational tools were used to legitimate the underlying economic interests, e.g., the ideology of the status quo, the communications media, a certain type of uncritical education from grade school to university, and so forth. All these tools were used to convince the people that the interests of a particular group were the true interests of the whole nation, that there was no other way to sociopolitical and economic progress. A shared consensus on the economic, social, and political level would cement the alliance between national elites and their counterparts in foreign countries.

In the 1960s the rise of political awareness and populist ideologies forced the ruling elites to give up the quest for consensus and integration. Military regimes based on force took control of the government in almost every nation of Latin America. This led to a third type of colonial pact rooted in the military-industrial-university complex. Brazil became an archetypal example of this development. A rapid process of economic development took place while structural dependence and underdevelopment were maintained. The armed forces and the bourgeoisie entrusted the task of national development to big business. The economic power center provided the national elite with technology, capital, and expert training for those bright people who accepted the ideology of the system itself. The gross national product underwent an astounding rate of growth, thus helping to bolster the ideology of the system. Income distribution, however, remained disgracefully inequitable and discriminatory. The function of the army became political. It was presented as the last resort of the western world in its fight against communism and other subversive forces. The U.S. Pentagon exported the relationships of the military-industrial-university complex to its satellite nations. Army officers, now scientifically trained, began to feel qualified to take over political power since civilian leaders seemed inept and ideologically disloyal. No longer simply military chieftains, they came to constitute a well-trained and ideologically homogeneous class.

The function of the army now is to guarantee order and security so that technology can lead to an economic takeoff. The Pentagon elaborated an ideology that was oversimplistic and Manichean, but that was also ideologically powerful for the very same reason. This was the doctrine of national security, which divided the world into two camps. On the one side stands the free, Christian world of the West. On the other side stands the oppressive and atheistic world of socialist communism. War prevails between the two camps. The nations of Latin America are part of the West, and so they must align themselves with the war strategy of that camp. Politics, too, is a form of warfare. The military forces of Latin America must overcome the forces of communism that are trying to infiltrate our nations through the channels of subversion, consciousness raising, populism, and church progressivism. In fighting this war, the military uses a political, cultural, and social methodology that is extremely effective. Exceptional tactics must be used because we are living in a state of war. The middle classes benefit from these implacable techniques of pacification because they establish the state of tranquillity needed to allow for big investments and lucrative profits.[10]

Government exercises tutelage over the nation. The common people participate in it minimally. They have been stripped of all the basic means required to make their legitimate grievances heard. To advocate structural reforms is to take a stand outside the system and risk dangerous repercussions. Technocratic military regimes are afraid of liberty exercised democratically by the common people.

In short, we can say that the system of domination that now pervades Latin America has been in the making throughout the region's history. It has always been dependent, first on Spain and Portugal, then on England, and now on the United States. Its whole cultural ethos is conditioned by this framework of dependence. Often this system is presented under the guise of nationalism, progressivism, or liberation. In reality, these are refined ways in which the system of domination co-opts the language of protest and maintains itself in power.

Latin America as a Product of Colonial Christianity and Ideological Manipulation

The pervasive system of dependence has also had an impact on the kind of Christianity that was planted here and allowed to grow. We must never forget that Latin America has been the only colonial Christian regime in history, and that it bears all the hallmarks of colonialism. European Christianity was not colonial but colonialist. It bore all the hallmarks of absolutism vis-à-vis truth, religious forms, and political ones. A quick glance back over the past few centuries of Christian life offers little in the way of an inspiring evangelical portrait. Exploitation and poverty have prevailed on a Catholic continent. As many official texts admit, the Catholic church must share responsibility for the present-day situation of domination and dependence. An imperialist ideology co-opted the messianic thrust, the eschatological hopefulness, and the revolutionary import of universal brotherhood that belong to the very core of the Christian faith. Thus the church became a religious counterpart of the expansionist ideology that characterized the Christian West.

On the one hand, we must confess that the Catholic church has been *a companion and an accomplice in the process of domination.* Though the church tackled the vast reaches of the landscape, planted the Christian message among the native populace, and preserved it among the European colonists, it also colluded with an imperial government that came here for baser motives. The latter wanted to exploit the natural resources of this area for its own selfish interests. The whole effort at conquest was marked by both a desire to spread the faith and imperial ambitions. Evangelization was marked by reactionary, warlike, and anti-Reformation tendencies in Iberian Catholicism.

The native Indian was an infidel to be fought and subdued. Mission work was a holy war. Instead of real human encounter, the Constantinian system of Christian Europe was imposed by fire and sword. No serious theological approach to the religions of the native civilizations was made. They were viewed as the work of the Devil, to be exorcised or extinguished. All too often the Indians were viewed as something less than human, as irrational and beastly creatures.[11] The European colonists felt every right to subdue these people and deprive them of their native resources. With prophetic courage Bartolomé de Las Casas went to the root of the matter:

The ultimate reason why Christians slew such an infinite number of souls was their greed for gold. They sought to get rich quick and attain higher social status than they deserved.[12]

The church accompanied this process of imperialist colonization. It transplanted the ecclesiastical institutions of Europe to our soil.[13] It made no real effort to build a native church. The whole process of dependence finds its ecclesial counterpart in the work of the Catholic church in Latin America; but this process is even more acute because it was upheld by dogma and an aura of sacredness.

It cannot be denied that the official church took the side of the elite during much of Latin American history. In the *Introduction* to its concluding papers, the 1968 Medellín Conference acknowledged as much:

The Church . . . must acknowledge that throughout the course of history all her members, clergy and lay, have not always been faithful to the Holy Spirit (n. 2).

The official church certainly was not at the forefront of any liberation movement, either from the centers of power, or from the bondage of slavery, or from the more recent bonds of social injustice. Its class status seemed to keep it from even taking cognizance of the social situation with its poverty and marginalization. The official church was an accomplice for the system of dependence and helped to solidify a discriminatory social order. At the 1974 Synod of Bishops Dom Helder Camara had this to say:

Without passing judgment on our predecessors, the bishops and priests of Latin America and the affluent countries, we must admit that we are so concerned to maintain authority and social order that we have not been able to realize that the existing "social order" is, for the most part, a highly stratified disorder.[14]

At the same time the Christian people as a group lived out the Christian faith in their own way, though they had been despised and somewhat abandoned by the official clergy and its orthodoxy. In a highly original effort at analysis Eduardo Hoornaert, a historian, recounts how the popular religiosity of Brazil sought to incarnate the principles of Christianity.[15] Popular religious practices are not a decadent form of the official religion. They are a legitimate and autonomous way of living the gospel message in the face of clerical elitism and its abstractions. Though it does contain ambiguities and alienating aspects, it also contains solidly liberative values. In the words of Capistrano de Abreu, our people have been bloodied and castrated time and again. It was through their own popular religion that they found the strength and meaningfulness they needed to survive, to go on being Christians without falling prey to despair.

On the other side of the coin, however, the Catholic church has also been *involved in the process of liberation*. Despite all its complicity with the centers of power, the church has also kept alive its evangelical awareness of the human dignity of the Indians, the blacks, and the poor. Throughout the continent we find a tradition of cassock-garbed patriots who fought hard for the freedom of their people and sacrificed their own lives in that cause. It is a tradition that stretches from Las Casas and Vieira to Camilo Torres and Dom Helder Camara.[16] The few who managed to get an education in Latin America are indebted to the clergy, as José Honório Rodrigues, a Brazilian historian, has pointed out.[17] The lower ranks of the clergy lived in the midst of the common people and shared their problems. They have been one of the most effective champions of social justice and libertarian ideas.

The great turn toward the people embodied in the Medellín Conference is part of a tradition that has always been there. Some have always put themselves solidly behind the project to liberate our continent. The new identification of the church with the poor and oppressed has given added impetus and unequalled publicity to the cause of liberation. The church has taken cognizance of its evangelical destiny, realizing that the latter is intimately bound up with the political and human destiny of the marginalized classes. If the latter do not attain their basic rights, then the church knows that it will have failed in its evangelical mission. The salvation it proclaims finds concrete embodiment in the concrete vicissitudes of history. Only in terms of the latter does it make sense to proclaim the fuller freedom of the kingdom of God. That is why theological reflection in Latin America has led to the elaboration of a theology of liberation, which seeks to link up our praxis of faith with the process of liberation going on all over our area.

CHAPTER 8

Experiencing Grace in the Reality
of Latin America: Responses

My reflections in the previous chapter presented a highly negative diagnosis, but that is only one side of the story. Heightened awareness of Latin America as a dependent reality has provoked much reaction on both the level of reflection and that of practice. Let us briefly consider some of these hopeful reactions.

Critical Analysis from the Periphery

The first step was a vivid realization of Latin America's situation vis-à-vis social realities in other parts of the world. We came to see more clearly how Latin America is characterized by backwardness, poverty, and marginality. Analysis was intertwined with various forms of diagnosis and interpretation that ranged from one end of the spectrum to the other. Some saw underdevelopment in terms of technological backwardness and urged industrialization. Some offered a more political interpretation. They saw the interdependence of numerous countries within one and the same politico-economic system and insisted that large investments of foreign aid were needed to overcome underdevelopment. Still others focused on the theory of dependence, regarding underdevelopment as a result of the one-sided growth of the metropolitan centers of power.

The theory of dependence was the first serious sociological attempt to ponder the situation from the standpoint of the periphery. It grasped the structural nature of underdevelopment, its pervasive and dialectical nature as a process going on with the western system itself. Dependence is not something merely external. It is also an internalized process at work within underdeveloped nations to maintain them in the context of periphery versus power center.

Latin American theoreticians of dependence offered political strategies for breaking the ties of oppression and proceeding on the road to liberation. Development would entail changing the existing social structure and creating a new society. There was renewed interest in native values, popular culture, and past historical movements that had vainly tried to effect liberation.[1] The creation of new forms of social coexistence would presuppose mobilizing all the various social forces and drafting new plans for the use of economic resources and production forces.

There was no reason to assume that the centers of power would give up their domination of their own accord. Hence the proposed strategy was obviously revolutionary. New forms of independence would entail the liberation of Latin America. This realization led to a vast effort at consciousness raising (conscientization) throughout our continent. Bold groups shifted to revolutionary practices, becoming urban and rural guerillas. The results were meager because they only exacerbated the countervailing forces of repression. Revolutions are not merely the result of willpower. As one author has put it: "Human beings can make only those revolutions that are themselves in the making."[2] People must submit to the inner laws and objective conditions of revolution. They cannot get far solely with the willed imperatives of some revolutionary ideology.

More moderate advocates of the theory of dependence showed greater historical sense. Aware of the mediating political factors and strategies in any revolution, they proposed to change the system by effecting changes *within* the system. They were not renouncing the ideal of full liberation; they were simply offering a realistic strategy for attaining it through concrete historical processes. Liberation is to be viewed as something already under way but not yet complete.

The shortcomings of the theory of dependence cannot be overlooked. It does not suffice to diagnose the structure of dependence and propose an alternative. We must ask whether objective historical factors exist that would make the alternative viable. A revolution confined to some region of the continent is politically impractical. The existing system has enough coercive force to bring rebelling nations back into line. The case of Chile is instructive in this regard. The political alternative of the theoreticians of dependence has not yet been implemented because it is inadequate. As was the case with many empires in the past, the present imperial system is able to restore its inner equilibrium and remain in force for a long time.

The politico-economic model adopted by Brazil poses serious challenges to the theory of dependence. By agreeing to ally itself with the economic centers of power, accepting generous amounts of foreign aid, and permitting multinational companies to establish themselves within its borders, Brazil has been able to attain high levels of economic growth. The idea is that the pie must first be made larger if it is to be shared equally by the largest number of people possible. In the case of Brazil it seems that economic growth can be strong enough to enable a country to compete with certain economic centers of power and even set up a subsidiary empire of its own. The greatly improved situation of the ruling classes will presumably create an overflow that will trickle down to the other social classes. Integrist theories of development, which support involvement with the centers of power, talk sympathetically about the "Canadizing" of Brazil as a model for the whole Latin American continent to follow. It seems more pragmatic and immediately viable.

The theory of dependence rightly grasps the *fact* of dependence. But dependence cannot be reduced to the economic factor alone as the sole cause of underdevelopment. Other social and cultural variables have something to do with underdevelopment even though they may not be directly related to economic dependence. Some peoples still live in a traditional culture where the categories of progress, reform, and liberation have no meaning or real impact. Those categories are usually meaningful to people living in typical examples of western culture. The problem of differing worldviews and cultural frames of reference has not been sufficiently thought through by the theory of dependence.

There are other problems of a biological and sanitary nature. For example, how will Brazil be able to maintain a rapid rate of progress and achieve liberation for its people when 70 percent of its people are sick? What is greatly needed is a national awareness that will enable people to elaborate their own project and then launch into the process of liberation while still taking cognizance of the interconnectedness of the modern world and the intertwined destiny of each country with all others.

An industrial society based on consumption prevails both in the capitalist world and in the socialist-communist world. It requires sophisticated technologies and access to large supplies of capital. Political liberation has certainly led to independence of a sort, but it has not led to development for satellites and former satellites because they lack technological resources of their own. No country can develop on its own, and so we face the dilemma posed by Comblin:

Either a country chooses to liberate itself and not achieve development, or else it chooses development and hence submission. . . . The third possibility is a compromise position. A country may choose to undergo limited development while still retaining a certain amount of autonomy, or to limit the degree of dependence by choosing to develop only certain specific sectors. But that takes us far beyond any simplistic theory of dependence.[3]

The question of social change is always a problem of scientific reasonableness and historical viability. All too frequently these factors contradict the humanitarian ideals of full and integral development. There are other more thoroughgoing reforms which are much more than developmentalism or refurbishings of the existing system. They are truly revolutionary reforms that pave the way for the gradual overthrow of a whole societal system.

Elaboration of a Native Theology

Theological and pastoral reflection in Latin America accepted the challenge posed by this modern, scientific analysis of our continental situation.

At great cost it managed to free itself from the confines of a theology centered around orthodoxy and antiseptic formulas unconnected with the historical praxis of the faith.

This theological reflection has begun to ponder its own concrete problems.[4] The poverty and marginalization of millions is not just a sociological datum. In the eyes of faith it is an embodiment of sin and injustice. In history and contemporary Latin American society it sees a rejection of God's plan for brotherhood, participation, justice, and solidarity. Doing theology no longer means looking for the rationale in adhering to abstract truths of faith. It means reflecting critically on the praxis of the Christian faith. As I noted earlier, one praxis of the faith in our area did not lead to more humanitarian transformations of the social order; it was easily manipulated to hallow a discriminatory situation. At the 1971 Synod of Bishops in Rome Barbara Ward commented on the shortcomings in earlier training of the Christian conscience. Such training was often limited to attendance at Mass on Sundays and obedience to the laws of the church regulating sex and marriage. No fault was seen in the fact that some Christians lived like the rich man in the parable while others grovelled outside the door like the poor man, Lazarus.

The 1968 Medellín Conference took cognizance of the need for a new and revitalized praxis of the Christian faith that would foster societal transformation and liberation. This gave rise to the theology of liberation, which is a critical attempt to spell out how Christian love may effectively commit itself to social, economic, political, and religious liberation. Here I should like to offer a brief description of this autochthonous theology and its main features.

Liberation theology begins with an *analytical, sociological, and structural reading of reality that is as scientific as possible.* To a large extent it has accepted the analysis offered by the theory of dependence, with the modifications injected by relevant criticism of that theory. However, liberation theology takes this sociological reading one step further by engaging in reflections of a philosophical and cultural nature. Sociological diagnosis of reality is not enough. Capitalism, industrialism, and socialist forms of government are embodiments of a more basic human option, of a whole cultural ethos that has its own history of concrete forms.

Human beings have opted for a certain attitude toward life and its meaning. This particular option seeks knowledge of, and power over, the world and other people. It has taken many concrete historical forms from the days of the ancient Greeks down to our own time. Today it takes the form of industrial capitalism as exemplified by the multinational corporations. No revolution is authentic if it fails to eliminate or change this attitude toward life that fetters human beings and prevents them from achieving fulfillment. That was the problem with the socialist revolution in Russia, which has produced the present Russian empire. We today are the captives of a cultural ethos. We are caught under the weight of its historical institutions and embodiments, which prevent human beings from blossoming as such. Progress is won at an inequitable social price; the blood of many must be sacrificed so that a few can

reap the benefits. This oppression has aroused people's yearning for liberation. It is a utopian project insofar as it is all-embracing and insofar as it
contains an eschatological dimension, i.e., total liberation from sin and death.

But it is not enough to offer a sound diagnosis of reality and elaborate some
utopian way out. The problem of concrete strategy and its implementation
must be faced. How is liberation to be achieved under the captive conditions
controlling the world right now? Proposed revolutionary approaches seem to
be too utopian and not viable politically. Revolutionary transformations
within the existing system would seem to offer us a way to arrive gradually at a
more just and equitable system.

Starting from the above reading of reality, liberation theology then proceeds to *its own theological reading based on the word of God*. It sees the various
aspects of reality as manifestations of grace and sin. In the interplay of human
interests people embody their acceptance or rejection of God's design. Thus
the Christian conscience feels summoned to take effective action that will
help people to get beyond a situation offensive to God and their fellows.
Stress is placed on the concrete practice of a liberative faith. Theology will be
a second-stage act of reflection on that practice in order to make the latter
more authentic and effective.

Such a theology then faces two tasks. First, it must liberate theology itself
from an excessively generalizing or universalizing tendency and from a
practice of faith that is completely uncritical with regard to its economic and
political presuppositions. It must then proceed to bring out the liberative
dimensions in the Christian faith and its major theological themes which have
been concealed by one particular way of understanding that faith and one
particular Christian life-style. This would include the social and political
dimensions in such themes as the kingdom of God, eschatology, sin, grace,
and the liberation brought by Jesus Christ. It would also embrace the liberative aspects of catechetics, homilies, and the sacraments.

Second, such a theology must also rescue and uphold the theological
perspective present in any authentic process of liberation, even though the
latter may be implemented by people who make no reference at all to the
Christian faith. The theological aspect of their activity does not depend on
their own ideological interpretation of such activity. It is to be found in the
objective liberation and creation of humanity which is implied in such
activity. In other words, praxis itself is fraught with Christian import insofar
as it is a truly liberative praxis.

Integral liberation is an eschatological reality. It falls under the heading of
utopia. But precisely because it is eschatological, it is anticipated here and
now in history through partial liberations, all of which form part of one single
liberation process. None of the partial liberations is full liberation, but
without them full liberation would be a figment of the human imagination
rather than an eschatological reality anticipated in history.

Thus eschatological liberation finds concrete embodiments in politics, economics, culture, religion, and so forth. Everything has something to do with the kingdom of God; hence everything can possess some aspect of salvation or damnation. As one fine Latin American theologian has put it:

God's eschatological salvation does not come solely through political liberation in history, but it cannot come without the latter either. The political dimension is not everything, but it is part of the salvation context.[5]

Liberation theology culminates in a *new praxis of the faith* that aids human beings in their liberation process. Obviously it is not for faith or the church to spell out tactics and strategy in the political arena. Its concern is to shoulder the basic options for liberation which Christians and other human beings live out in their lives. In the realm of pastoral theology its action is concretized in a strategy of action which will ensure effectiveness to the political and social dimensions of faith, evangelical proclamation, charity, and so forth.[6]

Certain pertinent questions arise at this point. How is catechesis to be organized so that it will effectively further religious enlightenment rather than impeding it? What concrete steps should the church take to help people overcome unjust situations that it regards as a break with God and our fellow human beings?

The mission of faith is to go to the root of problems. While respecting the various levels of rational thinking, it must make it clear to people that political and economic solutions are not enough in themselves. We must strive to create the new human being and adopt a more fraternal and just attitude toward reality. We must also seek out the mediations that will make such a project historically viable.[7] Here countless variables and questions of strategy come into play, and we must possess a sense of history. Existing conditions may rule out the possibility of proposing some radically qualitative leap. Liberation at any cost is not to be envisioned, since that may only aggravate the present situation of the oppressed. An attitude of patient hope is meaningful, and it need not deprive action of its efficacy. Faith is particularly obliged to see and live out the mystical dimension of liberation even within a general context of pervasive oppression.

Guidelines for a Theological Reading of Reality

The task of theological reflection is to try to discern the plan of God in historical situations. Here our concern is to discern the dimensions of grace and dis-grace in the reality of Latin America. To what extent is eschatological grace being anticipated and realized in time, and to what extent is it being refused?

Our reflections so far might well incline us to feel that the scale is heavily weighted towards the side of dis-grace. But is that really true? How does theology know that what appears as dis-grace in terms of social analysis is also dis-grace in theological terms? This question compels us to consider briefly the underlying guidelines for any theological reading or interpretation. The issue is a complex one calling for extended treatment, but here I shall simply discuss a few basic guidelines for our reflection.

To begin with, there are not two separate realities: one the object of sociological consideration and the other the object of theology. Reality is one. Hence the church and the world do not have two different ends or goals. The eschatological goal of the world is also the eschatological goal of the church. So we can conclude that grace and dis-grace are dimensions of one and the same reality; they are not isolated dimensions immured within the confines of the church.

It is a difference in outlook and experience that gives rise to two different readings. The outlook of social analysis sees the conflict-ridden aspects of the world. It detects poverty and misery, and it then explores their underlying causes. They are the result of the way human beings relate to the things of this world in a system based on private ownership of the means and products of production. Egotism and individualism imbedded in the very heart of the economic system are at the root of the tragic drama that characterizes western societies, particularly those in Latin America.

Faith contemplates reality as it is mediated to it by this socio-political reading. Where the latter sees the toll of social inequality, faith sees the presence of sin. Relations between human beings themselves, and between human beings and God, have become distorted. But faith does not stop with the reading mediated to it through sociological analysis. It has its own proper horizon and its own specific reading that need not necessarily come by way of scientific analysis. To use an expression of Lucio Gera, faith's perception of reality is symbolic and sacramental by its very nature.[8] At a glance the people of God intuit whether a given situation has salvific import or just the opposite. They see that a given situation contradicts God's design. Poverty and humiliation, the violation of human rights, and the exploitation of human labor do not mesh with God's project of salvation. Moreover, they realize that the yearnings to attain liberation and create a more just and fraternal society are the grace of God, motivating people to undertake a transforming praxis. In these signs of the times, which are sacraments and symbols, faith glimpses the road that God would want human beings to follow.

Faith has its own sources. The reflection of the believing community in history has ever tried to view reality in the light of God or of Jesus Christ. This reflection is preserved in Scripture and tradition, and it is still alive today. Thanks to this body of reflection, faith knows that evil endures in the world, that it takes structured shape both in the individual person and society, and that grace is also ever present in the form of historical liberation. In the light of faith the Christian also knows that, despite the ambiguous tension between grace and sin, there is always a surplus of grace. In the end no competitor can outdo it; it is always victorious. The human capacity for rejecting God and sinning is never the equal of God's offering of grace. Grace ever remains the greater, because even the refusal of grace is grounded on the gift of *being able to refuse it*. The latter ability was given to human beings by God, and he respects it.

In such cases grace finds other ways to operate, and meaning is achieved through other courses. Like water, grace will not let obstacles stand in its way. It knocks them down, or filters through them, or gradually wears them away. This realization gives rise to an invincible hope. What ought to be has a power of its own, and no one can keep it down. Some day justice will overcome, and historical grace will bear its full fruit in the midst of human beings.[9]

Thanks to the overriding excellence of grace by comparison with sin, faith is convinced that all evil and dis-grace can be reconverted into goodness and grace.[10] Everything depends on the attitude of human beings toward evil, misery, and sin. Because it is stronger than sin, grace at work in human beings can turn even poverty into a way to human exaltation. This is not to say that we should stop fighting evil in the world. We must create conditions that will stop perpetuating the cross of Christ and the martyrdom of the oppressed in history. But even if those events go on, human beings can be greater than they are. Humans can freely shoulder the burdens and overcome them, revealing a grandeur amid humiliation that far exceeds any grandeur created by humanity's will to power.

It is in that sense that Augustine talks about the "happy fault." It is not meant to be a justification of sin. Instead it is an apology for grace, which cannot be limited by sin. Thus the reconversion of evil into good can serve as a criterion of historical interpretation for faith. The age-old suffering of the Latin American people must have some meaning. It should be paving the way for a major turning point in history, for a more fraternal and humane type of human being. It cannot be totally without meaning.

The reality of Latin America brings out clearly the simultaneous existence of grace and dis-grace. Only a superficial or ideological analysis would make a neat division between the two, pinpointing grace here and dis-grace over there. In history we find an intermingling of liberation and oppression, salvation and damnation, the tares and the wheat. So it is with grace and dis-grace. No historical situation is so bad that it is pure oppression and leaves no room for grace. No historical situation is so good that it contains no traces of sin and oppression. Thus a truly coherent theological reading of reality cannot divide human beings neatly into oppressors and oppressed, or nations into developed and underdeveloped countries.

The relevance of some kind of sociological analysis remains undiminished, but we must also take cognizance of its limitations. Faith transcends these limitations. It cannot exhaust itself within such neat divisions without losing its nature as faith. It must say that every human being is simultaneously oppressor and oppressed, graced and dis-graced, however much this may offend political human beings and their desire to identify which is which. No one is so completely an oppressor that he or she can evade liberative grace completely. No one is so completely graced that he or she does not harbor inner traces of sinfulness and oppression.

Thus no matter how filled with oppression the history of Latin America is and has been, the presence of freedom and liberation can still be found in it. If it cannot be detected in the realm of politics or economics, we must look for it in other manifestations of human life. We must look for it where the common people can be themselves, where they can exercise freedom beyond the clutches of the powerful, where they can savor liberation in freedom from imperial control. If we seek the presence of freedom and liberation, we must look to the religious practice of the people, to their music and customs, to the warm-hearted human relations and qualities of Latin Americans, and to their ability to rejoice and celebrate amid pain and privation.[11] In the eyes of faith such manifestations are channels through which meaning is communicated and signs through which grace makes its presence felt in the world despite everything.

More than in most cases, the Latin American situation clearly reveals the structural nature of grace and dis-grace. One of the great defects of Christian reflection has been its failure to consider the structural side of problems. Theological tradition has engaged in minute analyses of the individual person and his or her conscious life in rejecting God or undergoing conversion. But it has done little to spell out the institutional and structural forms of grace and dis-grace. For this reason it is naive or voluntaristic when it tries to tackle the problems involved in social transformation.

In Latin America we see the profoundly structural dimensions of the human drama, which are largely independent of the concrete will of individual persons. The nicest and most well-intentioned people may still be living within a structure that produces oppression. They may be personally opposed to any and every sort of privilege, but still their class status may place them among the favored members of discriminatory society. Unwittingly, perhaps even against their will, they may be part of a structure that fosters structural injustice. This fact shows us once again that human beings in their present condition are both oppressors and oppressed, both just and sinful.

These basic guidelines should help us to examine the reality of Latin America in terms of grace and dis-grace. So we shall proceed to do that now.

Dis-grace and Grace in Latin America

From the standpoint of faith, the situation of dependence and underdevelopment that characterizes our continent cannot help but be seen as an enormous social and structural sin. The symptoms of dependence are clear and inescapable: hunger, infant mortality, endemic diseases, cheap manual labor, deteriorating pay scales, abandonment of the schools by young people who must help their families eke out a living, a lack of participation and freedom, an inability to gain recognition of the most basic human rights, political corruption, and control of the nation's wealth by a small but powerful elite. Such a situation produces an inhumane way of life, and marginalization prevents people from being real human beings.

These symptoms are manifestations of sin and give sin a structured place in the world. Yet there is nothing natural or inevitable about them. They are the result of an even greater sin, of a basic option that leads to the accumulation of wealth and power in the hands of egotistical minorities who have no social sense. The cultural ethos that informs and structures the capitalist mentality is profoundly antievangelical and inhuman. The aforementioned symptoms are embodiments of a mode of existence that cannot be upheld by faith. Indeed it must be denounced because it offends human beings and denies God, though the latter may often be on people's lips.

This structural sin takes on even more subtle forms when it is introjected into the minds and hearts of the oppressed themselves. Then they unconsciously accept the values of the prevailing system and the human image advocated by imperial governments and their agents. The ideology of the ruling class is passed off as a national value. It is taught in the schools and broadcast by the communications media. Failing to be critical enough, the intelligentsia gives up its own ideas and unwittingly plays the game of the oppressor. Individuals may personally have the best intentions in living their lives, but in structural terms they are the Herodian agents of sinfulness in the world.

Where are we to situate grace, on the personal level or the structural level? As we noted earlier, human beings live in both dimensions. Thus they show up concretely both as just people and as sinners. They inherit a history of sinfulness which they did not create, which has been taking shape in various ways ever since the rise of Latin America under European hegemony. They also inherit a history of grace that has been unfolding in that situation through the life-style of the common people, their concrete values in history, and their yearnings for liberation and human betterment.

When Christians take cognizance of the link between the personal and the structural levels, they can no longer rest content with a conversion of the heart and personal holiness on the individual level. They realize that if they are to be graced personally, they must also fight to change the societal structure and open it up to God's grace.[12] Insofar as the latter does not happen, their personal goodness will remain terribly ambiguous. It will generate both grace and dis-grace whether they will it or not. They will feel a need for pardon every day and they will not be able to rest content with a pharisaical reliance on a wholly inner Christian life.

This contradiction shows up even more obviously in the ecclesial sphere, where one would expect a keener awareness of structural sinfulness. As we noted earlier, the church in Latin America preached and lived the gospel message within a context that was strongly conditioned by political and imperial factors. Instead of stepping back and viewing these things critically, the church tended to become an integral part of that picture. This makes structural sin an even graver matter. Evil and wrongdoing attain their fullest form when they are committed by Christians who have the best intentions but who are naive and uncritical.

But faith can also see the eruption of grace in our area. Today it takes many forms. It can be seen in the present-day advertence to the situation of dependence and oppression that marks our area. It can be seen in concrete efforts to translate this new awareness into liberative praxis. It can be seen in the various signs of protest all over our continent. It can be seen in the renewed sense of social justice among young people and others who feel the urgent need for transformations.

The grace of God can be seen in the rise of a new kind of sociological reflection that unmasks imperial ideologies and fosters the ideal of liberation. The grace of God can be seen in the burgeoning pedagogy of the oppressed, which enables them to effect their own liberation, not in order to take revenge or oppress others but in order to take more responsible control of their collective destiny. The grace of God can be seen in the sense of solidarity with the wretched of the earth that prompts people to join them as human beings in the effort to facilitate love among human beings. The grace of God can be seen in the newfound awareness of the Latin American church, which now seeks to do penance for its past complicity with the status quo and to ally itself with the liberation process. The grace of God can be seen in the rediscovery of the common people, their culture, and their specific values. The grace of God can be seen in the emergence of so many prophetic figures who passionately fight for justice and are persecuted even unto death for their defense of those who have no voice. The grace of God can be seen in the effort of theology and the church to be faithful to the cries of the common people and to reincarnate the gospel message in the culture that is taking shape among them.

The victory of God's grace can be seen in the fact that the common people somehow manage to retain their freedom even though they are oppressed socially and politically. Oppression has not succeeded in dehumanizing them. They remain free in their popular culture, their religious practice, their music, their cuisine, and their language. They have not stopped being hospitable, gracious, and jovial in their music, their festivals, and their get-togethers. What may look like resignation and fatalism to the petit-bourgeois mentality may actually be the people's way of finding the strength they need to go on living and survive their burdens.

Finally, the grace of God is to be seen in our invincible certainty that we are nurturing a new kind of society more worthy of human beings and God. It will be born out of the contradictions of the present. In it all will enjoy greater participation, freedom, and justice. Sentiments of profound reconciliation can be found among those of loftier hearts and minds. They echo the sentiments which a Jew wrote out on a piece of wrapping paper before entering the gas chamber:

Lord, when you enter your glory, do not remember only people of good will. Remember also those of ill will. Do not remember their cruelty and their violence. Instead, be mindful of the fruits we bore because of what they did to us. Remember the patience of some and the courage of others. Recall the camaraderie, humility, fidelity, and greatness of soul which they awoke in us. And grant, O Lord, that the fruits we bore may one day be their redemption.

CHAPTER 9

Experiencing Grace in the Life of the Individual

So far we have tried to consider the experience of grace in the context of our scientific world and in terms of the concrete reality of Latin America. Now I want to get down to an even more concrete level, the life of the individual person. Though people are immersed in a sociocultural context, they nevertheless emerge as irreducibly individual. In some way each person is a totalization of the universe and hence possesses some absolute sense in himself or herself. All individuals live their own experience of grace, offering their own unique and personal yes to the supreme mystery of love.

As should be evident from all that has been said, we cannot get to the experience of grace unless we get beyond one obstacle posed by the modern mind. I refer to what might be called the spirit of geometry. We are accustomed to divide up reality into neat compartments. For example, at one pole lies God, at the other pole lies the world, and human beings stand somewhere in between. The Christian experience is neatly translated into dogmas, canons, traditions, commandments, and counsels. Such a mentality has its usefulness for the exact sciences, but it can be disastrous for theology.

God certainly does somehow enter into human conceptual categories, but he also causes them to break down. For holy things we have need of another spirit: the spirit of delicacy, cordiality, and courtesy. To the intellect we must add the heart, to the process of knowing we must add a sense of taste, and to instrumental reasoning we must add sapiential and sacramental reasoning. Through the qualities of sensitivity and cordiality we assume and transcend the divisions created by the spirit of geometry. We begin to perceive and savor the import of things that surpass practical ends and human interests. We arrive at a dimension that opens us up to the ultimate truth of the universe while still respecting its scientific truth. Sensitivity enables us to contemplate the world as something attached and reattached to a mystery. Christian tradition has referred to it as the mystery of divine grace present in things. This spirit of sensitivity generates cordiality and courtesy toward all the manifestations of life and the world. It opens our eyes to the additional dimensions present in every phenomenon. Things cease to be merely things and become sacraments of God and his love. The opaque immanence of the world and the abstract transcendence of God give way to the transparent presence of God in the world. When we Christians talk about grace, we envision something of that sort. We see God present in the world and at work transforming it. While preserving all its own solidity, the world becomes a sacrament, a vehicle for the concrete communication of God.

Our earlier reflections sought to bring out the theological reality of the world. It is imbued and suffused with the grace of God. Despite the presence of sin and the fact of human rejection, divine love never refuses or fails to communicate itself. God is ever fully present in the world, but the world is not always fully present in God. Human beings and the world do not always allow God to be transparent. They can prevent the presence of God from showing up phenomenologically. Such obstacles do not destroy the presence of God, but they do prevent it from historicizing itself in the world. They place obstacles in the way of the concrete experience of grace.

Humanity ever lives in the divine milieu of grace. It is, so to speak, the life within which we find ourselves. But what is life and how do we experience it? We cannot define life because we cannot step outside it. It is presupposed in any attempt to define it because one must first be alive. What we can do, however, is take cognizance of the structures of life that we find in ourselves and situate ourselves in the midst of life. Instead of trying to define life itself, we can try to define our position vis-à-vis life.

The situation is much the same with grace. We cannot pigeonhole it because it surrounds and envelops us. To experience grace is to experience the atmosphere of saving life that pervades us, to make way for the gratuitousness in which we move. We implicitly experience God and his grace in everything we think and do, but we are not always conscious of that fact. Our ignorance, on the other hand, does not destroy the reality; the latter is greater than the realm of consciousness. Consciousness is operative within reality, trying to lay hold of the latter, to accept or reject or modify it, to historicize itself in that reality.

One of the mistakes of the modern mentality has been its attempt to reduce reality to consciousness. The ontological began to predominate over the ontic. The ultimate mystery was reduced by consciousness to a mere problem or puzzle, and this led to an outbreak of anxiety. That is the way in which the ultimate mystery managed to remain present in human consciousness as something anonymous and unconscious. When the ultimate mystery is accepted, when reality is accepted as something "other" than consciousness, then there can be exchange, dialogue, opening out to the other in mutual self-giving, and joyous acceptance of novelty.

Now if we do live and move within the divine milieu of grace (see Acts 17:28), then any situation is capable of introducing us to the experience of grace. That is what I tried to show in the preceding chapters. Here I want to choose certain major aspects of personal living where the presence and import of grace are more clearly manifested. All such choosing is subjective to some extent, and we must remember that grace is not confined to the aspects mentioned here. Grace fills all life and the whole of life. But it is particularly transparent in the aspects discussed below.[1]

Experiencing Grace in the Specifically Spiritual Dimension of Human Beings

This kind of experience has been discussed sensitively and at length by Karl Rahner.[2] At some time or other we all have probably experienced the specifically spiritual dimension of a human being. Here I am not talking about the experience of thinking some thought, or appreciating some work of art or music, or even of enjoying some friendship. In such experiences we obviously sense the reality of the spirit and what it might mean. But there are other articulations which may well bring out more clearly what spirit is and can be as freedom and inner determination. There are certain situations which seem to be less human but which stand out as more truly human in the case of human beings.

Have we not had the experience of keeping silent when we were misunderstood and could have justified ourselves? Have we not had the experience of remaining silent when we were deeply and unfairly cut to the quick? Have we not had the experience of pardoning in all sincerity and gratuitousness? Have we not sometimes followed our conscience and maintained our purity of heart when we could have relented and won some personal advantage thereby? Have we not sometimes renounced certain benefits of a personal nature which others esteem highly because such benefits would compromise the path we have chosen in life? Have we not tried to love God faithfully in some fundamental option of the heart, rejecting an easier way which did not seem to be the right one for us even though it was legitimate in itself? Have we not perhaps accepted some personal limitation of an emotional or intellectual nature, or even some illness, without complaint? Have we not been willing to embrace and live an onerous existence courageously?

In such experiences we experience the specifically spiritual dimension of human beings. We experience a living transcendence that is greater than the world, more excellent than success, and more fulfilling than mere happiness. Spirit is not some part of the human being. It is the whole human being living in a transcendent way, capable of overcoming things and orienting itself above and beyond the pleasure principle. For those who live in this spiritual way, even calamity and dis-grace can be instruments of growth. The spiritual human being attains greater perfection through dis-grace while the foolish human being complains and sinks deeper into foolishness.

When we experience the spirit in this way, we also experience what grace and the supernatural mean. Here the spirit is no longer simply spirit; it is the Holy Spirit living in us and moving us.

We can entrust ourselves to the mystery of life. We can stop belonging to ourselves alone. We can stop putting ourselves first and give ourselves in loving service to others. We can believe and hope that nothing escapes the design of the ultimate mystery, that no evil or dis-grace can separate us from the love of God. When we do these things, then we experience the reality that Christianity calls grace.

Such an experience does not allow us to say: "Look! I have grace!" People who say that are already outside the bounds of grace because we cannot possess it. It is rather we who are possessed by it. We can seek and find it, or better, we are found by it, only if we forget about ourselves.

Experiencing Grace in the Fact of Existence

There is no reason why anything exists. Nothing in the world, not even the world itself, is necessary. Yet the world with all its things and facts does exist. It is pure gratuitousness standing before us as a brute fact and calling for some reason that transcends the world to justify its existence.

This experience is felt even more profoundly on the level of the person. A person does not emerge as an *en soi,* as a self-enclosed entity. Persons do not create themselves. Persons depend on others for their entrance into the world. Others loved them and accepted them when they entered the world at birth. Persons always find themselves to be created beings because they can only live as human beings insofar as they enter into the give-and-take of friendship, love, service, information, and so forth. In the realm of freedom, where the specifically human shows up more clearly, they experience the gratuitousness of encounter, the fortuitousness of love, and the unplanned nature of human reciprocity. The existence of the human person as such is absolutely gratuitous. We all experience the reality of our own contingency. There is no reason in the world why I should exist with all my personal, racial, cultural, religious, psychological, physical, and biological characteristics. And yet it is a fact that I do exist.

In dynamic and historical terms human persons do not possess a nature in all its fullness from the start. They must run their course, gradually winning their identity as they meet many other people. Freedom is the form in which persons express themselves in the world and thus fashion themselves. Speaking in historical terms, we can say that our complete nature as persons will be attained only at the end of our journey. Human persons create their personality through effort and the exercise of their freedom. It is not fated. It is not the automatic, mechanical consequence of some fixed plan. Instead it results from the interplay of freedoms that came as a gift from others, from unforeseen encounters, and from a history whose future is not always predictable. Herein lies the dimension of gratuitousness that is a component of every personal existence.

Modern human beings do not have difficulty experiencing that sort of gratuitousness on the personal level. The main problem in this area has been in connection with the image of the world that science has offered us at any given stage of its development.[3] For example, classical physics presented a closed system based on order, physical necessity, and the immutable laws of nature. Chance was a problem for the philosophy of science and for religion. People tried to tackle it in terms of the as yet undiscovered import of the laws of nature. In other words, chance showed up where we were as yet ignorant of the true cause of something. However, current science is more inclined to offer us open-ended systems. Atomic physics, biochemistry, Planck's quantum theory, and Heisenberg's theory of indeterminacy on the subatomic level put us in contact with a different kind of experience. Here the more basic experience is one of chance and probabilities, and it is against this new backdrop that we must interpret the meaning of natural laws. Physical laws are statistical laws. They are the concrete embodiment of one probability among many others. In other words, the world is not ready-made and finished once and for all, nor is it dominated by blind, inner necessity. If we set up certain artificial conditions, we can produce new configurations of atoms and molecules. Atomic processes are discontinuous, operating in bundles of energy called quanta, according to Max Planck. The various combinations cannot be completely predicted. A principle of indeterminacy prevails, so that chance combinations are possible.

This holds true in particular for the combination that is responsible for life on earth: the DNA chain. At some particular point in the history of our planet, one probability among millions was actually realized. Life arose, and it is characterized by the exact duplication of the chain. Differences in the forms of life are due to irregularities in the transmission of the DNA chain, which in turn stabilize and become necessary. This physical chance, which is present at the origins of life, endures throughout the course of life itself. Although the DNA chain has a tendency to maintain itself, certain casual irregularities begin to mount up; eventually the organism begins to decompose and finally withers away completely.

In the light of this scientific evidence, many would now say that chance and indeterminacy are the most universal and satisfactory categories for interpreting the world. They would seem to be far more suitable than such categories as order and harmony.

But chance is only one facet of reality. These chance combinations tend to constitute a relatively stable order or system. Ludwig von Bertalanffy, the great theoretician of general system theory, had this to say:

We can say . . . that in modern science the notion of isolatable units operating simply in terms of chance has proved to be inadequate. This explains the appearance of holistic, organic and gestalt concepts in every field of science. All suggest that we must think in terms of systems of elements interacting mutually. Similarly, the notions of teleology and finality once seemed to lie outside the range of science. . . . They were viewed as a false problem, . . . a mistaken projection of the spirit of the observer onto a nature governed by laws which had no finality. Yet those aspects do in fact exist. We cannot conceive any living organism, much less human society and behavior, without taking account of what is variously and somewhat imprecisely called adaptation, finality, intentionality, etc.[4]

By the same token, however, these systems cannot be deduced from some principle or inexorable law. The indeterminacy of unpredictable elements persists. This gives rise to new units that possess their own finality, but it can only be analyzed *a posteriori*.

Faith in a personal, provident God is not threatened by such an image of the world. God is not a category designed to offer a direct and immediate explanation of intraworldly phenomena. It is the word we use for the mystery embodied in the existence of the world as a total fact. As a fact it is not a scientific problem, though it continues to require some explanation for its existence. In the eyes of faith God is the one who has set everything in motion. This motion may well take the form of chance combinations and accidental processes that tend to form ever more complex units and systems. The latter in turn raise the question of some final, eschatological unity. Where is this journey heading, toward total disorder or toward some good, well-ordered end?

Chance does not suggest cosmic anarchy but an order open to new syntheses and systems. It is an anticipation of some potential order of an ultimate sort. Faith in God is faith in some ultimate meaning. Believing in God does not mean replacing the chanciness of intraworldly phenomena with some higher providence, because divine providence is not on the same level as phenomena. Believing in God means assuming that God lets the world alone insofar as its autonomy and the interplay of its combinations are concerned. This is not an assumption based on deism but one grounded on a correct theology of secularization.

God does not enter the picture directly as a worldly phenomenon might. Instead he is the principle and foundation that makes all things possible. The concrete and immediate operation of phenomena, however, takes place in the interplay of probabilities. It is that interplay which gives rise to units and systems which embody some meaning and finality. To believe in God is to believe that these meanings, which are shaped within the world, will not suffer absolute frustration; that they are anticipations of the ultimate meaning of the whole cosmos, which Jesus referred to as the kingdom of God. Luck and chance are thus enveloped in a higher meaning, while they serve as the forms in which intraworldly meaning is embodied and made available to scientific inquiry.

Neither does knowledge end within the possibilities of science. It, too, raises questions about the future and the whole. It, too, is brought face to face with the whole dimension of gratuitousness. The world as a total fact is gratuitous. Intraworldly phenomena are ruled by a scientific form of gratuitousness called chance. In turn, the latter is involved in the formation of units with systematic and teleological characteristics that suggest the probable emergence of some solid meaning for all creation.

The Christian faith also reckons with an exceptional precedent that breaks through the ironclad chain of life and death. It is the resurrection of Jesus Christ, which offers us hope and assurance that all reality will end up well. The grace of the beginning links up with the grace of the ending. But to perceive this we have need of sapiential reasoning, which transcends analytical and instrumental reasoning.

Experiencing Grace in the Unforeseeable

Imagine someone driving a car along the highway. Suddenly another car speeds past and cuts in front, forcing our driver to slow down. A few moments later the car in front crashes into some obstacle on the road and its driver is killed, while the car behind has enough time to come to a safe stop. Surely the driver in the rear car would realize that he might have been killed if the other car had not cut in front of him earlier. He might be inclined to ask: why was I spared this time? Why did that other car cut in front of me just when it did? Somehow it seems to be more than chance, and our driver feels that he ought to thank someone. In most cases people in such a situation are likely to thank God and his mysterious design. They feel that the thing that happened and their experience of unforeseeable gratuitousness are somehow connected with a Person who arranges everything. They can understand why G. K. Chesterton said that the worst moment for the atheist was when he or she felt the need to say thanks but didn't know whom to thank.

Certain happenings seem to be so charged with meaningfulness that they cannot be adequately explained in terms of "luck" or "chance." The grandeur of the happening seems to be of a transcendent and personal nature. Here we might do well to make a distinction between "chance" and grace. As we noted in the previous section, chance or luck can occur in the casual interplay of probabilities. Winning a lottery need not be experienced as a grace; generally it is experienced as a stroke of luck. Even if it is interpreted as grace, that would be nothing more than a subjective judgment; someone else might judge it to be a happy coincidence. The dimension of grace emerges when an event possesses such human, existential density that it provokes a person to a decision for God. The sense of fulfillment is so clear that it turns the person toward a higher court of appeal and invites some act of thanksgiving.

Paradoxical as it may seem, if grace is to be experienced as grace, it must break in as the crowning culmination of some effort, some quest, some pain-filled hope. Thus it was that Abraham and Sarah celebrated the birth of Isaac as the grace of God. The same was true for the parents of Samuel and John the Baptist. Having a child is one of the concrete possibilities for a fertile couple; it is not so for a barren couple. The latter are confronted with an insuperable barrier beyond their concrete possibilities. Then suddenly the barren couple gets the child they had yearned for so long. What had seemed concretely (not metaphysically) impossible suddenly became possible; it was the grace of God. Grace does not exempt human beings from effort and searching. Paternalism is "grace" given without any effort or suffering being expended. It does not enlarge human beings or open them to an act of thanksgiving. Instead it humiliates human beings because it leaves them in the same state of dependence and keeps them as charity cases. The grace that elevates human beings must be a gift following upon human effort. Then the whole work is that of God and of human beings simultaneously, and both can celebrate a grace-filled encounter. That is what grace is.

Experiencing Grace in Legal Relationships

The gratuitousness present in life is also manifested in the social and legal relationships of a community. A criminal is sentenced for his or her crimes. The penal code is applied to the case. If the sentence is shortened or commuted for some extralegal reason, then the convict feels that he or she has been graced. We even talk about "grace periods" in different contexts.

We can have the same experience in dealing with the civil bureaucracy. The laws have their own weight, but a lot depends on their interpretation. One person may interpret them very strictly, following the exact letter of the law. Another person may interpret them more benevolently, so that people are benefited by them. There is some truth in the remark that we apply the law to our enemies and try to do justice for our friends.

There is a difference between legality and justice, between following the letter of the law and following its spirit. True justice is not exhausted in the codification of laws. There is another factor which escapes the letter of the law, i.e., the particular human individual and his or her particular problem. When people feel that they and their claims have been given a respectful hearing despite the letter of the law, they feel graced. They have experienced what gratuitousness means.

Experiencing Grace in the Realm of Creativity

The realm of spontaneous creativity is certainly one of the areas of human experience where gratuitousness shows up most clearly. We stand in wonder at an uneducated poet who can string verses together in a wondrous succession of original thoughts and images. Idea and rhyme flow with what seems to be absolute spontaneity. The agile brush of a painter or the fingers of a violinist create a whole new universe of colors or sounds in a matter of moments. This creativity seems to well up like a fountain. It cannot be forced or produced by a sheer act of will. The person seems to be the locale where a daimon or a genie is at work. That is why we commonly refer to people of great spontaneous creativity as geniuses.

The poet, the musician, and the writer feel overtaken by inspiration. On the one hand, it is they who do the work. Their energy and their deepest selves are totally involved. The effort to express themselves often leads to complete exhaustion. On the other hand, they feel possessed by something that is above them, outside them, or within them. It drives them to create, compelling them to express their inner experience to the outside world. The poet exclaims that he is overtaken by words. The painter explains that forms and colors take possession of him. It is an experience of gratuitousness.

Artistic creativity does not dispense us from effort, serious preparation, and discipline. But these things merely pave the way for inspiration. Inspiration itself cannot be produced. It breaks in unexpectedly. This explains the importance of the right moment, when a host of imponderable factors come together to allow for the explosive emergence of creativity. That is why people make a distinction between technique and creativity. Technique can be exercised anytime. Creativity has its own time, and it cannot be compelled to show itself whenever one wills it. The sheer exercise of willpower produces work. The result of creativity is a masterwork. The latter, as we noted above, does not dispense us from work; but our effort and work is to give shape to the creative impulse, to channel it, to subject it to the rigor of an ascetic ordering process. Through this process artists succeed in expressing all that they can, without losing themselves in dionysiac enjoyment of the impulse that has seized them. Through effort and assiduous work people of genius can rise to an authentic universality and somehow speak for all human beings and all ages.

Linked to creativity is fantasy and creative imagination. Modern studies have shown convincingly that fantasy is not mere fancifulness or a mechanism for escaping from conflict-ridden reality.[5] It is the key to explaining authentic creativity even in science. Creative imagination enables us to break away from things that are taken for granted, to abandon accepted presuppositions and begin to think in unorthodox ways. It enables us to set off on a different road or head in a different direction. Fantasy enables us to unmask the limitations of reality. The latter is the concrete embodiment of one possibility, as we noted above. But all the other infinite possibilities are not thereby squelched. With them human beings can dream about and even construct what has not yet been experienced in reality before. They can be turned into reality because life is stronger than the structures that serve as its support and framework.

Thus the last and decisive word does not go to bare facts. The truly creative word has not yet been pronounced. Liberation has not yet been completely effected. Fantasy preserves the primacy of the future and of hope over the brutal reality of facts and the heavy weight of the present. Through it human beings manifest their innermost essence, their capacity to transcend and to keep on living above and beyond all limits. As Harvey Cox has pointed out, fantasy is the soil in which humanity's capacity for invention and innovation flourishes. Fantasy is the richest source of human creativity. Theologically speaking, fantasy is the image of the creator God in human beings. With fantasy human beings, like God, create entire worlds out of nothing.[6] It is fantasy that nourishes the principle of hope in human beings and the utopian dimension that keeps history moving forward. It keeps opening humanity to the future and revitalizing history, liberating both from the sclerotic hold of their own prior constructions. It is within the horizon of imagination and fantasy that gratuitousness shows up for what it truly is.

Experiencing Grace in Success

Success is the fruit of a gift and of human effort. Without the gift and the initial motivating force there would be no creative will. Without effort and struggle there would be no victory. It is the happy conjunction of gift and effort that turns life into a gratifying experience and grants it fulfillment. We feel personally fulfilled, glad to be alive. Life seems to be filled with meaning. The element of gratuitousness is revealed in the fact that we have attained success amid the manifold variables that seem to lie beyond the manipulative power of human beings. We are led to give thanks. We rejoice over the fulfillment attained. We share our success within the circle of our friends, rejoicing, celebrating, and partying.

The element of grace in all this appears on the scene when human beings recognize the element of gift in all their efforts. As Pelé, the great soccer star, put it: "Please let me play the game that God has granted me." Recognition of the gratuitous element generates humility, simplicity, and a feeling of being inhabited by Someone greater than ourselves. Success does not make us proud nor close us to the most basic dimensions of life, e.g., being open to others, knowing how to while away time with our friends, retaining an eye for an unselfish appreciation of beauty, affection, and the obscure reaches of day-to-day life. Such an attitude evokes corresponding reactions from others. It evokes their sympathy, their human admiration, and a personal transparency.

When the gratuitous element is not recognized, when success is attributed solely to our own human efforts, this gives rise to ostentatious display. An inflated sense of self and an overweening pride prompt people to put themselves first at all times. This gives rise to artificiality, to theatrical airs, to masks, to complicated wheelings and dealings, and to a neurotic preoccupation with our own self-image. We can admire the success of such a person, but we begin to develop an antipathy toward the person in question. Such people begin to lose their luster and their ability to communicate with others. Isolation and loneliness are the punishment inflicted on those who have succeeded indeed, but who have fallen prey to vanity and pride. In the latter example we can readily see what dis-grace means when a gift is not recognized as such by its recipient.

Experiencing Grace in Festive Celebrations and at Play

Festive celebrations represent a high point in life where gratuitousness shows up clearly.[7] Festive celebrations are not characterized by selfish interests and practical usefulness but by pure gratuitousness. They possess their own intrinsic meaning as occasions for celebrating the joy of living. Festive celebrations proclaim the goodness of the world. During the time of festivity we celebrate the reconciliation of human beings and of all things. Clock time is suspended, and so are the conflicts between human beings. We rejoice in anticipating paradise. A festive day is a holiday, a day free from servile work and its focus on selfish interests. For a time we break with our day-to-day routine. That is why a festive day is different from other days.

Celebration implies a certain excess. It breaks through common standards, formalities, and our habitual frugality. It is, in short, a phenomenon of affluence and wealth. This is not to say that we possess a lot of money. The wealth of festive celebration is the wealth of the heart, of joy, of affirming the goodness of the world. That is why this type of wealth does not permit our excess to degenerate into an orgy as so often happens with people who are rich in money. Joseph Pieper, the great student of festivity, reminds us what the real reason for joy in festivity is:

The reason for joy, although it may be encountered in a thousand concrete forms, is always the same: possessing or receiving what one loves, whether actually in the present, looked for in the future, or remembered in the past. Joy is an expression of love. One who loves nothing and nobody cannot possibly rejoice, no matter how desperately he craves joy. Joy is the response of a lover receiving what he loves.[8]

Or, as St. John Chrysostom put it: "Where love rejoices, there is festivity."[9]

Human beings are always looking for occasions to indulge in festive celebration. Fully realizing this, the liturgy turns each day into a reason for celebrating the goodness of the world and human beings as well as the reality of redemption and God's presence. Everything culminates in an act of giving thanks.

The festive quality of such days of celebration does not depend on our preparations for them or on the mere will of the participants. It is something wholly gratuitous. It depends more on the purity of our intentions and the ability of each and all to let themselves be overtaken by this sheer gratuitousness. It is then that the festive occasion reveals its nature as a gift, letting us taste the pleasure of eating and drinking together, of dancing and singing, and of opening our hearts to each other.

Experiencing Grace in Loving Acceptance
of Life's Joys and Sorrows

Few realities manifest grace more than life itself with its spontaneity, its contradictions, and its richness. In its initial stage life is the exuberance, agility, flexibility, liberty, and spontaneity that sparkle in all living things: plants, animals, human babies, and so forth. It is an explosive force that moves out to conquer space and express the joy of being. At a later stage, however, life runs into obstacles. It must overcome resistance and face up to pain and death.

Life is both joy and sorrow, but it is difficult for human beings to accept both as dimensions of one and the same phenomenon. They want joy and they try to evade sorrow. Grace appears as a force that synthesizes both and makes them a part of life's richness. There is grace in life's joys, as all can readily see: but there is also grace in life's pain and sorrow, as all too few recognize. Here is how Leonardo Coimbra put it: "Before suffering and sorrow grace is the smile of joy, and afterward it is unity and integrity regained."[10]

That there can be grace in suffering is something which can be appreciated only by those who do not seek joy and happiness for their own sake and at any price. Joy and happiness are always the fruit of something else. We must seek what is right and just and good and true. Joy and happiness will follow as a result. We cannot enjoy the latter if we have not worked for the former. In this effort we may encounter obstacles that cause pain and suffering. In this case, however, the latter are noble things possessing real meaning. They arise out of the struggle to overcome the causes of suffering. The capacity to endure them courageously as meaningful things is itself the work of grace.

Christianity has always stressed the close link between suffering and love. The fact is that love makes sense only in connection with suffering. It is not that love is rooted in suffering but rather that suffering finds its real roots in love. It is not the community of the cross that creates the community of love but vice versa. Thus asceticism has no meaning in itself. It is not a norm but a technique. We must know how to endure suffering if love demands it of us. Love which endures suffering brings us happiness and a secret joy. It is the presence of grace.

Only human beings who are graced, who are caught up in the mystery of God, appreciate the fact that we can happily endure suffering. It is evident in the writings of Paul and in the songs of martyrs undergoing torture. They do not speak with any thought of recompense. They simply know that they are in possession of the good and gracious God who makes them feel happy. This is quite different from any quest for happiness for its own sake, in which people look for happiness and find only tears. Christians possess happiness (God) and hence are willing to endure suffering, for the latter results from their struggle against the temptations that would rob them of God. They may even seek suffering to fortify and purify themselves. Such suffering is gratifying because it is inhabited by love. Dante glimpsed this dimension of grace when he spoke of intellectual light that is filled with love of truth and hence transcends any other sort of happiness:

> Luce intellettual piena d'amore,
> Amor di vero ben pien di letizia,
> Letizia che trascende ogni dolzore. (Paradiso 30:40–42)

Experiencing Grace in Authentic Human Encounters

The basic experience of festivity for human beings lies in human encounters.[11] Here grace may well be most transparent. In real encounter there is nothing planned or premeditated. It is the fruit of some chance happening, e.g., a late bus or a conversation on some street corner. It may lead to a mutual opening up of two human freedoms to each other that marks the beginning of a long history and fulfills their lives.

Real encounter is not just any type of being together. It does not take place when two people remain anonymous, when they are simply two people among many in the world. Real encounter makes them unique. They can now exchange thoughts and feelings and confidences. They can divulge their deepest secrets, certain that they will now be understood and that they can bear the burden of life together. Real encounter takes place when people indulge in mutual commitment and self-giving, going beyond mere sympathy and a show of personal kindness. It takes place in an atmosphere of freedom which allows the other person to be other. This mutual openness is experienced as grace because it is not demanded or forced. It allows me to free myself from my own ego, to enrich my life, and to expand the horizons of communication. We experience joy and a fullness of meaning that frees our energy to engage in sacrifice and to accept other people and life.

Encounter can take place on many different levels: in our personal, professional, and family life; in any human situation or social setting. We can even experience such a high point in our daily round of activities. It occurs when we truly accept another human being, or offer sincere pardon, or make a noble gesture of help. We can also have encounters with people who are humanly and spiritually mature, and whose lives become a guiding light for many others. Making contact with such people, we may be able to discern solutions for our own inner problems and find light and strength for our own journey. In such situations we can experience the grace of spiritual elevation, feeling sure that there is another living, personal world as well as deep affection and unselfish gratefulness.

Every encounter between two human beings takes place in a particular situation, at a particular point in time and space that has its own specific content. Every encounter clearly has cosmological, social, and economic dimensions; these help to make up the concrete reality of the human person. If the scene is Latin America, for example, people may encounter a whole pervasive situation of poverty and misery. They may choose to love and unite themselves with the destiny of an oppressed class. This encounter may represent a real conversion, in which people open up to a new and unsuspected world of different values, challenges, and demands. Such an encounter gives the lie to a different kind of encounter that is glorified in societies which are wrapped up in their own egotism. They would reduce the Christian faith to the realm of private life. They would evade the demands of Christian praxis as a love committed to the liberation of other human beings from inhuman and unjust conditions.[12]

The kind of encounter which entails conversion, in the sense described above, does not relate to an isolated "you." It relates to a situated "you," to a multitude of people caught up in the same drama. This was the kind of encounter typified by Jesus Christ, who gave up his life for all, not just for a few intimates. In such self-surrender we see clearly and fully what the gratuitousness of love and what liberating grace mean.

Experiencing Grace in Love

Love is the most thorough kind of encounter. Here grace does not just shine through; it appears as itself, because it is identical with love. Love is either gratuitous or it is not love. That is why grace is described as the communication of God's love to human beings. Human love is the consequence of divine love. It is the response of human nature to the divine love which created it. We love because we were first loved. All love is divine because God is love. In Homer's time people used to say that there was a deity in all love. Love is alluring and maddening. It takes people outside themselves, because it breaks through merely human bounds. In it the divine shows up in the human.

There is always some "other" in love. Loving always means loving another. In the last analysis it means loving the great Other: God. As one great mystic writer put it: "Love is a unitive and concretive force."[13]

If they are to unite, however, the two must remain two. Though two, they become as one. The otherness of love does not lie outside the person. It lies inside the person; it is the person himself or herself. Loving means first and foremost loving *oneself*. The love which we have for ourselves is the measure of our love for others. Jesus said: "Love your neighbor as yourself." But why is it that love of self is the standard of love for others? Because the "other" closest to hand is yourself. One who loves himself turns his "I" into a "you." Initially love is a love of self: "If you do not know how to love yourself, you will not be able to truly love others."[14] Or, as Augustine said in another place: "*Pondus meum, amor meus.*"[15] I carry my own burden, and I do so out of love for myself. To love oneself is to hail one's own existence.[16] We rejoice in our own existence and feel at play in it, for it is wholly gratuitous. Instead of rebelling, we enjoy the gratuitous reality of our own existence.

But love of self is not synonymous with egotistical love centered wholly on our own ego. Self-love does not mean love of our own ego just as it is. After all, what does "yourself" mean in Jesus' statement above? What is the specific nature of true self-love? What is the real nature of this person who loves himself or herself? The reality of the person lies in the fact that it is a web of relationships extending outside its own ego. The human "I" is always inhabited by many "yous"; it is not closed up in itself. It is an authentic human "I" only when it opens up, transcends itself, and communicates with others. To love oneself means to love this Abrahamic obligation to break away from one's own inner homeland and keep moving out toward others. Love of self does not mean love of our own ego. It means loving the other person who makes possible our ego and creates it. Thus the more I give *myself,* the more I am; the more I renounce myself, the more I receive; and the more I open myself, the more I am fulfilled. The economy of the person is a paradoxical one. It is an economy of self-giving rather than of accumulation and holding back. Thus the other rises up within my own "I."

I can truly love others because of the love I have for myself as an "other," because I as a person am open to others. When I love others, I hail their existence and rejoice in it even as I do in my own. This applies to those who do not seem so lovable also, and even to my enemies. The more I can accept and hail my own existence, with all its perplexing and contradictory aspects, the more I will be able to accept and welcome the existence of others. By the same token, to reject others is to reject the other inside myself.

Not everyone can welcome the existence of others in deed and in truth, particularly the existence of those who persecute and hate them. It can only be done by those who are able to hail the supreme being, God, who creates and sustains all living things. Everything is possible for those who love God. Goethe said: "A heart that loves someone cannot hate anyone."[17] When Beatrice came into Dante's life, he tells us that there were no longer any enemies for him.[18] When this other someone is God, and Beatrice symbolized the Absolute, we can readily see how love for God involves loving all those whom he himself loves. We must also love our enemies because God loves the wicked and the ungrateful too (Luke 6:35).

To love others is to give them a reason for being. There is no reason for existing because life is a gratuitous gift. Loving a person gives that person a reason for being. Love makes one person important in the eyes of another person. As Gabriel Marcel put it, to love a person is to say to that person: "You will never die." We tell that person that he or she *ought* to exist and cannot die. Such a person now has a reason for being because he or she is important to another person. That is why someone in love has the sensation of starting life all over again.

The whole complex phenomenon of love is framed in the horizon of gratuitousness, of grace. Indeed grace and love come down to the same thing. Human beings need love, but it must be free, gratuitous love. Only such love can bring fulfillment, joy, and indescribable happiness. Only those who know true love can comprehend the most sacred words of Christianity: that God is love (1 John 4:8–16); that love comes from God (1 John 4:7); and that love will never cease to exist (1 Cor. 13:8). It is the grace of God in the grace of human beings.

Grace Anywhere in the World

Christian thought articulated clear-cut moral and religious situations to exemplify the action of grace in the world. In this effort, however, it was easy to forget the fact that grace, as God's love in the world, is ever present in the world—even in thoroughly ambiguous situations.

God's love (grace) does not depend on our love or our inner purity. God gives himself continually and gratuitously. Sometimes we are surprised by its appearance somewhere where we least expected it, because all we can see is some terrible distortion of the moral order and upright habits. Jesus Christ scandalized the pious people of his day by drawing examples from areas which seemed to overstep the boundaries of good taste and correct behavior. For love of neighbor he used the example of a heretical Samaritan. For prompt obedience he used the example of a pagan Roman. For confidence and trust he used the example of a pagan woman from Syro-Phoenicia. For compassion he used the example of a prostitute, Mary Magdalene. He criticized his Jewish compatriots for being unable to see God at work beyond their sharply defined boundaries.

Here I should like to offer two examples of grace and love at work beyond the normally accepted boundaries of moral behavior. I am not trying to justify abnormal situations. I simply would like the reader to join me in going beyond the accepted categories of good and evil so that we might see how the presence of God can be at work in secret anywhere.

The first story takes place in the interior of Brazil, where God walks unencumbered by the hallowed laws of religion. A man, Severino, comes to get holy water and the local priest asks him why he wants it.

"It is to bless my house," Father.

"But I am the priest. I will come and bless your house."

"That would not do, Father. I hate to say so, but I will tell you the truth. I live with a woman whom I did not marry in a church. I have made two mistakes in this case. First, she is black. Second, I took her from a life of prostitution. I am going to try living with her. I will give her understanding and affection. If she mends her ways and proves able to be the woman of one man only, then she will be my wife. You cannot come to the house yet because there is still sin there. That is why I am going to bless the house. It is up to God to help her. If things work out, I will ask you to marry us."

This man loved. He voted his confidence in the black prostitute, believing that she could be rehabilitated. Here there was a basic project of great purity, and it counted for more than certain acts taken individually.

Some months later the priest went to Severino's house. The marriage ceremony took place, and a small celebration followed.

John tells us that Christ is the true light who enlightens every human being coming into the world (John 1:9). He enlightens one person in one way, another person in another way. All are enlightened in the context of their concrete situations, which often have profound limitations and ambiguities. My light does not enlighten Severino. Can I then say that the light which enlightened him does not come from God?[19] Much was pardoned him because he loved much.

The second story concerns an incident that took place between a woman and the little sisters who serve God so heroically in the Amazon region. For several days the nuns had been tending a man in their quarters who had micosis. But what were they to do with him, after all? One day a nun happened to be passing an alley at the far end of town when she saw a sign over a building: House of Charity. She found out that it belonged to a woman, but the woman was not there at the moment. The nun went back to her convent. A few hours later the proprietress of the House of Charity showed up on her own at the convent.

"What's up, Sister?"

"You own the House of Charity?"

"Yes, Sister."

"Who is it for?"

"It is for all those who are ill or who have no place else to stay."

"You see this man we have here."

"He has leprosy?"

"No. Only micosis."

"Then I will take him to my House of Charity."

"But how do you manage to keep it going?"

"Sister, please try to understand me. I have a dance hall. One has to live. The women around here have no jobs. They have to live. Many of them are prostitutes. So am I. They work with me. I know it is against the law of God, but isn't the law of life accepted by God too? It hurts me to tell you this, but there is no other way out for me. I and the other women live off the dance hall. Everything that exceeds what I have to live on goes for the House of Charity. In that way I can take care of many sick people. They pay nothing. I cook their meals, wash their clothes, and buy their medicine. They can stay there for free until they are well. It is my way of making amends for my sins."

There are no limits to God's love or his presence. He goes where he wills.

He comes to whomever he wishes. He can be present in the midst of any situation.[20]

The various situations analyzed above do not lead us to the threshold of grace. They themselves are already forms of its presence in the world. They do not invite us to catch a fleeting glimpse of some divine grace that is somehow different from the gratuitousness that occurs in our own lives. Divine grace is communicated in those very situations, appearing as gratuitousness, goodness, *joie de vivre,* and meaningful fulfillment.

Grace is all this, but it is much more as we shall see later. It is also the indwelling of the Trinity and participation in the divine nature. These are the ultimate articulations of experiences which human beings already live here and now and which I have tried to describe above. In the light of the ultimate depths revealed to us by faith, our earthly experiences may seem to fade into nothingness. But we must always remember that the latter experiences are true anticipations of the ultimate depths that give grandeur and fulfillment to human existence.

PART THREE

THEOLOGICAL REFLECTIONS ON THE GRACE EXPERIENCE

CHAPTER 10

The Universality of Grace
and Its Embodiments in History

Our reflections on the various manifestations of the grace experience have made it clear that access to this experience is not reserved to a select few. It is the atmosphere surrounding the existence of all. In its ontological ground human life is suffused and supported by the goodness and love of God, who creates and moves everything. To be a human being is to live in the divine milieu, to live amid transcendence in every move we make. In their history human beings can accept and nurture this reference to the fundamental ground of their lives and to the living transcendence that is manifested there. When it is accepted at every level of our personal journey, of societal organization, and of our immersion in the world, then grace can manifest its presence and even create its own history. We get the history of grace's concrete embodiments in the world, of the ways in which God's presence has suffused the lives of human beings.

No one stands outside this atmosphere. All are grounded in God and supported by him. What human beings can do, by virtue of their freedom, is relate positively or negatively to God within this pervasive divine milieu. God can ensure openness and fulfillment to all, offering them a fully realized future. To say that is to affirm the universality of grace as something offered to all. There is thus a real possibility that all can attain salvation.

The Witness of Christian Experience

Christian awareness has always adverted to the universality of liberating grace. The God of the New Testament is a God of love for all human beings. He is the savior of all human beings because he is the God of all human beings (1 Tim. 4:10). In the life of every human being he shows up as meaningfulness, love, goodness, hope, and a future offering infinite fulfillment to the human heart. This, then, is the pristine sense of God. He is the mysterious, all-embracing reality who offers fulfillment and complete meaningfulness to human existence.

The New Testament is filled with expressions that convey the experience of God's universal love and his indiscriminate offering to all: "For he wants all men to be saved and come to know the truth" (1 Tim. 2:4).[1] The universality of human decadence finds its counterweight in the universality of God's salvific offering (Rom. 3:23–26). As all died in Adam, so all can receive life in Christ (Rom. 5:12–21). Light is shed on the meaning of all history in the journey of the resurrected Jesus Christ. He is the personal mirror reflecting the collective destiny of humankind and the cosmos (Eph. 3:9; Col. 1:26). All that exists in heaven and earth has been placed under one head, as it were, taking on meaning in the light of what happened to Jesus (Eph. 1:10). Thus meaningfulness and salvation are ensured for reality as a whole.

The "good news" is precisely this affirmation of God's universal offer of salvation. All are lovable in God's eyes and hence all can reach him. However, they do not reach him by some magical step or some merely physical mechanism. Salvation is a human reality, and so it is realized within the horizon of human freedom. God's love does not do violence to the latter. Instead it invites a loving response from human beings. It does not subjugate anyone. Instead it invites all to undertake a journey where God and human beings unite to make history. This is the history of salvation, the fruit of two freedoms at work and the product of two loves.

Several passages in the New Testament do talk about a blasphemy against the Holy Spirit which can never be pardoned in this life or the next (Matt. 12:31–32; Mark 3:28–29; Luke 12:10).[2] They should not be viewed as an attempt to set limits on God's power of forgiveness. Instead they should be interpreted in terms of the personal dispositions of the human subject. Some may recognize the presence of grace as such and yet refuse to give it a welcome place in their real lives. The people's rejection of the person and message of Christ is pardonable. The humble nature of Christ's origin, the frail nature of his proclamation devoid of all ostentatious trappings, and his seemingly "unmessianic" attitudes might easily have led the people to miss the hidden mystery, i.e., that he was the Son of God and the messianic envoy of the Father. Blasphemy against the Holy Spirit presumes that people have recognized the divine character of Jesus and his activity. Although they knew that his works were God's, the Pharisees attributed them to Satan. Here we have the maximum in human perversity and the most direct and conscious rejection of God's offer as embodied in history. So long as such a basic attitude persists, there can be no saving encounter. Here we catch a glimpse of what absolute rupture and damnation might be.[3]

Aware of the unlimited nature of God's love, Christian tradition could join Augustine in saying *"Deus non deserit, nisi deseratur"* [God does not abandon people unless he is first abandoned by them] (*PL* 44: 935, 942). In 835 A.D. the Synod of Quiercy offered this assertion:

The omnipotent God wills to save all human beings without exception (1 Tim. 2:4) even though not all are saved. In the case of those who are saved, salvation is a gift; in the case of those who are damned, damnation is their own fault (DS 623).[4]

Trent felt obliged to reject the radical position of Calvin. According to that Council, he divided humanity into two groups: those predestined for salvation and those predestined for eternal damnation. As he saw it, history is the setting for divine judgment; it shows who the damned and the already saved are. The damned are revealed by their poverty and laziness; the saved are revealed by their affluence and their dedication to work. This conception, as Max Weber would stress in his much debated thesis, generated the capitalist mentality, the unrestrained quest to accumulate wealth as an assurance of eternal salvation.

Those who take their guidance from the words of the gospel message can readily see how far we have moved away from Christ's own promises. He tells us that the kingdom of heaven belongs to the poor (Luke 6:20), and he has harsh warnings for the rich: "How hard it will be for the rich to go into the kingdom of God!" (Luke 18:24); "that is the way it works with the man who grows rich for himself instead of growing rich in the sight of God" (Luke 12:21). Trent teaches:

A person puts himself outside the community of faith if he says that the grace of justification is granted only to those predestined to life, that all the rest, . . . even though called, do not receive grace because they were predestined to evil by God's power" (Session 6, Canon 17: DS 1567).

Catholic theological reflection has always tried to take due account of all the data and avoid going to one extreme or the other. It has tried to break down any false sense of security on the part of human beings that would excuse them from shouldering their own history of salvation. On the one hand, it has always refused to accept Calvin's twofold predestination (to salvation and damnation). On the other hand, it has also rejected the theory of apocatastasis, which proposes that all human beings will eventually be saved. Both these extreme interpretations try to offer some kind of complete assurance to human beings, whether it be about salvation or damnation. Both fail to respect human freedom. They do not pay serious attention to the element of unpredictability in human history. History, after all, is not the endless repetition of the same thing. It contains an element of novelty and unpredictability. There is growth in the direction of the kingdom or a turning aside from it. Salvation depends on human beings too, on their love or lack of love, and on the way in which they exercise their freedom in history.

Christian tradition formulated two basic propositions to guarantee the fact that grace and God's gratuitous love are universal:

1. To the nonbaptized and to adults who never hear the Christian message God grants grace that is truly sufficient for their salvation (DS 2305 against Jansen; DS 2425–39 against P. Quesnel).
2. God never denies his grace to sinners, however blind and hardened they may be (DS 1542–43; Trent, Session 6, Chapter 14).

On the basis of these two propositions we can now advance a critical conjecture; it was a metaphysical representation of God as a supreme being living outside the world that created false problems which puzzled theology and terrorized the faithful with thoughts of predestination.

God's Salvific Will Versus Human Freedom: Theological Systems and the Approach to Grace

Within the framework of a metaphysics about God and his eternal decrees one could legitimately raise a question that hardly seems worthy of him insofar as he is a mystery of love, i.e., how can we seriously talk about God's salvific will when not all human beings are saved? If grace and divine omnipotence take priority, then must we not say that God can effectively save all even while respecting human freedom and motivating it into action? And if some people are damned anyway, how can we excuse God?

We know that this was the great *quaestio disputata* that vexed Augustine. In the sixteenth century people sought to resolve the problem by elaborating differing systems of grace. They gave rise to interminable disputes and kept theology in turmoil for at least a century.[5]

God as the starting point. This theological system falls within the Thomist tradition. It was elaborated by Domingo Bañez, who died in 1604. Thomist thought is basically characterized by a brilliant interpretation of Greek metaphysical reflection within the framework of salvation history provided by the Bible. God is the center of the Thomist vision of the world. All understanding must start from God if it is to be truly *theo*logical. God is the ultimate, transcendent cause of all being and all activity.

God's universal salvific will is historicized in the world through sufficient grace and efficacious grace. Through sufficient grace God gives all the capability of being saved, the will to be saved. Through efficacious grace he enables this willing to pass over into action. God penetrates the salvific action of human beings in such a way that he becomes the cause responsible for salvation. Without the interior action of God it would be impossible for human beings to go from simple willing to effective doing. That is why this view holds that God physically predetermines human beings for salvation. Of course, God does not suppress human freedom; he enables it to be even more free. But the presence of God in human activity is such that it is infallible. God's presence is always efficacious and triumphant.

Then how can human beings be damned? There are two possible ways of answering this question. One is to say that all are saved. The other is to say that only those predestined to glory are saved. Bañez puts it this way: only those predestined to eternal happiness in absolute terms are saved. For this reason they receive both sufficient grace and efficacious grace. The rest are not predestined to glory. In other words, God does not step in to alter the fact that the latter, on account of their evil lives, do not attain salvation. They are not predestined to damnation. Thanks to his foreknowledge, God foresees their refusal. They receive only sufficient grace, which does not pass over into efficacious grace. They do not receive efficacious grace, which is God present in human activity and hence is always infallible in its saving effects.

This theory preserves the absolute priority of God's initiative. But we must ask ourselves whether it pays due respect to the real universality of God's salvific offer. Isn't sufficient grace a superfluous construct, since it does not really produce any effect? It proves to be insufficient, and God's project does not seem to give rise to any human project. From this standpoint the history of salvation is not human, nor is it the fruit of human freedom. It is simply the history of God's freedom. God predestines some to share in his love while others are left to their own devices. Even though God could prevent their damnation, he does not.

This theory, it would appear, falls short right at the point where it should provide some enlightenment. It starts off from the premise that God's activity is always infallible and efficacious. Then, recognizing that there are wicked people who can be damned, it admits that God's action is not infallible and efficacious. So it has recourse to another principle, i.e., predestination to glory. The logic of the system breaks down. Damnation does seem to be a human work, but salvation definitely is not.

Human beings as the starting point. In the face of the aforementioned difficulties, Luis Molina (d. 1600), a Jesuit theologian, elaborated another theological system concerning grace. Its starting point is clearly grounded in the spirit of humanism that typified his era and that placed much value on human freedom and human responsibility in the world.

Sufficient grace, which is offered to all human beings by God, is transformed into efficacious grace through the collaboration of human beings. Salvation is the result of a gift and an achievement. In his foreknowledge God sees who will open up to the mystery of his love and who will refuse it. He predestines those who will decide for him after foreseeing their merits. He excludes from glory those who will reject him, again foreseeing this rejection, but he does not deny to them the grace that they will reject. According to this theory, then, human beings must act as if everything depended on them and trust as if everything depended on God.

The Thomists raised questions about this solution. How is the absolute primacy of divine grace preserved in it? Since salvation seems to depend more on human beings than on God, how can we say that salvation comes from above? For now the criterion of predestination seems to lie in human beings, not in God.

Concrete salvation history as the starting point. Following the tradition of Augustine himself, the Augustinian school refused to indulge in metaphysical ratiocination. It views human beings in terms of the concrete human situation, where people are attracted by two possible alternatives. One is life according to the flesh, the other is life according to the Spirit. The real-life situation of human beings is one of concupiscence. They are torn between dynamisms that draw them to the flesh, egotism, and self-concentration and dynamisms that draw them to love, encounter, and communion with God and their fellows.

Sufficient and efficacious grace triggers and bolsters the latter dynamisms. It gives human beings an inclination that is stronger than the inclination toward carnal concupiscence, gearing them toward love for God and their fellow humans. The taste and affection for good overcomes the negative forces of fleshly concupiscence. Augustine refers to the *delectatio victrix,* the victorious delight in the gifts of the Spirit and the proper order of things as God wills.

Thus the work of grace is not grounded on metaphysical considerations about God's efficient causality. God's activity permeates human activity. Rather than taking the place of the human being, it helps the latter to act with greater intensity and affection. This view talks about freedom and grace in concrete rather than abstract terms. It talks about the free human being living in a situation of grace *and* dis-grace, shouldering that situation, overcoming obstacles, and trying to get more and more in tune with the concrete will of God as it is manifested in the mediating circumstances.

Rephrasing the whole issue in terms of the primacy of divine love and the divine mystery. All of the above systems, and particularly those of Bañez and Molina, suffer from insufficient reflection on the fact that the mystery of God cannot be turned into an object.[6] The transcendence of God's activity is not respected when we assume that God is a secondary cause on the same plane of meaning and reality as created causes. This point of departure, it seems to me, is inadequate. It talks about God as an objectifiable factor vis-à-vis human beings, failing to take due account of the differences between human logic and divine logic.

In that respect the debates of the sixteenth century are based on the same understanding of being that typified the early period of modern history, and they lead to the same consequences. In that era being was viewed in terms of infinite being, and God was the Supreme Being. This led people to turn God and his mystery into an entity, to reify all nonobjectifiable reality as God, Grace, Mystery, and Salvation Plan. The consequences are evident in the discussion of predestination that occupied the schools. The capabilities of speculative reason were strained to the utmost, but no clear-cut reasoning could resolve the antinomies encountered. Reason proved incapable of maintaining the polarity between human freedom and God's activity; it was forced to choose for one side or the other.

Another line of thought is possible, however. Instead of taking reason as the last court of appeal, it can appeal to the mystery of God and allow reason, to do its work within the context of that mystery. It can maintain the polarity between God and humanity because it sees this polarity as a manifestation of the mystery that lies hidden underneath it. God is not the being we call God.

God is a mystery, the supreme mystery. What we call God is a representation of the true reality of God. The God of theological language is a projection of our reason; it is an image and representation. It is the only way in which human beings can draw near to the divine mystery without dying. But a line of thought that maintains its rigor as such must always remember that its representation is not God but only a way to God.

Theological discourse deals with our representation of God, not with God himself. We cannot discourse about God. We can only focus on God insofar as we are touched by the ineffable reality of his divine mystery, which ever remains in hallowed silence. Theology then ceases to be theology; it is reborn as mysticism and the experience of God.[7] We thus reject all the rationalism latent in the systems described above. Reasons begin with reason, but reason itself has no reason for its existence. It is a mystery. So we cannot make the mystery of God intelligible through the use of reason. Any such pretence would be human hybris and cryptoatheism.

However, we can be touched by the divine mystery. It can be the most profound and gratifying experience of our lives. Within the bosom of this experience there is room for rational discourse, not to eliminate the divine mystery or replace it with some created concept but to catch a gleam of light from its luminous depths. In this way the divine mystery ever retains primacy over human reason. It becomes the Reason of human reason rather than the agonizing limitation of the latter.

The reification of God and the metaphysical interpretation of his salvific will in terms of eternal decrees had to lead to what it did in fact lead to: to an impasse for theological thought and to a false alternative between the primacy of divine grace on the one hand or the primacy of human freedom on the other.

When we view God as the supreme mystery, divine foreknowledge need not be interpreted in terms of chronological priority: as if to say that God were on the same level as human beings, moving in a succession of moments that entail a before and after. Our human talk proceeds like that, but God does not. As the supreme mystery, God is the foundation of all. God is ever present. For him, before and after are an eternal now. We are speaking in purely anthropomorphic terms when we talk about eternally predetermined decrees and as yet undecided human choices that exist in the future in God. In an act that is eternally simultaneous, God knows the potential modes that imitate his own essence and the temporal succession in which they are to be realized.

The reification of God and divine grace also affected people's understanding of freedom. Human freedom became an abstract freedom in the face of an equally abstract divine grace. What is involved here is the free person living within a defined, concrete area of freedom. Within this area we find concrete grace being given to human beings, inviting them to accept God in the manifold mediation of concrete situations. Grace is not some attribute of

God. It is God himself, communicating himself and offering himself as meaningfulness, hope, love, strength, etc. What is called "divine concourse" is not something external that impinges on the action of the creature. As the living, ontological foundation of every action, God enters into the whole specification of such action and sustains it. Liberty, too, depends on God. He makes it what it is. The activity of the divine mystery does not replace or diminish human freedom. It makes that freedom what it is.

Thus actions are not produced partly by human beings and partly by God. To say that would be to place human beings and God on the same level. God always retains his character as supreme mystery and transcendence. On that level actions are totally God's. Human beings retain their character as created beings and immanence. On this level actions are also totally those of human beings. Hence every action is at once totally divine and totally human. The distinction is not to be sought in the act but in the agent. One agent is the creator, the other is the creature who has been created to be a creator. Ontologically there is an absolute distance between them. But human beings are not just creative creatures. They are also children of God in a dialogue with the supreme mystery and hence in absolute proximity to it. The eschatological epiphany of this fact occurred in the incarnation of the Word.

In the ontological dimension of reality no action is bad in itself, for it depends on God. Evil appears only in the moral dimension. Created freedom is summoned to dialogue. It is created and hence dependent and imperfect. It can choose freely to withdraw itself from its dependence on the divine. It cannot do so ontologically because it can never exist without God. But in its freedom it can will the impossible, and that is sin:

Thus the absolute beginning of sin lies in the creature. This beginning is not a coming-to-be but a partial ceasing-to-be, a void introduced into the texture of being. When people perform a good action, they enter into even deeper dependence on God because they share more in God's perfection.[8]

With liberty, it seems to me, we get something of the absolute in human beings. Hence there is the possibility of absolute fulfillment or of absolute frustration. This absolute quality of freedom is really absolute, and so mysterious. In other words, there is no possibility of it being justified on rational grounds. Whenever we find arguments for freedom, we run into determination rather than freedom. Access to freedom comes only through freedom itself, not through reason. Of course, freedom does have its element of rationality, but its true identity does not surface there. Only those who exercise freedom know it, just as only lovers know what love is. Freedom is a bare fact, present in all its gratuitousness. It is spontaneity, despite all the conditioning factors amid which it is exercised. Though immersed in reality, it creates reality. It creates the positive or negative self-fulfillment of human beings insofar as they accept or reject the divine mystery which fashioned created freedom.

The various systems described above also raised the question of salvation on the level of the individual: How can I be saved? How can I save my soul? Today we know that we must go deeper to give a full answer to this question. Thanks to the return to biblical sources and our new-found awareness of the social and cosmic dimensions of the human person, we now realize that the salvation of the individual cannot be severed from the salvific meaningfulness of reality as a whole. The human being is not an atom lost in a chaotic world. It is a part of world and cosmic history. In it is revealed the meaning of the whole, and through it the whole takes cognizance of its latent meaning.

Personal predestination must be viewed in the broader context of universal predestination. Predestination signifies a destiny ordained in advance for all creation by God in his love. It is through love that all things, particularly human beings, were called into existence and given a destiny. It is because God wanted companions to share his love that all beings were called out of nothingness and given the ability to love as God does while living outside him. In human beings, however, love is not ontologically fated nor a created inevitability. It is the result of freedom and a gift from God. Herein lies the risk at the core of free creation. In its nonrationality freedom can refuse this encounter. The ultimate end is attained because the person, despite this refusal, is ontologically tied to God and chants the love of the eternal even in the act of refusal. But on the moral plane of freedom and its exercise we now get total frustration as the result of human refusal. It is the hell which God did not will or create but which exists by virtue of humanity's rebellious freedom.

The essential truth at stake. Despite the criticisms voiced above, one question deserves consideration: what was the point of the various theological systems dealing with grace? That basic question may have been buried under an inadequate approach and a plethora of disputes. Perhaps we would do well to reformulate it today in terms of our own context, setting aside the sense of desperation which it once evoked. In this way we may be able to salvage the truth underlying theological tradition in the past four centuries.

The basic truth at stake here is an enlightening one for us. It has to do with the absolute primacy and reality of God's love, which is shared with all and touches everyone. God wills supreme happiness for all creation, and for human beings in a most particular way. God offers himself to all, and he himself is supreme happiness. This love of God is not a reaction to the good deeds of human beings. Prior to any good act on the part of human beings, God loves us because his inmost being is love and cannot be otherwise. We are good and lovable because God loves us. By the same token, however, this love would not really be love if it did not offer itself to freedom. It does not do violence, and it is not structured as power. Instead it takes the form of fragility and vulnerability. The latter, in fact, constitute the real strength and grandeur of love. In creation human beings are the creatures who can heed the proposal of divine love and assume the responsibility of responding to it. Because human freedom is a created, limited one, this response is not fated.

Human beings possess the terrifying capacity to reject the offer. This is their grandeur and their drama. In history human beings have exercised their freedom in terms of refusal. Hence they can freely be lost forever. God makes himself vulnerable once a created freedom exists. Yet despite this denial of his love, God does not stop loving, pardoning, and renewing his offer. The doctrine of predestination reaffirms the absolute primacy of God's love and the abysmal radicalness of human freedom. The aim of Catholic doctrine was always to maintain this polarity without any sort of reductionism.

Obscurity still persists, but now it is located where we, in all humility, should see it: not in the refusal to engage in intellectual effort but in the recognition of the latter's limitations. Reason must realize that the divine mystery cannot be completely framed within the bounds of reason. Instead of rebelling and setting itself up as the measure of all things, reason must recognize its dependence on the mystery of God. To acknowledge that mystery is to accept the illogical arbitrariness of facts as conveyors of a divine meaning that escapes the logic of reason and science in their vaunted efforts to universalize and absolutize concepts.

Reason is exercised within the bosom of the divine mystery, not outside its sway. It feels itself illuminated by the impenetrable depths of the divine. Herein lies the theologic character of theology itself insofar as the latter is reasoning in the bosom of faith. Theology does not seek to abolish the divine mystery. It hymns the unlimited depths of that mystery, thereby turning into doxology:

How deep are the riches and the wisdom and the knowledge of God! How inscrutable his judgments, how unsearchable his ways! For "who has known the mind of the Lord? Or who has been his counselor? Who has given him anything so as to deserve return?" For from him and through him and for him all things are. To him be glory forever. Amen (Rom. 11:33–36).

But this can be understood only by those who get beyond the spirit of geometry and take guidance from the spirit of delicacy, who go beyond the instrumental, analytical reasoning that prevails in our scientific and technological world and make room for sapiential, sacramental reasoning.

Historical Embodiments of Universal Liberative Grace

We cannot talk in abstract, universalizing terms about the presence of God in the world (grace). God is the inmost presence in each being, and each being is a concrete one. Therefore the divine presence is always concrete for each and all. As R. Bacon put it in a striking formula: *"Unum individuum excellit omnia universalia de mundo"* [One single individual is worth more than all the universals in the world].

Concrete life as the locale of salvific encounter. Grace and salvation do not fall like a bolt from the blue. They come along the byways of humanity. Each human being lives in a particular cultural and historical milieu, participating in a collective destiny. Individuals share in the opportunities and achievements of the communities in which they are immersed. Our personal journey is freighted with all sorts of influences: archetypal, psychological, educational, family, and so forth. Then there are our associates in life and school and work. All of these are vehicles and sacraments of grace or dis-grace. Our culture, the traditions and values of our people, the concrete form of their religion, the works of their thinkers, poets, humanists and religious figures— all these go to make up the concrete way in which divine grace fleshes itself out in history for us as individuals. They are the ways in which the goodness and sympathy of God reach down to the individual, despite all the sinfulness that may be conveyed through the same channels.

God's salvific will is not an abstraction on some eternal plane. It is the most concrete sort of historical reality, mediated to us by history itself and turning the latter into a history of salvation or perdition. Grace and salvation are a joint effort of persons and their worlds, of persons and the communities with which they share life. One is responsible for the grace of the other. Each must be a sacrament of salvation for the other. Herein lies the deepest meaning of love for neighbor, which is to embrace even our enemy. Grace and salvation entail universal solidarity. The concrete course of divine love passes through human love and everyone that I approach. This is the privileged way in which God chose to reveal who he is: a mystery of love communicating himself to others, causing other loves to exist and enabling them to love even as he himself does. The grace of God becomes history in the history of love at work in the world.

Religion as a celebration and communication of grace. In their most pristine and positive form religions are the institutional forms that translate humanity's relationship to the Absolute. Religion is always a reaction to a prior action. It is the human response to God's proposal. It is an original phenomenon that cannot be reduced to something more basic. It bears witness to humanity's openness to some transcendent reality, to something of definitive importance, to a transcendent meaning that transfigures reality with all its contradictions.

Religion itself is already an acceptance of grace. It celebrates an encounter with divinity. Hence, without denigrating any Christian claims, we can say that religions are the ordinary pathways to God. In other words, every human culture has worked out its response in history to God's offer. In the concrete, all human beings find themselves in a religious tradition, the tradition of their people. In that particular byway individuals are given a glimpse of God, and saving grace is turned into a sacrament for them.

This theological valuation of religion does not mean that everything in that religion is legitimate. It can contain diabolic elements that do a bad job of translating the demands of God and the mystery of humanity into words, deeds, and ethical requirements. Yet despite all the ambiguities of the world's religions (including the religion of the Bible and Christianity), they are vehicles that communicate grace, forgiveness, and the future that God promises to human beings.[9]

The historical embodiments of grace also have a history. They are instruments of inspiration and concrete grace for the human beings who make contact with them. Such was the case with Chuang-Tzu, Lao-Tzu, Buddha, Gandhi and others in the Orient; with the letters of Seneca, the Stoic maxims of Marcus Aurelius, and the philosophy of Plato in the Occident. In faith they can and should be regarded as vehicles of grace. They were the work of grace and, in the course of history, they turned into an enduring atmosphere of grace for countless people. Through contact with these privileged witnesses of the Spirit, human beings feel summoned to arise and entrust themselves to the mystery of God, to discover the mysterious design of divine light in their own lives.

Something similar took place in the Christian sphere. Jesus of Nazareth is revered as God's grace in the world in a definitive way. The history of his life, death, and resurrection is the concrete way in which human beings of all time, including non-Christians, find the meaning of their lives and the future deciphered. Francis of Assisi, following in the pattern of Jesus Christ, was the work of God's grace in the world. His example, his cordial relationship with all creatures, his universal sense of brotherhood, and his sense of reconciliation with all realities (including suffering and death) became an envigorating light for other human beings. In him they rediscovered the hidden dimensions of their lives. The perennial presence of works of grace through the centuries attests to the permanence of divine grace in the world and its import as an inspiring, motivating, healing, elevating, and sanctifying reality.

Christianity as a sacramental expression of grace. Among the religions of the world Christianity stands out. Basically it does not regard itself as a religion but as the divine life itself penetrating human life. The religious expression of this divine life does not exhaust the latter's richness; it should also have temporal, secular expression. In Christianity human awareness, touched by the grace of God, came to full lucidity. This awareness has a history and it has been set down as such. The Old and New Testaments are written testaments of the self-awareness of a people who allowed themselves to be led by God's presence and fidelity. Jesus of Nazareth arose within this tradition and the decisive event in world history took place: the resurrection. It was an anticipatory manifestation of the eschatological end promised to all the saved and the whole cosmos. In Jesus, God fully revealed his plan of love and the destiny of all things as the kingdom of God, where God would be all in all (1 Cor. 15:28). In Jesus, God said yes and amen to all the yearnings for fulfillment that are nurtured in the human heart (2 Cor. 1:20). In Jesus, God was present in absolute immediacy and man was present in total communion.

That is why Jesus is viewed and loved as the eternal Son of the Father dwelling among human beings, as God himself incarnate.

In Jesus Christ and his community (the church) the grace that suffuses the world attained its most solid sacramental expression. Christ emerges as the primary sacrament of God, and his community as the radical sacrament of Christ.[10] In the world the church is to be the sign of God's universal grace and unbounded love. It is to be the sacrament of the unheard-of hope that was fleshed out in the resurrection, and of the *joie de vivre* to be found in the realm of the Father when all shall live as brothers and sisters in union with all creation.

As a historical achievement and a social phenomenon, the church is the incarnation of Christianity. In the very process of incarnating it, the church sets limits on itself. It must use a particular language, particular signs, and a particular form of presence in the world that bears the marks of a particular culture. Human beings of other cultures have need of a special vocation if they are to enter into this concrete incarnation of Christianity. All are called to live Christianity, but not all are called to express it within a particular church which is bound to certain cultural elements by the very fact that it is historical. Though all are meant to be Christians, each within his or her own culture, not all are called to be sacramental, ecclesial signs. To be a member of the Roman Catholic Apostolic church is a special grace. Yet this grace does not establish privileges that set its members apart from other human beings. Instead it establishes a more demanding function in salvation history. They must be the sign and instrument of Jesus Christ and his liberation in the midst of the world.

The specific reality and function of the church do not lie in being a vehicle of grace and salvation. That is offered universally to all, and all are touched by the universal sacraments of life, religion, and culture. The specific function of the church in salvation history is to make visible the presence of grace in the world, to turn it into awareness and history by serving as the sacrament of God's unrestricted, universal love for all human beings.

Death as the truly universal sacrament of grace. Finally, there is one thing that is a truly universal sacrament of grace because it touches all, i.e., death. Viewed in its human dimension, death is not just the end of terrestrial life. It is also the opportunity offered to human persons to reach the end of their journey in history. And here "end" means goal, point of convergence, and full meaningfulness. Human history is the realization or destruction of meaningfulness. Death is the possibility for human persons to fashion their ultimate overall synthesis, to bring together their whole past and then move on to the realm of the eternal God.

Every free act is a synthesis of the life history of the person. It sums up a journey that comes out of the past and opens up to the future. At death human beings are given the possibility of making an act of love or an act of closure that gathers up their own earthly past and stamps some ultimate, definitive character on it. And the latter is ultimate and definitive precisely because at death we are given the last chance to decide our fate. Unlike other acts, this act has a quality of its own: it is the ultimate one, and hence it is the one that allows for an ultimate synthesis. After it comes eternity. Thus at death there is the possibility of a decision that sums up everything. Precisely *at the point of death*—not before because there is still time, not after because that is already eternity—the ties of a human being with this earthly situation are ended. A new celestial situation begins. There is now the possibility of a total liberation from the bonds of earth. There is now an opportunity for the spirit to reach its light, for the will to exercise its freedom totally, and for the human project to become fully and totally explicit.

Granting the dense and critical nature of this moment by virtue of its ultimate, structuring character, we can accept one hypothesis as reasonable and in accordance with the goodness of God. It is the hypothesis that at the moment of death there is a radical encounter with God, with the risen Lord, and with the ultimate Truth of creation; that acceptance of this encounter signifies saving grace and rejection of it means eternal frustration. Because all die, all are confronted with this offer from God. All are touched by his saving grace. Thus grace would be the universal sacrament *par excellence*. For it would truly reach all indiscriminately, embodying God's offer to human beings and hence a universal opportunity for salvation.[11]

At death all have the opportunity to become Christians, i.e., to become like Christ. All can become the church, i.e., the community of those who are Christ's. Thus all can be saved. It is in this sense that we should interpret the repeated assertions of tradition about the necessity of the church for salvation and, in particular, about the church as the universal sacrament of salvation. At death there is the real possibility of the church becoming truly universal. In the eschatology of the individual we see in miniature what the reality of the universe's eschatology will be: there will be only one flock and one shepherd, only one redeemed humanity and one church, living in glory with God.

At death, when all is at stake and the eternal destiny of a human being is decided, the church is present. At that moment the import of God's universal salvific will takes on its full density. As Clement of Alexandria put it so pointedly:

Just as the will of God is one single act called the world, so his only divine intention is the salvation of human beings and is called the church (*Paidag.* 1.5).

In life and in death the divine foundation, which is light and love, is at work in all. It stimulates and inspires the thirst for life and the yearning for liberation, happiness, and goodness. In all there are underlying forces sufficient to impel them to full realization in the areas of encounter and absolute meaningfulness, which are the existential names for God. That is the concrete form in which God's salvific will is manifested to the individual person and the human community.

Later on we will see that in the eyes of Christian faith the ultimate foundation on which all subsists and exists is Jesus Christ. He is the savior and universal liberator. In him salvation is incarnated and offered universally to all. Through him we also have access to the ultimate mystery of creation, the holy Trinity, which dwells in the world and in the heart of the just human being. In the mystery of the Trinity God's universal salvific will attains its full, transcendent meaning. We find that human salvation is the presence of the Father, the Son, and the Holy Spirit in the world, and the presence of the world in the Father, the Son, and the Holy Spirit. This is the meaning of all creation, which is the precondition for the self-communication of the Trinity and the celebration of that communication. While creator and creature preserve their distinctive identities, God ultimately becomes all in all (1 Cor. 15:28).

CHAPTER 11

Habitual Grace: God's Grace
in the Fundamental Project of a Human Being

God's salvific will planted us in an atmosphere where divine love takes priority over any capacity for humans to refuse it in history. God continues to love humanity at all times, and his love finds historical mediations through which it can visit all human beings in their concrete life situation. It penetrates the historical project of humanity, of a nation, of a political and economic system, and it touches the heart of individual persons and society.

Habitual grace is the enduring presence of God's concrete salvific will and his love within the world. But if this presence is to be effective, God's gracious sympathy is not enough. The presence of the human being in God is also necessary. It is in this profound encounter that the enduring presence of grace is made real. Catholic tradition has designated this reality as habitual grace.[1]

Need for a Correct View of the Human Person

Theological investigation contemplated the reality of habitual grace within a rather limited horizon. It treated it on the level of the human person insofar as the latter was viewed as an individual. And even then it considered the individual almost exclusively in terms of the soul. Here we face the urgent task of deepening our conception of the human being.

The concrete human being is a network of operative relationships that extend out in all directions. The person and his or her individuality are of the utmost importance, but they are immersed in a biological, genetic, social, and cultural infrastructure. The person is never a *tabula rasa,* a virgin entity, a zero. Persons come already fashioned by a whole preceding history that culminates in them. Persons do not relate to others by mere juxtaposition. They are organic relationships. Persons live in organisms that range from the more simple to the more complex, from the family to the school and the socioeconomic system. The same is true with regard to nature, of which the human being is a part. Human beings relate to nature only insofar as they humanize it through their work and modify it through science and technology. These relationships are not mechanical ones. They are active, conscious, and historical. In relating to all these realities, the person alters others and the world even as others and the world alter the person. Concrete human persons are this complex network of relationships. They cannot be understood if we abstract from these realities that help shape them in a concrete and basic way.

This interrelationship between the person, others, and the world must be kept in mind when we talk about human persons in terms of their fundamental projects inhabited by divine grace. Otherwise we will "mystify" our understanding of the human being, giving the false impression that human beings can exist as isolated atoms with conditioning factors and without a biological and cultural past that has a profound effect on both body and soul.

Granting all the above considerations, however, we must also say that there is a totally irreducible dimension in human beings. It is the nucleus of all the aforementioned relationships, the free human ego. Human persons are not just the sum of their conditioning influences or the product of history; nor are they merely a cultural result. As persons, individuals are absolute beginnings. They are not means to ends but ends in themselves. They cannot be understood on the basis of anything prior, but only on the basis of their own spontaneity and interior freedom. Through the latter they can attain full self-realization or succumb to absolute frustration. Nothing in the world justifies the fact that I exist as I am, with my particular stance toward the totality. The totality can influence, condition, and mark me deeply, but I am not a robot. I react and assimilate in my own distinctive way. I reject things and fashion my own personal synthesis of the universe, however rudimentary, curious, consistent, or inconsistent it may appear to be. Thus the category that elucidates the mystery of the person is the category of presence. Human persons are there, present to view. I can accept or reject them, but they are the presence of a challenging mystery.

The question facing human thought and organization is how to maintain these two poles: the human person and the world, the human person and others, the human person and God. How are we to view persons so that we always include the social element present in them, and how are we to view the social element so that it always includes the personal element present in it? For person and society intermingle with each other in a basic and central way.[2] On this matter there have been two basic temptations in history.

One temptation has been to dissolve the person in society and culture. The individual person counts for nothing. We develop an image of the human being based on his or her conformity to the proper social roles. The human being becomes a robot, a cog in a totalitarian system without morality and freedom. The human being is a raw datum to be manipulated.

Society is viewed without any thought of the person, so that we end up in the imperialism of social roles, social structures, and social functions. We get a nonhuman image of human society. This temptation is much in evidence in all modern forms of structuralism and functionalism, especially in those inspired by scientific and technological models. But as Ludwig von Bertalanffy, the theoretician of general system theory, points out, human society is not a community of ants or termites governed by hereditary instincts and laws stemming from some higher totality. Society is based on the fulfillment of the individual, and it is doomed if the individual becomes a cog in the social machine:

A theory of organization . . . is not a manual for dictators of any sort . . . so that they can more effectively subjugate human beings through the application of ironclad scientific laws. It is a warning that the Leviathan of organization cannot engulf the individual without inevitably sealing its own ruin.[3]

The other temptation is to reduce the human being to the unique and unrepeatable aspects of the personal ego. Traditionally western and Christian thought has tended toward this extreme. We then get a picture of humans in terms of their ability to protest and say no, to overcome and transcend the alienating factors in the mechanisms of history. We see humanity as totally creative and absolutely free, subject to no fetters at all.

But such a human being does not exist. For that human being must also eat, drink, sleep, and submit to the daily struggle to get food in a world which no longer belongs to the first person who sets eyes on it. For now the land is already in someone's possession under some sort of political and economic system. The concrete human person is enmeshed in a given infrastructure and the conditioning influence of sex, race, culture, religion, class, age-group, and profession. All this is part of the person as well.

Neither of the two images just described above is realistic. Neither has existed in history. Only if we try to maintain both dialectically can we move toward a more adequate understanding of what a person is. In a human being we find reducible and irreducible elements. There is a human history that can be described and narrated, and there is a history of inner personal life that will never be told in words. There is the reality of an absolute presence among us, and there is an immersion of that presence in our all too tangible world. There is an infrastructure we can touch and manipulate, and there is something sacrosanct in human beings that we can never manipulate. As Ortega y Gasset put it: "I am me and my circumstances. If I do not save those circumstances, I will not save myself."

All this has a great deal to do with the theme of habitual grace. To what does it relate? What does it touch? Only the irreducible element in human beings? How are we to picture the state of sanctifying grace if a human being is not just the inmost region of the heart but an active network of relationships that go to make up the *essence* of what its nature is? What if a human being is, in fact, a spirit fleshed out in society and a particular set of relationships with the world? Grace touches the whole human being, which means that it also touches these relationships with others and the world. The sanctification of human beings necessarily implies the sanctification of all these relationships, and vice versa.

Human Life as the Historical Construction of a Project

The above considerations should help us to get a better view of human life in the concrete. The life of a human being is not the mere sum of isolated, single acts. Those acts relate to the structure of the person who performs them. In one sense they are unique and irreducible; in another sense they are immersed in the web of surrounding societal life. The concrete person is the synthesis of this dialectic, because we are talking about unity and synthesis when we talk about spirit.

As a spiritual being fleshed out in the world, a human being is one who lives by fashioning an ongoing synthesis of all that it finds and thus fashions its own world. The life of a human being is a oneness of meaning, a history. There may be breaking points and ruptures, but they can always be taken up in a new synthesis. Taken individually, the actions of a human life both concretize and reveal the unity of a person's life.

This "unity of life" is called the "fundamental project" of a human being in these pages. It presupposes some fundamental option that somehow sums up the various manifestations of life and joins separate human acts as does the chain of a necklace. It need not be operative on the level of explicit awareness. Rather it is the import of a personal journey that is gradually taking a certain course and weaving a human life into oneness.[4]

This fundamental option is articulated in the deepest yearnings of the unconscious and in our personal inclinations. It is made more explicit in the educational process, where learning material and influences and encounters have a great impact on our basic orientation. They greatly help define the main course and give shape and context to our fundamental project. The dreams of childhood, the conflicts of adolescence, the personal experiences of family and work life, and the stream of individual life as it is lived are other factors that help give shape to this fundamental project.

Since a human person is not an island but a continent involved with nature and others, the resultant relationships have their impact on our personal project. The aims embodied in institutions and the thrust of events at a given juncture in history also imply certain basic projects that the individual person will accept or reject in terms of his or her own personal project.[5]

This basic option need not be spelled out in a given act. A particular act need not, indeed will not, be our fundamental project in life. Rather, it is one embodiment of that project. The fundamental project itself is a unified thing that precedes the individual acts rather than evolving from them.[6] It is more like the surrounding atmosphere or horizon that makes individual acts possible and serves as their backdrop. It is a world view, a lifestyle, revealing both the inner personal dimension and the sociocultural dimensions of a basic option. Taken individually, the various acts are manifestations, confirmations, or falsifications of the latter option. But none of the individual acts as such is definitive or irreversible, however good or bad it may be. So long as human beings are moving in space and time and the material world, no individual action can express or define them in a definitive way. People can change their mind, alter their outlook, and set out on a different track.

Each action is a more or less intense expression of the fundamental option. There is an interaction between the two. The fundamental option underlies the individual acts, even as the latter give concrete expression to the former. There can also be acts which undermine the fundamental project, which diverge so sharply that they eventually give rise to a wholly different project. In any case we must not view the fundamental option as we might view the work of an architect. We do not first work out the whole plan and then gradually put it into execution. The overall plan takes shape with each concrete step we take, developing and unfolding in the process of living itself. Born of the dialectical interaction between our inner and outer life, it is the thing that gives unity to our human journey.

Habitual Grace as Fidelity to a Basic Option Open to God

Now we can raise another question: what can we say about a fundamental option that is open to God and that remains so throughout a person's life? Isn't that precisely what western theological tradition has called habitual grace? After all, this fundamental option possesses all the characteristics of a habit as the latter was described by Thomas Aquinas and Aristotle. A habit is not a passing disposition or capability.[7] It is an enduring quality and possession of the human person.

A fundamental option for God has a weight and impact of its own. Following in the footsteps of the Old Testament, Jesus Christ described it as loving with one's whole heart and soul and mind and strength. In short, it is an unconditional love that embraces the whole of life and entrusts itself to God as the absolute reality that confers meaning and fulfillment on human beings. An option for God is not just another choice. It is an option for that court of appeal which relates to us unconditionally and which thus becomes both the motive force and the purveyor of meaning behind our lives. This love is a love for God above everything else. In the concrete it can demand renunciation and sacrifice. It can call human beings to a course of suffering if they wish to remain faithful to it. It is a supremely active effort on the part of the human person, a profound exercise of human freedom.

This option for God can go on gaining in intensity throughout life. It can keep maturing and developing until it reaches the point where one feels inexpressible harmony with God, as the saints and mystics have testified: "The life I live now is not my own; Christ is living in me" (Gal. 2:20).

One point deserves stress here, however. People need not explicitly voice the name of God in order to have a basic, authentic, consistent option for God. What matters really is the reality that lies hidden under the hallowed word "God." Thus the project of a given person may be wholly directed toward the supreme values of human life without the name of God ever being mentioned. This person may be wholly dedicated to truth, justice, and the sacred dimensions of the human person that are open to transcendence. He or she may fight for these values and sacrifice other legitimate facets of life in the process. In fact such a project touches the supreme, ineffable reality that we call God. The person lives in communion with him and thence draws strength to remain loyal, firm, and persevering to his or her fundamental option.

The ability to live out such an option is what we would call living in the state of sanctifying or habitual grace. Such a life is permanently immersed in the *divine milieu,* which is the historical manifestation of divine grace.

The permanence of habitual grace survives even though human beings may occasionally perform acts that deviate from their fundamental project. Of course such acts must not strike at the very heart of the fundamental project, either by destroying it or by expressing some very different basic option or personal identity. The acts of deviation are truly sins and acts of betrayal, but they are not so substantive that they imply a definitive break with God (mortal sin). The habit of love, of remaining open to God and searching for him, remains; and hence the person remains in the state of sanctifying grace. Living in this dimension and persevering in it through the temptations of this world is the work of grace. Here grace is present in an enduring form, sanctifying human beings and their network of relationships.

This habitual grace manifests itself *in operation.* It helps human beings achieve ever greater harmony between their fundamental project and their concrete, individual acts. It also plays a *formative* role, perfecting and unifying human beings. It elevates them to deeper communion, ensuring the victorious dominion of love, understanding, mercy, forgiveness, and sincerity in their lives. They become more and more tuned to all that is truly human and divine.

Here we cannot yet say what habitual grace means in terms of relationship with the Father, the Son, and the Holy Spirit. These aspects of the fundamental human option will be the concern of Part Four of this book.

Merit and Fluctuating Degrees of Habitual Grace

The above considerations will help us to understand what classical theology has to say about such things as merit and the increase, decrease, or loss of sanctifying grace.

Merit. Here we will not deal with certain issues raised by the Bible. For example, in the Bible eternal life is described in various ways as some sort of recompense (Matt. 5:12; 20:8; 1 Cor. 3:8) for the good works performed by the just (2 Thess. 1:5; Luke 20:35; Rev. 3:4). It is a reward (1 Cor. 9:24), a crown (2 Tim. 4:8; 2:5; Rev. 2:10), a remuneration (Col. 3:23–24; Heb. 10:35). Nor will we go into various theological debates associated with the Protestant Reformation.

Let us simply say that the term "merit"[8] is an attempt to express the dialogic character of grace. In other words, it is God's love for human beings and the corresponding love of human beings for God. Merit, then, is grace considered from the standpoint of humanity's effort and collaboration with God. The fundamental project directed toward God (habitual grace) is carried out in history. It is animated and pervaded by God, but God does not exempt human beings from moving on their own. They were created to be creators and to collaborate with God. The motive force behind the journey is God; but humanity, the wayfarer, must move out and take the journey.

We might interpret "merit" to mean an obligation in terms of commutative justice to recompense someone for the good services he or she has rendered. In that case we can state unequivocally that no one can have "merit" before God. Human actions

are not the works of another vis-à-vis God because God is the author of these works [i.e., as the one who grants man the possibility of acting, the impulse to act, and the reality of the act itself] in the natural order and, even more, in the supernatural order.[9]

Merit is understood here in terms of God's promise to grant the happiness of the kingdom to all those who live in conformity with his will and who persevere in a basic project that is oriented toward him. Scripture is full of passages that tell us that good works will be rewarded and evil deeds punished (Matt. 5:12; 6:1–6,16,18; 10:32–33; 25:31–46; Mark 9:41–43; Luke 14:12–14; 19:11–27). In the eyes of the supreme judge a cup of water given to a disciple (Matt. 10:42) or a bit of compassion for the lowly (Matt. 25:31–46) makes a person worthy of the kingdom. The notion of merit underlines the fulfillment of God's promise to those who hear his voice and put his commands into practice.

Merit is not the precondition for supreme happiness. It is the presence and joy of that happiness already existing in the life of the just person. Good works do not attain a future heaven. They translate what heaven means into the present time. Heaven begins to be a reality here on earth in the upright life of human beings and their world; it culminates in eschatology.

Many false problems about merit arise from a false picture of heaven and its causal nexus with good works. We tend to think of heaven as something distinct from good works. In fact, however, heaven is concretized, even within the bounds of time, in our good works. It is in gestation within human history as the latter moves toward the final days of eschatology.

Official Catholic theology has asserted two things that are two aspects of one and the same reality of grace. One thing, merit, looks at the matter from the standpoint of human beings. The other thing, grace as a gift, looks at the matter from the standpoint of God. Heaven is a gift from God on the one hand, and something merited by human beings on the other. Good works are a divine gift and a human achievement. In the latter respect they are the result of our fidelity to a right-minded basic project.[10] A celebrated text attributed to Pope Celestine (422–32) puts the matter elegantly: "So great is God's goodness to human beings that he wants his gifts to be our merits" (*Indiculus;* DS 248). Merit, however, does not justify any self-boasting on the part of human beings. It simply expresses the dialogic nature of grace and stresses the aspect of human participation.

What actions are meritorious? Here again we must not fall into the temptation of treating actions as isolated atoms. It is the fundamental project of a person's life, which unifies it into a totality, that is meritorious. All concrete acts are meritorious to the extent that they express this fundamental project in varying degrees of intensity.

Classical theology distinguished between merit *de congruo* and merit *de condigno.* This terminology arose in the twelfth and thirteenth centuries. It can be found in the works of Alain of Lille and William of Auxerre,[11] and it is not without its problems. It has been debated right up to our own day.[12] In the light of God's absolute transcendence, human beings do not seem justified in claiming any merit in the strict sense, except in the light of the divine promises which are so evident in Scripture.

Merit *de condigno* implies that there is a proportion (*condignitas*) between God's project, humanity's fundamental project, and merit by virtue of God's promise. Because of the promise, a person merits total fulfillment in God if he or she faithfully lives in the love of God. In the light of God's promise there is a real-life basis for heavenly fulfillments, namely, a fundamental human project that is oriented toward God.

Merit *de congruo* implies that it is fitting that God should be more generous than any good human project would let us dream of. It accords with God's magnanimity that his benefits and love should exceed the bounds of any human merit. The notion of merit *de congruo* does embody a profound human experience. It is a frequent human experience that the scope and import of an action can escape the person responsible for it. An artist may spontaneously introduce new features or nuances into his or her art, never realizing that they will give rise to a new school associated with his or her name. A person may make some little gesture of understanding of an ordinary sort that will profoundly alter the life of its recipient. A poet may dash off a little poem that captures his or her feelings at the moment, and that poem may inspire many others to turn anew to God. These consequences are not the merit of the author. It is God who injects them into the work. He is the real agent who moves both the author and the author's readers. The neat proportion between cause and effect is broken through the superabundant generosity of God. He communicates to human beings through human works, causing the latter to produce greater effects than might have been expected.

De condigno and *de congruo* simply reaffirm the encounter between God and human beings, stressing the fact that it is always God who takes the initiative and holds primacy. God's project does not destroy a human project. It assumes the latter into itself, making it its own and "eternally rewarding what God himself granted" (DS 248).

Increase and decrease of grace. The notion of a fundamental project open to God (habitual grace) also helps us to understand what increase and decrease of grace must mean.[13] Here we must get beyond the quantitative innuendos suggested by the words "increase" and "decrease." As we have noted many times before, grace is not something different from God. It is the encounter of God and human beings in mutual love. Gratuitousness exists in both poles of the encounter. God can communicate himself freely and gratuitously in a way and a degree that suits each individual (what is called the "distribution of graces"). In like manner human beings can give of themselves freely to the extent they are open to God. The fundamental project of a human being can be oriented to God in such a way that it welcomes the divine mystery with ever increasing intensity as life unfolds. In that case we can talk about an increase of grace. We are talking about a person's increasing openness to God, which presupposes and implies increasing self-giving on God's part as well. Grace is not something other than this openness; it is this openness itself. Never empty, it is increasingly inhabited by God and is capable of indefinite, infinite growth.

It is in this sense that the New Testament refers to growth as a basic category in the relationship between human beings and God (Mark 4:28; Matt. 6:28; 13:32). It is God who grants growth and increase in the elaboration of our life project (1 Cor. 3:6), thereby allowing the fruits of our true identity to grow as well (2 Cor. 9:10). This growth does not undermine human effort; it inspires it. We can thus understand the exhortations of the New Testament:

Grow rather in grace, and in the knowledge of our Lord and Savior Jesus Christ; let us profess the truth in love and grow to the full maturity of Christ the head (2 Pet. 3:18; Eph. 4:15).

Decrease of grace means that a human project is moving further and further away from God and drying up. Vices begin to take over and deviations in the moral life undermine our basic option. We begin to develop a different basic project in which God will no longer be the radical meaning of life or the culmination of existence. Here again Scripture testifies to this tragic human reality: "I hold this against you, though: you have turned aside from your early love" (Rev. 2:4; see Gal. 3:11; Heb. 10:32; Rev. 3; Isa. 3:15–20).

Loss of grace. The continued closing up of the human person to any higher destiny and the ongoing betrayal of God's appeals in reality can give rise to the total loss of God's grace. Nevertheless we must remember that no basic option within present history can be regarded as definitive and irreversible.[14] So long as human beings are on their journey, they are not capable of defining their stance toward God in an absolute, irreversible way; for no act and no basic option can exhaust all the possibilities of life in history. This applies both to good and to evil. So long as a human being is alive, there is always a chance for salvation. While a human being moves through life as a pilgrim, no loss can be definitive. There is always room for conversion.

As we noted earlier, however, death does provide the occasion for a synthesizing act that sums up a whole fundamental project. This last synthesis does have a definitive and irreversible character. Here there is a real possibility of an absolute loss of grace. It is not the result of a bad act. It is the outcome of a whole human project that gradually was frustrated and took definitive formal shape at the moment of death. In that sense we can say that there is only one mortal sin, i.e., that which leads to death and absolute frustration and hell. It becomes a reality in death, signifying the complete loss of grace, of relationship with God.

Doubt and Certainty About the State of Habitual Grace

One of the much debated questions at the time of the Reformation concerned the degree of certainty we could have about the state of habitual grace.[15] The Council of Trent set forth this teaching:

While a pilgrim in this mortal life, no one should seek to penetrate so deeply into the hidden mystery of divine predestination as to be able to say with certainty that he has no doubt about the number of the elect; as to suggest that a just person could no longer sin or, if he did, could be sure of another conversion. For without a special revelation from God, we cannot know whom God has chosen for himself (DS 1540; see Canons 15 and 16, DS 1565 and 1566).

This affirms that there is no certainty about either damnation or salvation. While they live, human beings are suspended between the possibilities of good and evil, of saving dialogue and damnable refusal to dialogue. In careful studies two theologians[16] have shown that the theologians and bishops of Trent interpreted certainty exclusively as intellectual certainty about one's state of grace. The Scotist thinkers at the Council had another point of view and it was not condemned. According to them:

from the evidence of their own experience human beings can know their own good inner dispositions in receiving the sacrament of Penance and thus arrive at the certain conclusion of having received grace.[17]

The "certainty" in question here was the "certainty of faith." The teaching of Trent is consistent with the concept of faith it worked out. It described faith as an intellectual assent to the truths revealed by God. Faith implies that dimension, but it is much richer. In biblical terms faith also means profession, obedience, and trust placed in God rather than in human effort.

In the realm of faith, then, there is a certainty based on hope, as Paul himself states (Rom. 5:5; 8:14–16).[18] Human beings can have moral certainty that they are in a state of habitual grace by virtue of the inner certainty they have about their fundamental project and its orientation to God. Knowing that they are in loving openness to the Father, human beings can know that they are experiencing the state of habitual grace. However, they can never be certain that they will continue in this fidelity to God. That is why they must ask for the gift of perseverance and fidelity (Trent, DS 806). The certainty we possess now has to do with our basic striving for salvation.[19]

Paul took note of this wayfaring situation of human beings, of the reality of a false conscience and the masks we may use to delude ourselves. He has this to say about himself:

Mind you, I have nothing on my conscience. But that does not mean that I am declaring myself innocent. The Lord is the one to judge me, so stop passing judgment before the time of his return. He will bring to light what is hidden in darkness and manifest the intentions of hearts. At that time everyone will receive his praise from God (1 Cor. 4:4–5).

Despite this strain of self-criticism, which ever remains necessary, Paul still professed his certainty of salvation:

For I am certain that neither death nor life, neither angels nor principalities, neither the present nor the future, nor powers, neither height nor depth nor any other creature, will be able to separate us from the love of God that comes to us in Christ Jesus, our Lord. . . . If God is for us, who can be against us?. . . Who shall bring a charge against God's chosen ones? (Rom. 8:38–39; 31–33).

The Christian faith and the presence of the risen one in our midst offer us joy, peace, security, and the certainty of being loved by God. It exercises all the fears that inhibit good actions:

I do not run like a man who loses sight of the finish line. I do not fight as if I were shadowboxing. What I do is discipline my own body and master it, for fear that after having preached to others I myself should be rejected (1 Cor. 9:26–27).

Hope-filled certainty that we are in the grace of God does not excuse us from working and persevering in "fear and trembling" (Phil. 2:12). It does, however, create a different atmosphere. Though our struggle is a dramatic one, we carry it out in a spirit of deep serenity and with a touch of joy and good humor.

The certainty of being in the possession of grace can easily be dulled. We have ties with other people and the world. We can see the underlying structures of sinfulness that pervade reality and that make us accomplices in its sinfulness. Thus we share in the mystery of the world's salvation and its damnation. We cannot be sure of our degree of responsibility for the world's sinfulness. But Christ shouldered that sinfulness to redeem us. He thereby created space for greater certainty and for God's consolation. Through the resurrection God showed us that he was also the Lord of the darker dimensions of the world: "You will suffer in the world. But take courage! I have overcome the world" (John 16:33).

CHAPTER 12

Actual Grace:
God's Grace at Work in the Execution
of a Person's Fundamental Project

The fundamental project of a human being, which in this case is oriented toward God (habitual grace), is a totality that ultimately unifies his or her life. This totality takes shape step by step. Successive individual acts give form and expression to it. Indeed the fundamental project exists in real life only insofar as it becomes historicized. Therein lies the importance of individual acts. Each individual act contains the human being in varying degrees of involvement, revealing his or her inner depths to a greater or lesser degree. The moral quality of these acts and their moral evaluation cannot be based on the assumption that they are isolated, self-subsistent actions. We must pay more attention to the person's fundamental project in evaluating the individual acts that embody it.[1]

One does not pass directly from the fundamental project to individual acts. A whole gamut of mediating factors and mechanisms can intervene, and they may have a relative autonomy of their own. Poorly assimilated experiences and distorted hierarchies of value may result from the socialization process at home, or in school, or in social life. Some dimensions of the human person may be as yet poorly integrated, so that they seem to stand as a parallel ego even without taking any recognizably pathological form. In other words, we may not always find harmony between a person's fundamental project and a given individual act that is meant to flesh out the project.

Underlying many actions that are viewed as morally evil or dubious there may be a good basic project. Underlying others that are considered good there may be an evil project. Aware of this fact, theology has always taught that not all the deeds of the just are just, and not all the deeds of the sinner are sinful. And we ourselves are more readily inclined to see malice in good actions than goodness in evil actions. It is harder for us to admit that there might be a good project underlying seemingly evil acts than to say that there might be an evil project underlying good acts.

Granting, then, that we must always take note of the ambiguity surrounding human actions, we can still say that human actions usually are the expression of a fundamental human option.

Two Aspects of One and the Same Grace

So long as individual acts do embody and harmonize with a basic option that is open to God, we can talk about actual grace.[2] It is not really different from habitual grace. Actual grace is really habitual grace being implemented and fleshed out in reality. Just as individual actions are expressions of a fundamental option, so actual graces are expressions of habitual grace. They are not two different realities, though they can be conceptually distinct. Grace is a single movement that can be viewed from two standpoints, as it were. Viewed in terms of its overall thrust, it is habitual grace; viewed in terms of the concrete actions that make up its movement, it is actual grace. The grace of God is one, not many, because there is only one love and one salvific relationship insofar as God is concerned.[3] Actual grace is habitual grace at work in the process of history through concrete, individual acts. It is a process of spelling out the underlying thrust. It is aimed toward the future. It moves from encounter here and now toward full realization in God eventually. Viewing it in this light, we can preserve the oneness of human life and the oneness of God's grace.

Alternative Names for Actual Grace

If we choose to use various names for actual grace because we perform various acts to flesh out our fundamental option, we can come up with something akin to the scholastic designations.[4] The whole of human life is immersed in divine grace, and grace makes its presence felt in even the slightest manifestations. Nothing in human beings fails to be loved and permeated by God. Thus it is said that even the preliminary actions that prepare human beings to open up to God (*initium fidei*) are already manifestations of grace. So too are the actions that express faith and humble surrender to God (*affectus fidei*).

Freedom is not some last human instance apart from grace, some ultimate residue that belongs exclusively to human beings. It, too, is immersed in the movement of grace; the latter makes the former more truly itself, more truly free. Various passages in John's gospel should not be taken to mean that God's grace emasculates human initiative, e.g., "Apart from me you can do nothing" (John 15:5); "no one can come to me unless the Father who sent me draws him" (John 6:44); "no one can come to me unless it is granted him by the Father" (John 6:65). These passages express the fact of salvation history that concrete human beings cannot be adequately understood apart from their immersion in grace. It is a part of their life and milieu *de facto,* though it need not have been that way *de jure.* The fact of *history* is that human beings live amid the reality of a permanent summons from God; they can only accept or reject it. Every decision of theirs is made within the horizon of salvation (grace) or sin (the rejection of grace).[5]

God's grace accompanies human beings in every life situation. This explains the traditional division of actual grace into a number of different terms, which we shall briefly describe here. But we must remember that they all represent the *one* habitual grace of God taking concrete shape in the various moments of human life:

1. *Gratia preveniens:* God always *anticipates* human beings and retains primacy. It is God who triggers the human desire for self-improvement, openness, and the quest for greater light.

2. *Gratia concomitans:* the grace which *accompanies* the human act that expresses a basic option for God, be it in thought, word, or deed.

3. *Gratia consequens:* the grace that *endures* in human beings as fidelity to the option taken and the acts already executed. Thus we see that grace accompanies human beings before they act, while they act, and after they execute concrete acts.

4. *Gratia excitans:* the grace that *incites* human beings to do good. The prodigal son rose up and set out to return to his father's house. That is the work of *gratia excitans.* So are dreams of betterment, good resolutions, and the quiet summons of hope in the recesses of the human heart. They all are tiny but effective manifestations of God's grace at work turning the human desert fertile.

5. *Gratia auxilians:* the grace that *helps* human beings perform the acts that dovetail properly with their fundamental project.

6. *Gratia sanans:* Human beings experience their own weakness and failure in trying to carry out their basic project. Grace reveals itself as a *healing medicine* that gives new life to their flagging strength. It cures their sickness and spiritual anemia.

7. *Gratia elevans:* the grace that *elevates* human beings from their decadent situation and restores them to their true nature as human beings. Now they can shoulder their basic option in a truly human way.

8. *Gratia sufficiens:* God communicates himself *adequately* to all so that they can save themselves. He does not deny himself to anyone, however terrible their plight may be. Any inadequacy resides on the human side, not on God's side.

9. *Gratia efficax:* grace that is *infallible in its effect.* It touches human beings and really transforms them, making them more human and more divine.

10. *Gratia perseverantiae:* Theological tradition has always maintained that "in the actual reality of the fallen human condition the just person cannot persevere for long in justice [i.e., in fidelity to his or her fundamental option] without special divine help" (Trent: DS 1572). This proposition makes sense in the light of our day-to-day experience of sinfulness, for which we are to ask forgiveness in the Our Father (Matt. 6:12). As the Letter of James

puts it: "All of us fall short in many respects" (James 3:2). That is why the Council of Trent also declared that without some special grace from God, some special divine self-communication, no creature can avoid all venial sin (DS 1573). Thus Trent made it clear that even the just commit some faults daily. The *grace of perseverance* is the special presence of God that makes it possible for human beings to stick loyally to the road that will lead them to the kingdom and hence arrive there without getting seriously sidetracked. Trent calls this grace a great gift (*magnum donum:* DS 1566).

We see, then, that the most simple and the most demanding of human actions and virtues are bathed in divine grace. Classical theology discussed this aspect of daily life in terms of humanity's need for grace in order to observe the natural law.[6] Grace must not be viewed as something outside human beings that does not belong to their historical reality. As we have noted time and again, there is nothing natural that is not also *in fact* supernatural.

Here the vast horizons of grace and its universality open up before us. It is offered to all human beings, whatever their historical or religious situation may be. Even without any direct contact with the Christian and Catholic expression of this truth, all human beings can be in communion with Jesus Christ, who is grace made human in history. We all live in the same salvific community because we all are passionately loved by God.

No Total Uprightness or Sinfulness in Human Actions

From the above observations it should be clear that not all the deeds of the just are just. Humanity's fallen situation means that human beings are always under the dark shadow of their own basic alienation, i.e., sin. Their fundamental project, though open to God, is stifled here and there. Though it may not be suffocated completely, it is injured in ways that offend God and shame the human beings involved. The latter do not fully execute the basic resolution they have set for themselves. Thus a deep dialectics runs through human life. Human beings resolve to undertake a project that is wholly open and loyal to God. Then they experience the painful fact that they cannot carry it out in a consistent way in history. They need pardon every day, and they require patience from their fellows.

It is equally true that not all the deeds of sinners are sinful. Insofar as they are still wayfarers who have not completed their trip, their fundamental project never becomes so evil and closed to God that it suffocates the Spirit and can isolate itself completely from God's grace. Even the worst sinner can still perform good acts, which bear witness to the remnants of goodness in the heart. The Roman church never failed to condemn pessimistic positions which maintained that sin could totally destroy free will and so becloud human understanding that a human being could do nothing but commit sin.

And so it passed condemnations on the views of such people as Jan Hus, Luther, Baius, and Quesnel.[7]

The teaching of the Roman church, then, is that despite sin human beings retain a basic, invulnerable goodness that signifies the victorious presence of God in them. This basic (ontological) goodness, though obscured, makes human life gracious and gratifying. It means that human history is not just a story of humanity's Promethean rebelliousness but also a symphony of love and truth on both God's and humanity's part.

Faithful in their quest for God, human beings can always count on his grace-filled benevolence. The point is put well in a classic axiom: *"Facienti quod est in se, Deus non denegat gratiam."* [If one does what is in one's power, God does not deny his grace].[8] Let us consider this axiom more closely, so that we do not interpret it in semi-Pelagian terms. We cannot divide things up neatly, figuring out what belongs specifically to human beings and what belongs specifically to God. *Gratia praeveniens* and *gratia excitans* inspire human beings to move toward the level of God. If they open up to God and remain faithful to him in spite of all provocations, then they can be certain that God will grant them the grace of final perseverance, save them, and bring them into his kingdom. If they do what is in their power, with the help of divine grace, God will grant them the grace of perseverance.

CHAPTER 13

The Social Structure of Habitual and Actual Grace

Our previous reflection on the basic project of a human being and its embodiment in concrete acts should not delude us into thinking that grace is something that works solely in the inner life of the divine I and the human Thou. Such an idea is based on an erroneous conception of the human being. As we have noted several times, the human being arises as a reality that is essentially social as well. The fundamental project of a human person is intimately bound up with the fundamental project of the culture in which he or she lives. Inhuman and antidivine dimensions in that culture cannot help but infiltrate and undermine one's personal project.

In earlier chapters we considered the experience of grace in our scientific and technological world and also in the geopolitical context of Latin America. We noted the inevitable link between the overall project of a culture and our own personal project. Here I should like to pick up that train of thought and focus on the social dimension of habitual and actual grace.[1] This dimension is seriously neglected in the theological tracts on grace and in homiletic discussions of it. The traditional Catholic conception, for all its good points, is excessively individualistic. Even when dealing with sin, conversion, and the earthly commitments of Christians, it considers them from a highly individualistic standpoint.

The Ontological Roots of the Social Dimension in the Individual

The social structure of human beings does not lie solely on the psychological level. It is not simply a matter of breaking our absorption with ourselves and opening up to liberative, therapeutic communication. This dimension is real enough, but it is not the most fundamental one. It retains a trace of dualism that sets the outlook of the individual over against that of society. To halt our reflection on that level would be to concentrate on moralizing sentiments that urge solidarity, communication, and the formation of a community.

In fact the social dimension of the human being is ontologically rooted in the very core of the human being as a person.[2] It does not arise after the individual dimension. It is not merely the sum of various juxtaposed indi-

141

viduals who happen to form a community or society. It is not a mere byproduct that is reducible to a more basic reality. Ontologically speaking, we can say that the social dimension is fundamental. It exists prior to the will of individuals or their encounter with each other. It is a structural reality that helps constitute the human person. Either a person is social or is not a person at all. Even if there was only one person in the world, that person would be social and communitarian by the very fact of being a person. Such a person would coexist with himself or herself, and with his or her world, ideas, projects, and interpretations of the surrounding, interacting world. Thus the social dimension is a web of relationships that constitute the very being of a person. We relate to ourselves by objectifying ourselves; we relate to others by communicating ourselves; and we relate to nature by transforming and humanizing it.

There are not two conscious awarenesses, one individual (I) and one social (we). There is only one human awareness that finds elaboration and expression amid the reality of shared life with others (we). Individualism is a false understanding of the human being. The ego is always inhabited by others.[3] The individual is always an abstraction. In concrete reality the person always shows up as a complicated web of active relationships.

In social terms, then, this means that the human person moves out to perform certain roles. Those roles are associated with certain patterns of behavior, certain social expectations, certain rewards and sanctions.[4] Human persons participate in the destiny of their society, in its achievements and its crises, in its opportunities for salvation and its temptations to perdition.

The Fundamental Project of a Culture and That of the Human Person

These basic anthropological considerations should help us to get a better idea of the tie-up between the basic project of a given human person and the overall project of a given society. There is an irreducible element in the individual ego, and each person can assimilate or reject the overall project of a culture. But in some way or another the basic project of the individual does reflect that of the culture. The former shares in the achievements and the limitations of the latter. The individual participates in those cultural dimensions that open up to God and others, but it also participates in those dimensions that close up and refuse to accept God. Vigilance and a certain amount of critical awareness are required so that cultural mechanisms do not engulf the person and turn him or her into a merely passive mirror of the situation.

Culture, the ethos of a society, implies some *way of being with and relating to* others, nature, and the transcendent. Hence it implies a particular way of living out political, economic, and religious relationships. The resultant values both express these relationships and serve as their ideological justification. And the relationships are perpetuated and legitimated by social institutions (which are both functional and symbolic), juridical bodies, ethical codes, and a given hierarchy of values.

Some ways of organizing societal life do not reveal the truth about human beings. They are based on inequalities in culture, race, and access to production and consumption goods. Some people are born black, poor, illiterate, or under a different ideology. This very fact puts them in a certain place within the societal structure. Prior to any considerations of a personal nature, their function and role in society is determined for them.

Other ways of organizing societal life have a high social cost. A heavy price must be paid for the enjoyment of cultural and economic goods. In many instances that price is paid by an impoverished majority, who are left to shift for themselves.

The way people approach material goods establishes a particular way of organizing property ownership, work, and economic transactions. Thus it affects the way people relate to each other socially in terms of justice, dignity, participation, and fraternal solidarity. The economic base serves as the foundation for the structuring of political relationships and the sharing of decision-making and power. A society may place all decision-making power in the hands of a small elite who control the means of production. The rest of the population takes orders. Over the economic and political edifice is erected an ideological structure. It lays down the hierarchy of values designed to legitimate the existing socioeconomic relationships and to reinforce continually the consensus that is ever threatened by those who feel maltreated and alienated. These values are inculcated socially by the schools, communications media, and other channels. They are structuring structures that convey certain patterns of perception and thus make it possible to achieve societal homogeneity.[5]

All these complicated social mechanisms, which have been only briefly touched upon here, have their impact on our personal project. Indeed the latter may simply mirror or reproduce the societal image. But the societal image can also be assimilated in a critical vein, so that it is purified of its alienating dimensions and perhaps even challenged openly. However, when a critical spirit and discernment are lacking, human persons may be so transfixed by the prevailing ideology that they erroneously feel free when in fact the values of the ruling class hold sway over them.

It should be evident, then, that it is not easy to talk about the state of habitual grace or about actual grace in such circumstances. Social and structural determinisms usually work on the unconscious. They can be good or bad. They can be the fruits of grace at work in the world or the consequences of sin. The ongoing process of *conscientization,* which entails both consciousness-raising and critical, transforming action, enables us to throw out the schemas that are oppressing us. We do not do so in order to replace them by equally alienating and dehumanizing ones. We do so in order to free our enslaved liberty for its true role and activity, i.e., communion, participation, and the creation of new forms of societal life in which it will be easier to love both God and our fellow humans.

The Project of the Modern Age and Grace

In Chapter 6 we considered the project of the modern age and its relationship to grace and dis-grace. Here I want to bring out its intimate link with the project of the individual person. By the "modern spirit" I mean here the cultural ethos that arose in the sixteenth century in conjunction with the scientific spirit and the formation of the bourgeoisie as a social class. It arose in Europe, and today it has made its way around the world, thanks to colonialism, imperialism, the growing oneness of the world economy today, and the rise of multinational corporations. It proposes a certain project for humanity as such, a certain project for society, and a particular type of reasoning that will make this project both feasible and legitimate.[6]

This reasoning is predominantly analytical and instrumental. It takes priority over dialectical and sapiential reasoning. Indeed it may even claim to be the only valid way in which to express the whole of human experience. It has created awesome works, such as the whole undertaking of science and technology that seeks to dominate the mechanisms of nature and to guide relations among human beings. This ethos has now come into crisis. Humanism, social structure, ecology, and the quality of life are in jeopardy. Underneath its will to power, this ethos has revealed its rapacious quest for profit, stockpiles of wealth, and rule by force.

Knowledge is power, the dominion of the subject over nature or human beings or society. Excessive concentration on the scientific method, efficiency, and the exploration of all that can be known and manipulated for one's purposes are some of the characteristics of the modern ethos. Western capitalism and communist state capitalism, the systems that govern most human beings today, are framed within the modern ethos. On the structural level communism is no alternative to the capitalist model. It has assimilated and accepted the analytical and instrumental style of reasoning, rejecting sapiential and sacramental reasoning as nonhuman. It views relations between humanity and nature as equivalent to those between human beings themselves, and so it has produced a predominantly economic view of social problems.

The wielders of science and technology, and hence of world power, are a small group of nations. They maintain other nations in a state of dependence and oppression. Slowly but surely they manage to impose their cultural ethos on others, pretending that it is the only one that is truly human and civilized. Other modes of access to reality have been confined within the boundaries of scientific rationality and efficiency.

This modern mode of being has led to structural conflicts of the most severe sort. The sophisticated growth of the affluent consumer nations must be bought at the high price of social inequality, and the price must be paid by the poor peoples of the world. Today people everywhere are conscious of the crisis this has produced, for the modern ethos has undermined the quality of life for all.

In the early stages of modern history Christianity rejected the modern ethos. At that time it did so for conservative reasons. It looked back nostalgically to the earlier period of Christendom, when it held power. Then, between the days of Leo XIII and Vatican II it moved toward open dialogue with the world. Some circles exalted modern progress and its autonomous scientific reason to the point where one could no longer see what Christian experience and faith might have to contribute on its own. There was no overall structural analysis of the spirit of modernity and its cultural ethos. Other circles, bolstered by sound theological and pastoral reflection in Latin America, began to take cognizance of the deeply rooted conflicts in the structures of the modern age, and also of its lack of openness to transcendence. This criticism was not based on nostalgia for a distant past. Its approach was a postmodern one, interpreting and evaluating reality in terms of the sapiential reasoning of the common people and the symbolic-sacramental character of humanity's relationships with nature and its fellows.

This new kind of awareness does not denigrate the anthropological, political, and historical project of the modern age. Moving beyond the narrow confines of reactionary versus progressive thinking, it seeks to elaborate alternative models for the future. It goes back to the national history of various peoples, looks at their distinctive way of thinking, living, and evaluating in sapiential terms, and accepts their differing rhythms of transformation and liberation. It offers an understanding of human beings and society based on faith, viewing the former as creatures, children of God, brothers and sisters, and people ever open to others. Faith thus becomes a force structuring a new meaning of life that will serve as the backdrop for social, educational, scientific, and technological practices.

This new attitude of faith does not just seek to salvage the true values of the modern ethos and justify them. It hopes to convert the modern ethos at its very core. It has a different vision, an alternative vision. Rather than adapting to the given horizon, it seeks to create a new horizon grounded in a better sense of justice, humanity, and communion with God. It offers an alternative image of humanity based on faith:

Faith entails a new view of the meaning of life and the world, liberating humanity's freedom from all the earthly bondages of sin. Faith offers people a new horizon of understanding. With it they can perceive, judge, and purify their cultural ethos and their understanding of life, death, nature, humankind, and God. For a people's understanding of life and its meaning is the ethical and transcendent core of every culture and of every personal or social action.[7]

Viewing the matter in this light, we can see more clearly the relationship between an overall historical project and the project of a given individual. The latter shares the pain and drama of the former. We glimpse the deeper truth of Jesus' parable about the wheat and the chaff growing up together. To a greater or lesser degree every human being shares in the salvation or damnation of the world. Habitual grace makes its appearance in our world insofar as we persist in willing to overcome the contradictions in the existing system and to make the world more human and divine. Actual grace makes its appearance in the concrete steps we take at every level—theoretical and practical, within ourselves or within structures—to achieve that goal.

No one is wholly inhabited by grace alone. Sin resides in all. That is the way it will be until we can get beyond this profound ambiguity at death. However sanctified we may be within ourselves, we all stand in need of God's mercy and our fellows'. We are in fellowship with one another, not only in grace with the new Adam but also in sin with the old Adam.

God's Plan and Human Projects

These considerations suggest that the human journey is a very mysterious one. The personal ego does not feel like the agent of its own destiny. Instead it feels like an actor on stage where the history of the world is being played out; and the overall plot seems to defy our analytical reasoning. Each actor plays his or her role and has his or her own part. But all must live with a basic insecurity in history. Whom, in the end, are we serving? For whom is the whole play? What point is it trying to make? It is sapiential reasoning that most readily glimpses the fact that no one happening or coincidence or structure in history is the point. It is the overall meaning of the whole that summons us to move on. All the individual elements are revelations of that ultimate meaning.

What is the meaning of it all? Is it perhaps that institutional and cultural events mark the advent of some radical and ultimate meaning? Might not our openness to intrasystemic meanings, which can be grasped by instrumental reasoning, be a sign or sacrament of some ultimate meaning that transcends all the others? Might not history be the revelation and demonstration of some ultimate word that will unveil everything? What is that ultimate word or meaning? Is it not what theology has always referred to as the mystery of God and his plan? Faith, which takes root and grows in the bosom of sapiential reasoning, offers an answer to our historical insecurity and our inability to know what we are really fashioning. It tells us that we are aiding and carrying out the plan of God through our own fundamental projects; and his plan is one of love, not of destruction. Nothing can prevail against it, not even the gates of hell or all the traits of nazism in every human heart.

We fashion projects. God has his own plan. We can see the latter clearly only through faith. Through faith we also know that his plan took concrete shape in Jesus Christ. His journey led to life, death, and resurrection. It is preserved as a living memory in the church and celebrated daily in the Christian community.[8] This plan, I repeat, is not clear to anyone. In particular, it is not clear to those who regard themselves as the bearers of light: the holders of decision-making power and the authors of plans for national security and world salvation. They are little more than actors on the stage. They are not agents of the plan, because it is God's alone. But though they may not even know it, they are in the service of this eternal plan of love. They find themselves within a movement they did not initiate. Though they pretend to be the prime movers, they are borne along by the movement itself. As I suggested in the little parable about the train at the start of this book, we are all borne along by the movement of God and his grace though we may react in various ways to it. His mysterious plan is sovereign, and history is moving inexorably toward the full realization he has in mind.

CHAPTER 14

The Course of Grace in the World

The profound ambiguity of the personal and social project of human beings has revealed to us the complex course of grace in the human heart and the world. In the concrete, the gracious design of God always entails an element of permanent crisis for the human project, which is always tainted with sin. Grace impels human beings toward a process of liberation from those dimensions that are hostile to the saving encounter and it tends to establish a new situation: the freedom of the children of God.

Human individuals and society have the following paradoxical experience: on the one hand they feel oppressed by all sorts of oppressive factors; on the other hand, they feel ardent yearnings for liberation. They see that oppression is of such a sort that they cannot attain liberation in isolation from others or by their own initiative alone. They must be liberated by someone. On the other hand, freedom cannot be handed to someone. It can be won only in a process of liberation that requires effort on the part of human beings. No one frees anyone else, and no one can free himself or herself by working alone. We liberate ourselves by working together in the same liberation project. Thus freedom derives from a force that liberates our captive liberty, but at the same time it is the fruit of a human effort effected by freedom.

Experience also convinces us that all liberation possesses a dialectical structure. In short, it contains contradictions. The attainment of freedom means the overcoming of prior oppressions, yet it also generates new forms of captivity in turn. The latter call for liberation in turn, and hence for even more freedom. Thus liberation is an action that seeks to conquer freedom over and over again. It is a process whose ultimate destination, in the eyes of theology, is God: the supreme freedom above and beyond all dialectical structures.[1]

Grace as Crisis

Breaking in on sinful humans, God's love (grace) acts as a catalyst. It awakens them to a process of liberation *from* their project of habitual sin and *for* a project of habitual grace. Here the word "crisis" has an eminently positive sense.[2] It comes from the Sanskrit *kri* or *kir,* a root which means to "clean" or "purify." As gold is purified of its dross in a crucible, so a crisis purifies human beings of their taints and prepares them for their true identity. God's grace (love) acts as a crucible in which human beings are transformed from sinners into just people.

The gospels depict Jesus as the crisis of the sin-laden world (see Matt. 10:34; John 3:19; 5:19–30; 12:31, 47; 16:11). His presence, light, and love purifies the world, causing it to go through a painful but grace-filled process of conversion. The Council of Trent, speaking in process-oriented terms, presents the justification of the sinner as the active passage of human beings from the sign of the old Adam to the sign of the new Adam (DS 1524). Justification results from the loving action of grace that triggers a process of conversion. In it human beings freely act to "accept the inspiration that they might just as well have rejected" (DS 1525). Sinful human beings, who had been living out a fundamental project closed to God, now become just people living out a fundamental project open to God.

Grace also appears as crisis in another sense. Crisis can also signify divisiveness and rupture within a given order. Every process of purification implies leaving something behind and assuming something new. The grace of God breaks in on sinful humanity as a ray of light on darkened eyes. The order of sin, which is a detour from the pathway leading to heaven, is challenged at its roots by grace. It enters into crisis, and this can give rise to a new orientation that serves as a *criterion* (which comes from the same root as "crisis") for distinguishing the false from the true.

In Greek *krisis* (verb *krinein*) means decision. It presupposes an array of options that offer various possibilities and generate tensions and conflicts. We overcome these tensions by deciding for *one* alternative that gives new direction to our basic project in life. Grace is a crisis insofar as it urges us toward conversion. We must take a stand vis-à-vis God's love, and this decision will involve our whole destiny as a person. As crisis, grace checkmates the human order and invites us to open up to self-transcendence. We are invited to undertake the experience of Abraham. It is the chance for a new life. As crisis, grace also passes judgment on a human being. We must make a decision, snapping out of our lethargy and moving away from the things we had taken for granted in our life project. Like any crisis, this entails ruptures that can be painful. But it also offers a great opportunity to grow, to give new direction to our life, or to solidify our trust in the path we have already chosen. Crisis is a normal part of human life, not a pathological element in it.[3] Grace as crisis is a constant in the religious life of every human being.

Crisis places human beings and society in a purifying process. Before we say more about this process, however, we must consider the scope of the ontological and moral alienation of humans.

The Limits of Human Decadence

In trying to interpret the human drama, the Catholic faith has always tried to avoid both exaggerated optimism (Pelagius) and exaggerated pessimism (the Reformation thinkers, Baius, Jansen, and Quesnel). God's grace never wholly abandons the realm of human beings, nor does evil ever take complete control of them.

The present situation is profoundly ambiguous. As Augustine put it, *"Omnis homo Adam, omnis homo Christus"* [Every human is Adam, every human is Christ].[4] Under this elegant formula, however, lies the whole tragic story of misery, oppression, and exploitation. From the depths of a hell created by some human beings other humans yearn unceasingly for liberation. The experience of torture chambers on our oppressed continent, of concentration camps in totalitarian regimes, and of dire poverty and hunger in the chains of an economic system give many good reason to doubt about the remnants of goodness in the human heart. Even more than other centuries, our present century offers us the crucifying experience of evil planned out in minute detail, systematically destroying thousands of people, manipulating millions of others, and maintaining whole continents in a state of oppressive dependence.[5]

Despite all this, our faith assures us that our solidarity with the new Adam, Jesus Christ, is even deeper than our solidarity with the old Adam who sinned. Despite all the evils that cannot help but remain a mystery for analytical reason, there remains an inexhaustible capacity in human beings to react against them, to struggle for more fraternal forms of societal life, and to die for a just cause. The history of anonymous people who suffer and die seems innocuous and meaningless to those in power; but God takes note of it all and will one day make a reckoning. The seeming anti-phony of history will be seen to be a true sym-phony from God's standpoint. A foretaste of this truth has been revealed to us in the resurrection of Jesus Christ, which celebrates the absolute future of a person lacerated on a cross.

If bad will and evil had taken such a hold on the human essence as to make us the complete enemies of God, there would be no place for redemption or any process of liberation. To talk about salvation is to profess that not everything in humans and the world is lost or inexorably fated; that there exists a kernel of goodness which can be redeemed and liberated (not merely inserted as a replacement). That is why there is a real, pristine continuity between creation and redemption, among protology, soteriology, and eschatology. God is the one who can transform the old into the new, the sinner into a just person. It is not *another* creation but a *new* creation out of the womb of the old that is promised us by Christian faith and hope.

Christian faith, then, is not merely a phenomenology of ambiguous existence under the sign of Adam and the sign of Christ. It is also a phenomenology of *homo redemptus et liberatus,* of human beings who can truly recover their identity before God. Otherwise there would be little sense to Christology, which talks gaily of the breaking in of the *novissimus Adam* (1 Cor. 15:45) in the risen Jesus Christ.

The recovery of humanity's religious identity (justice and justification) does not occur with the stroke of a magic wand. It entails a painful process of liberation.[6] This process is not simply a preparation for grace; it is grace itself making its way through human history.

Grace as a Process of Liberation Leading to God

In theological tradition we do not find any treatment of grace that spells out this liberative dimension in a personal and social perspective and deals specifically with the fundamental projects of the individual person and society.[7] Tradition elaborated the lengthy tract on justification from a totally individualistic standpoint. This is the dogmatic core of the Council of Trent (1545–63).[8] Sinful humanity and its justification are considered apart from any thematic reflection on humanity's immersion in a fallen world and the impact of the latter on its personal project of conversion. Moreover, due to the theoretical tools of late scholastic theology and ontology that it employed, Trent did not consider justification as an evolving process akin to the ongoing process of conversion. It did not see it as a slow but steady rejection of a project turned away from God and acceptance of a new project centered more and more on God and Jesus Christ. It viewed justification in fairly watertight compartments. Each phase had its own self-contained meaning, e.g., the preparation for justification, justification itself, and the effects of justification. Thus the Christian experience was elaborated in ontological terms. This is legitimate enough. But if the Christian experience is not considered in historical terms, in terms of a process, then it tends to remain in abstract formulas wholly apart from living experience. The idiom used seems to have no connection with a concrete praxis of conversion and the living out of the Christian project.

If the Council of Trent did not spell out the justification of the sinner in historical, process-oriented terms, this does not mean that theology need limit itself to the confines of the doctrine as defined. The task of theology is to ponder and enunciate the truth of faith. Obviously it must take due account of official teaching; but it must also go further than such teaching when it becomes necessary. That is what I shall do in this chapter, basing my remarks on the *Decree on Justification* that was approved at Trent's sixth session on January 13, 1547. We will ask for more than the texts themselves can provide, preserving but also prolonging their original sense even insofar as they are obligatory for the Catholic faith. Instead of using the term "justification" (a key word in the theology of Paul and the Council), I shall use the term "liberation." It is the same reality, but now elaborated in terms of its dynamic, historical dimensions.

Introducing the theme of justification in Chapter 4, Trent itself insinuated that it constitutes a process. However, this implication was not developed as such. Trent says:

The justification of the sinner is described as a passage (*translatio*) in which a human being, born as a child of the first Adam, passes to the state of grace and adoption as a child of God (Rom. 8:15) through the second Adam, Jesus Christ our Lord (DS 1524).

This "passage" (*translatio*) can only be interpreted in terms of a process. People leave one state and gradually acquire another state. And the whole process is the work of grace, from its start as conversion to its culmination in divine filiation and the indwelling of the Holy Trinity.[9] Trent puts the matter very well, though it does not reflect on it systematically:

The Council declares that the *beginning* of justification in adults must be sought in the prevenient grace of God through Jesus Christ, that is to say, in the summons by which they are called without any merit existing on their part . . . (DS 1525).

However, this "beginning" is not *formally* viewed as justification itself in process or in actuality. Rather, it is a "disposition or preparation for justification" (DS 1528). Justification itself comes afterwards and possesses its own distinct formal nature. The Council fathers could only say so much insofar as they were using an ontological set of concepts rather than an existential or process-oriented set.

Recognizing this epistemological break and translating their ontological language into historical, process-oriented terms, we might express the Catholic teaching of Trent in the following updated terms:[10]

1. The process of human liberation is the historical concretizing of God's liberation. Out of sheer gratuitousness and love God is the one who initially "disposes, stimulates and helps" (DS 1525) human beings to make the liberating transition from their situation as enemies of God, offenders against their fellows, and alienated beings in the world. Liberation is human because it is effected freely by human beings (DS 1525: *"libere assentiendo et cooperando"*). Yet it is God who motivates and penetrates human action in such a way that liberation can be called God's liberation.

The historical process anticipates and paves the way for definitive liberation in the kingdom. Thus human forms of liberation acquire a sacramental function. They have a weight of their own, but they also point toward, and embody in anticipation, what God has definitively prepared for human beings.

2. "Aroused and aided by grace" (DS 1526), human beings accept faith. Faith is not just total openness to the transcendent God and humble, generous-hearted surrender to the supreme mystery that ontologically alters the situation of human beings before God. It is also trusting faith, fiducial

faith, not in a moral sense but in an authentically ontological sense. In other words, it is faith as an attitude that embraces and covers the whole of life. Trent condemned fiducial faith insofar as it is a "vain confidence remote from any and all piety" (DS 1532). But it did not condemn fiducial faith in its ontological sense, which has solid roots in the Bible.

Faith, however, is not just this basic ontological attitude of openness to God and acceptance of him. It also signifies a historical project. It entails things revealed by God and it announces divine promises to us (DS 1526) regarding human destiny. In particular, it tells us of those promises regarding the sinner, who can be liberated (DS 1526), who is called to a new order of life, and who has a vocation to be inhabited by God himself. The theological project, precisely because it does pro-ject ahead, has a utopian function. Here "utopia" is not to be interpreted in a pejorative sense. It does not mean vain fantasy, escape from reality, or futile dreams. Here it has the more positive meaning that has been salvaged by modern anthropology, sociology, and theology. It refers to the ultimate, fulfilling eschatological reality which is historicized only at the end of the historical process but which is also anticipated in time and concretized bit by bit with each step forward. It thus keeps history open for a fuller capability which is truly possible though not yet experienced as such in reality.[11]

God's liberation is what ought to be for human beings. It is *already* a reality in anticipation, but it is *not yet* fully realized. Trent rightly stresses that this sort of faith is really God's project for human beings. As such it moves toward realization, unleashing a process and seeking its fulfillment in the future as the realization of utopia. In this sense utopia goes hand in hand with reality rather than being opposed to it; it is the total realization of the potentialities latent in reality.

3. This utopian project must be embodied in stages, so that liberation becomes a process in history. *Initially* it operates as a phase denouncing the gap between a given concrete situation and God's project. It brings a human project into real crisis: "Sinners are disturbed for their own benefit" (DS 1526). Their typical points of reference are shattered in a process of criticism leading toward conversion. The sinner reacts against sins with hatred and scorn (DS 1526).

This already constitutes a process of transformation, involving both personal and social dimensions. Viewing it in social terms, for example, we can see here the possibility of a revolutionary process that will destroy an iniquitous situation which generates structural sinfulness and will elaborate an alternative project which facilitates fraternal love and the practice of justice. It is not just the individual human being who must be liberated and justified. The same must happen to the whole network of their active relationships that keep them bound to socioeconomic and political realities and their structured sinfulness.

At a second stage, which is equally decisive, human beings articulate a new, renovating praxis. They begin "to love God as the fountainhead of all justice, . . . to live a new life and to carry out God's commandments" (DS 1526). This new project fleshes out God's project in history. It is liberation and justification in process.

4. This process aims at increasing the space of freedom *for* a new life and a concomitant praxis. Liberation is not complete if it is centered wholly on overcoming an iniquitous situation (i.e., through the forgiveness of sins). This would be only a liberation *from* something; it would not yet be a liberation *for* some better alternative. Thus Trent rightly insists that real liberation is something more than the remission of sins. It is also "the renovation and sanctification of the inner human being" (DS 1528). Here we have the new fundamental project oriented toward God that restores authentic identity (justice) to a human being.

Thus the liberation process is not just directed against unjust situations. It also creates new situations, generating a new, transforming outlook in human beings. The tyrannical ruler and the iniquitous society do not just become more permissive or flexible while still retaining their basically sinful structures and their mechanisms of institutional or personal sinfulness. The process of creating a new being is under way. Focusing on the personal level, Trent has this to say: "The unjust human being is turned into a just person, the enemy of God into a friend" (DS 1528). Further on it says: "We are renewed in our innermost spirit. . . . We are not simply deemed just; we really are just and can call ourselves that" (DS 1529).

The liberation involved is a liberation *for* something new even more than it is a liberation *from* something old. What Trent calls for is a real revolution on the personal level. And since a person is never just a person in isolation but is essentially social, we can conclude that a structural revolution of the world is necessary if the conversion of the nuclear person is to be real and effective. But how? What tactical steps must be taken? When? Under what conditions? To try to answer those questions is to engage in a different type of reflection, to seek out the tactical and strategic steps that will mediate an effective transformation. Trent did not engage in such reflection. It stayed on the doctrinal level, offering no suggestions for effective praxis. But such reflection is proper to the pastoral function of the church insofar as it is immersed in the world and seeks to be the leaven of transformation. I have already alluded to such reflection when I considered the experience of grace in the light of Latin America and its concrete problems.

So we see that the grace of God is not present in the liberation process as some parallel reality. It is not that the liberation process stands over here while grace stands over there. The liberation process itself, seeking to produce a human life that is more fraternal and open to God, already constitutes the presence of liberating grace in the world. God's liberating grace is incarnated in the pain-filled but liberative course of human beings.

God and human beings collaborate to bring about the birth and growth of the kingdom of God in history until it attains its final fulfillment.

Liberation as an Unfinished Process

Despite the freedoms won in the liberation process, *homo viator* does not step outside the ongoing process of liberation. Historical liberations anticipate eschatology but they do not establish the eschatological state, for that would amount to the end of history. History lies open to an unforeseen future. It can advance toward the kingdom, retreat, or even lose the right track. What does it mean, then, when the Catholic teaching of Trent affirms that human beings really are justified and liberated?

First of all, this must be interpreted in a basic, ontological sense. Something really does take place in the fundamental project of a human person that situates that person in a new way vis-à-vis God and eternal salvation. At the same time, however, Trent adopts a concrete, historical perspective. By comparison with their previous state of sinfulness, human beings are now just. But this situation is not the definitive one of eschatology:

When a human being looks at himself and his frailty . . . he can well fear for the remission of his sins, since no one can know with the certainty of faith subject to no error that he has obtained the grace of God (DS 1534).

So long as history goes on, the liberation process is ever threatened from within and from without. With a sound, realistic sense Trent teaches that "no one is promised anything with absolute certainty. . . . Anyone who thinks he is standing upright must watch out lest he fall (1 Cor. 10:12) and work out his salvation in fear and trembling (Phil. 2:12) . . . knowing that his birth is a birth unto *hope* of glory (1 Pet. 1:3), not unto glory itself. . . . He must still fear the struggle that remains with the world, the flesh, and the devil" (DS 1541). So we are liberated in hope; and hope implies both something *already* present and something possible that does *not yet* exist and is ever threatened.

So we are confronted with a real course of ongoing, gradual liberation. Concrete humanity in history is simultaneously oppressed and liberated (*"simul oppressus et liberatus"*).[12] This formula must be understood correctly so as not to lose the insight we gained above on the authentic liberation already achieved. To assert that a human being is *simul oppressus et liberatus* is not to make a metaphysical statement. We are not dealing with some reality viewed in static, abstract terms as if it were closed up in itself and outside the liberation process. Such an affirmation would be a contradiction in terms. Viewed on one and the same level and in a univocal sense, a human being cannot be simultaneously oppressed and liberated. He or she would have to be one or the other.

To understand the statement correctly, we must frame it in a historical context. In the dimension of history there is a before and after, there is continuity in a process that has various phases of realization. Liberated persons of now are not the oppressed persons they were before. That is why we can say that these persons are liberated. They have overcome a situation that held them in bondage earlier. At the same time, however, these persons do not stand outside the process of history. They are open to the future, can be threatened, find themselves limited. They have won a field of achieved freedoms, but the latter contain new contradictions within themselves that also call for liberation. Liberated human beings are not free from all oppression and sin. Though their fundamental project is firmly oriented toward God and they themselves live in a state of habitual grace, certain actions and dimensions of their lives may completely escape the sway of this fundamental project. These actions may not go so far as to destroy or seriously jeopardize the fundamental project, but they can taint it and obscure its orientation toward God. Paul tells us that "in hope we were saved" (Rom. 8:24). Salvation is not realized in such a way that it freezes history; it keeps the latter open to all the unforeseen possibilities of grace and dis-grace. Thus a human being is *oppressus in re, liberatus in spe.*[13]

As I noted above, the Council of Trent alludes to this liberative process when it points out that we are not yet in glory but on route (DS 1541). We are exposed to all sorts of setbacks, especially because the negative manifestations of concupiscence maintain their hold on us. What, then, is concupiscence? In its original anthropological sense—which has always been upheld by the Franciscan school—concupiscence is not an evil dynamism; it is basically good. It is the underlying dynamism of human life by which every dimension of our personality strives to realize its inclination in the most intense and perfect way possible. Thus there is a dynamism aiming at such things as heaven, other human beings, intimacy, the domination of the earth, the flesh, the spirit, and God. At the dawn of humanity human beings possessed original justice. They managed to order all these forces into a harmonious project even though it had its tensions. Insofar as God was concerned, they felt they were his children; insofar as other human beings were concerned, they felt themselves to be brothers and sisters; insofar as nature was concerned, they lived as its masters. One of the consequences of sin was to destroy this harmony. Now in history every passion, which is good in itself, seeks its own road outside of the basic human project. Only at the cost of effort and sacrifice can we manage to tame the angels and demons that dwell within us. Originally a fine dynamism, in history concupiscence came to signify the factor of tension, conflict, and rupture within human beings. As Trent rightly noted, concupiscence is the "fuse for sin" *(fomes peccati:* DS 1515). It is closely related to sin because it derives historically from sin and tends toward sin (DS 1515). We can really fall into sin, against which we have the sacrament of Penance (DS 1542). When the Council said that concupiscence comes from sin, however, we must remember that it is speaking in historical rather than ontological terms. The lack of control over concupiscence which we detect today derives from sin.

Because of this agonizing situation, the freedoms achieved by human beings must be confirmed continually. The best way to do this is to persevere in an open-ended process of liberation, to "increase the justification received" (DS 1535). There is no absolute certainty in faith that we will persevere to the end without a special grace from God (DS 1533, 1540). Without a special privilege from God we cannot live without small oppressions at least, i.e., venial sins (DS 1539 and 1573).

In the life of faith our daily experience convinces us that we always stand in need of pardon. The New Testament reiterates the point:

When you pray, say . . . forgive us our sins; if we say, "We are free of the guilt of sin," we deceive ourselves; the truth is not to be found in us (Luke 11:2,4;1 John 1:8).

That is why the church constantly asks for pardon. Mass begins with an acknowledgment of our situation as oppressed beings, even though we may be on the road to liberation. People who think they are just are sinners. People who deem themselves sinners are just. This is the lesson to be gleaned from the parable of the Pharisee and the publican (Luke 18:9–14). The saints and mystics possessed a keen sense of this ambiguous situation. The holier they were, the more distant they felt from God. When John of the Cross was on his deathbed, the attending priest sought to comfort him by recalling the fine works he had done. John replied: "Don't tell me about them, Father, tell me about my sins."

So long as human beings live, they stand in need of liberation. They are oppressed and liberated at the same time, and they live in an open-ended process of liberation.

Grace as an Anticipation of Authentic Utopia

The above reflections on the simultaneous coexistence of oppression and liberation in history—because the eschatological dimension requires this—must not blind us to an essential aspect of the liberation process, i.e., the creation of authentic freedoms. Because of the eschatological stipulation, we know that these freedoms are not definitive. They carry within them the seeds of other oppressions. At the same time, however, they are real freedoms. Liberation tends to generate new freedoms and a new state of affairs in which humans can better reveal their truth and God can appear more clearly as our Father and gratuitous love. This state of affairs is a real anticipation of the definitive state of liberation.

So there is a whole field for celebration, festivity, and *joie de vivre.* Class struggle, conflict, and uncertainty about our end are not the only realities. They reveal the "not yet" of future reality, but there is also the emergence of the "already" in history which gives ground for Christian joy and optimism. To talk about eschatology is to stress the two aspects of present and future. The present is the concretization of a future that is anticipated. The unexperienced future calls the present into question, ensuring that the latter will not bask in self-sufficiency or degenerate into orgiastic celebration of itself as the fullness of eschatology.

Thus the liberation process does create real freedoms in history. Trent itself stressed two of them: the forgiveness of sins and the sanctification and renewal of the inner human being (DS 1528–1531). Let us consider them briefly here.

1. When grace touches the reality of human beings, it generates a crisis, a liberation process, and freedom *from* a situation of enmity with God. Through God's initiative and grace human beings enter a process of conversion. The prodigal son rises, sets out for his father's house, and draws near to his father. This new direction of life signifies the forgiveness of sin. We do well to recall that sin is not just a bad act. It is an interior disposition which the Bible sums up in the word "heart." This disposition, this fundamental option, is abandoned and destroyed to make place for another. The evil acts as such cannot be destroyed. Once they have been committed they take on the air of eternity. *What is pardoned, undone, and destroyed is the basic project of life which repeatedly generated such acts.* Human beings now find a guiding light in the sky of their lives and know that they are being led toward God.

The forgiveness of sins takes place in the midst of a great inner conflict. The orientation of years is not erased in a day. Hence the forgiveness of sin, insofar as this sin is a habitual situation of sin, is really a grace. It is a victory over temptations and impulses that were wont to be satisfied within the context of a certain life project. The effort is all the more difficult when we take due note of the social aspect entailed in sin.

2. Forgiveness is focused on some past *from* which human beings are liberated. It is liberation *from* something. Liberation or freedom *for* something is equally important, however. *In this case it is freedom for a new basic project that is oriented toward the future and that translates into a new praxis in the present.* Humans do not just turn toward God. They adhere to him, enter his house, establish a saving dialogue with him, and enter the intimate communion of friendship and love. Humans are *sanctified* down to the very roots of their being.

Sanctification should not be interpreted in merely moral terms as the doing of good works. Even the wicked person can do good, as we noted earlier. Sanctification implies an ontological dimension. Something in human beings is altered. The whole complex reality of human beings is penetrated by divine grace, turning them into new creatures, i.e., their basic project oriented toward God, their core as a person now open to the mystery of love, and the basic, underlying attitude that defines them as human beings.

This fundamentally good attitude produces concrete works and actions that are good, good because they express the radical goodness of the underlying project. Trent expressed this same point by using Paul's terminology: the renewal of the inner person. The creation of a new project rooted in God turns a human being into a new human similar to Jesus Christ, *novissimus Adam*.

Sanctification means "to make holy." Holiness is a trait of God and his mystery (Isa. 6:3; 12:6; 30:11; Ezek. 49:7) and of all that belongs to the divine sphere. Everything is holy insofar as it is related to God. We cease to be holy, we turn profane and sinful, insofar as we try to withdraw from this relationship with God. "Holy" people are those who come *from* God, exist *for* God, and live in relationship *with* God. The sanctification of human beings is a process, an increasingly intense assimilation of divine reality by human beings and of human reality by God. When people make God the reference point of their lives, they live with God *as their starting point*, see themselves as people *of* God, and exist *for* God. To be sanctified, then, means to be consecrated to God, to become his property, and thus to share in the sanctity that is God himself.

Baptism expresses humanity's consecration to God. It sanctifies the roots of human life, freeing it from the worldly situation of sinfulness. It is a sacrament of initiation, which starts a process of progressive liberation from worldly sin, extends through life, and can ultimately win complete victory over sin in death. Consecration, however, does not just mean surrender to God. Being infinite and omnipotent, God has need of no one. Consecration also implies mission. God draws people to send them out into the world as his missionaries. They are to bear witness to his love and live out the work of grace in the world, liberating people from all oppressions and for all true freedoms.

Worship of God highlights the theme of consecration and sanctification. In it God is venerated explicitly as the Sun of all things and the ultimate meaning of all human projects in history.

Sanctification does not just restore the human project and its course toward God. It also signifies God's coming into humanity, which culminates in the incarnation of his first-born Son. The incarnation is the work of divine grace. It signifies the definitive consecration of the world and human flesh. Perfect and eternal freedom suddenly explodes and implodes in the world. What this means both for humans and for God will be the object of study in the next section.

PART FOUR

GOD AND HUMANKIND
AS REVEALED
IN THE GRACE EXPERIENCE

CHAPTER 15

The Varied Manifestations
of God's Grace in Human Beings

A fundamental project oriented toward God and its concretization as liberation amid the conflicts of history profoundly alters a human being. Now, inhabited by the grace of God, the human being is a new creature (Gal. 6:15; 2 Cor. 5:17). This new being implies a correspondingly new way of acting. The fundamental option oriented toward God (habitual grace) finds expression in basic attitudes and ways of acting that translate into a new life. Paul refers to them as the fruits of the Spirit (grace): "love, joy, peace, patient endurance, kindness, generosity, faith, mildness, and chastity" (Gal. 5:22–23). Theology refers to them as "virtues":

They are, so to speak, further developments of our fundamental project. As a ray of light splits up into the color spectrum when it hits a crystal, so our single basic option is moved by divine grace to assume many different forms in order to express itself in the complex reality of human existence.[1]

Being as the Ground of Doing

We must understand the virtues correctly. We do not want merely moralistic or psychological explanations that have been responsible for so many distortions in the Christian way of life. The moralistic approach examines doing detached from being, virtues detached from the fundamental option (new being), instead of regarding the practice of the virtues as the concrete embodiment of the new creature and the dynamic expression of the presence of divine grace. It degenerates into inhuman legalism; its Christianity does not get beyond pharisaism. As the great German mystic Eckhart put it: "We should think less about what we ought to do and more about what we ought to be."[2] To put the point in other words, doing (virtues, obligations, commandments, and precepts) must be rooted in the authentic being of humans. Their actions will be what their being is since deeds are merely being-in-action.

The virtues are varied and they can be studied separately in terms of their distinctive characteristics. But they derive their life from a deeper, underlying unity. They all are related to the single, basic fundamental project of habitual grace. Considered individually, they are different colors of one and the same ray of divine light.[3] All of them without exception are theological because all of them, in their foundation and thrust, come from God and are ordered toward God. Even when they pass through human mediations—and it is a basic thesis of this book that all of them do—they do not lose their immediate reference to God. And this immediacy must be viewed in ontological rather than psychological terms.

Let me explain. Acts of faith, hope, and love must not be considered the only ones with immediate reference to God simply because people consciously and deliberately relate them to God. Every *authentic* act of virtue—of hope, love, patience, temperance, and so forth—immediately touches God even when we love a human being or hope for some earthly good. The structure of every virtue is such that we do not just focus on a single thing but on the totality. In hoping for a particular thing, for example, we are also hoping for the Absolute who lies hidden beneath the fragility of temporal goods. Taking cognizance of this ontological dimension, we can echo the sentiments of the great medieval masters such as Bonaventure and Thomas Aquinas: whenever human beings think, they think of God; whenever they love, they love God; whenever they hope, they hope for God.

In the light of this point we can also say that no virtues are merely acquired by a succession of repeated acts: they always are infused by God as well. The notion of "infused" virtue signifies the ontological dimension: the new being. The notion of "acquired" virtue is its expression in terms of effort and concrete action. Here we must recall the point brought out earlier. God is always involved in human action. *Historically* speaking, there is no neutral ground for human beings to operate apart from God. Humans are always immersed in the divine milieu of grace. In the concrete, then, this means that virtues are human and "acquired" because they are born of human effort to flesh out their fundamental option for God; but they are also divine and infused because God is the force *(virtus)* in humans who triggers, sustains, and fulfills everything.[4]

Having clarified this basic point, we can now move on to consider some of the principal ways in which God's grace is revealed in human beings.

Grace as Faith

In the ontological sense just discussed, faith is basically a radical attitude of openness to the supreme mystery of our existence and of loving acceptance of it so that our human course is altered. To believe in God is to live life as a confident surrender into his hands. Our interpretation of the world and all our experiences are seen in the light of God's design and linked to his divine reality. This is the pristine sense of believing in God. We live in total openness to an absolute Thou, who is the Light in which we see light. This "Thou" abandoned its obscure mysteriousness and became our brother in Jesus Christ, the incarnate God. In Christian terms believing in God means opening up to the holy humanity of Jesus of Nazareth, in whom we encounter the absolute mystery that is the meaning of our living and our dying.

But believing is something more than total, ontological entrusting of self to the divine Thou. It also means opening up and accepting what he has to say to us. It means heeding his historical project for human beings and his revelation on the destiny of the world *(credere Deum)*. We hear and heed what he has to say to us in our awakened conscience. With our senses sharpened by his light, we discover him in the signs of the times and read his message in the history he makes with the privileged Judeo-Christian people. That history is attested to by the Scriptures, and it is read and interpreted in the light of the history of the Christian faith. It reached its culmination in the concrete journey of Jesus of Nazareth, his words, and his liberative praxis.

This attitude of openness and acceptance, which is universal on the one hand and singularly concrete on the other, is a manifestation of what grace might be in each human being. The grace of faith is not restricted to this personal dimension, however. It also has an impact on the social dimension. The grace of faith as a fundamental attitude reveals its potentiality insofar as a social system is organized in such a way that it opens up to a transcendent being and breaks the absolutism of ideologies based on power, self-interest, and profit. By the same token the community of faith, insofar as it has its own vision of faith, possesses a tool that can liberate it from all intraworldly absolutisms and destroy all the idols fashioned in the place of the one God who is Lord. Because of the grace of faith, Christians are responsible for the kind of society and the quality of life they create as human beings. Will their society leave room for the emergence of God or will it suffocate him under its own claims to absoluteness?

Grace as Hope

In its pristine reality grace is not simply a psychological state of openness to some longed-for thing that is possible but that has not yet been experienced in reality. Human beings can live in hope insofar as the structure of hope goes into the "construction" of human beings as such. Humans are not simply beings that exist; they are a web of possibilities seeking to realize themselves in the concrete.

In recent times modern thought has coined the phrase, the "principle of hope."[5] Rooted in human beings, it is responsible for their hopes and expectations of all sorts. It is responsible for their historical efforts at dissent, transformation, and the construction of utopian models of reality. These models are not escape mechanisms. They are forces stimulating people to make alterations that will bring their forms of life ever closer to utopia. And utopia itself is part of reality insofar as it is the future fulfillment of that reality.

Hope translates the openness of human beings to tomorrow, where they hope to find some meaningfulness that will fulfill the life they are living today. Hope is not just the future as future. It is the future as *already* present, tasted, and experienced but *not yet* received and fully realized. Hence it is also future. Thus in hope there is always a tension between being (the present) and what can be in the future and is desired now. The present is lived as an anticipation of, and preparation for, the future; hence it ever remains open-ended. Because the present is not a present in all its fullness, there is an element of sorrow in hope. Paul calls it a "sorrow for God's sake" (2 Cor. 7:10). It is the tearful aspect of things that the ancients referred to as *lacrimae rerum*. This sorrow is not born of despair or distress. It is born of a hope that is not satisfied with the present and that looks forward impatiently to the full revelation of reality which it can only glimpse now in desire.

The principle of hope is not exhausted in the future that human beings can plan and construct. It goes beyond all human constructions in history. It ever remains metaphysically unsatisfied because it always feels called to better things. Only the absolute future, the realization of utopia, can quiet the heart steeped in hope. God is thus seen as utopia, as the absolute and total concretization of all that can be.

Historical hopes and the future that can be constructed by humanity are viewed as a preparation for, and anticipated realization of, this absolute future. The kingdom yearned for in dreams and ardent vigils will not arise with the stroke of a magic wand: nor will it arise on the ruins of human kingdoms. It is the culmination of a historical process, which will give fulfillment to all that humans have constructed by the grace of God: "On this earth that kingdom is *already* present in mystery; when the Lord returns, it will be brought into full flower" (GS 39).

Living in grace, human beings live grounded in the absolute future, God. They encounter God in their concrete hopes for a more humane life, for better housing, and for a more just and fraternal society. Eschatological hope (God) is not inimical to historical hopes. Quite the contrary is true. As the absolute future of humanity, eschatological hope must be able to translate itself into historico-political hopes that will lead society ever closer to its fulfillment. Pondering and hoping for an absolute future makes sense only if this future proves to be the culmination of human hopes beyond our wildest dreams. As Vatican II put it:

The expectation of a new earth must not weaken but rather stimulate our concern for cultivating this one. For here grows the body of a new human family, a body which even now is able to give some kind of foreshadowing of the new age (GS 39).

By virtue of this absolute hope, Christians do two things. On the one hand, they involve themselves in the work of concretizing human hopes because they see their relation to the absolute hope. On the other hand, they see these concretizations as relative because they are not absolutely identical with the Absolute that is to come. Hence they are critical of all totalitarian regimes that pose as the realization of the promises made to humanity. Hope as the grace of God gives us strength to erase the note of ineluctable fate from history, to fight those who wish to freeze history and deny it a future, to combat those who seek to repress all who challenge them in the name of a better future. Here hope reveals itself as sovereign courage *(parrhesia)*, which endures and confronts everything in the certainty that it is fighting for the only thing that has a future and that will one day be revealed as the truth of all things.

Grace as Love

Like faith and hope, love too is an ontological structure in human beings before it is a psychological reality. Humanity is not just structured as openness and as a web of relationships extending out in every direction. Human beings do in fact continually enter into communion with reality. They can identify themselves with it and make history with all those with whom they establish a relationship. Love is this pristine capacity to freely communicate oneself to another who is different, to accept that other inside oneself, and to involve oneself in some definitive way with that other.

Viewed in this light, love too is an ontological structure in human beings. It can be articulated in many different concrete forms: as eros, libido, friendship, a love universal enough to cover one's enemies (Matt. 5:43–48), or even agape. The last-mentioned form is not really so much the sublimation of love as the radicalization of its thrust that ends up in God as supreme love. In any case the various forms of love are different concrete embodiments of one and the same root principle. Far from being inimical to each other, they are ordered to one another in a single movement that keeps seeking the other and finally ends up in the absolute Other, God.

This pristine sense of love stretches much further than sympathy. In itself the latter is selective and focuses on a few. Love also goes beyond benevolence toward those who are benevolent in turn. It embraces everyone and everything because nothing can be excluded from a human relationship. With love human beings can draw near to all and make them their neighbors. There are no limits to the human capacity for loving. Jesus himself alluded to this fact: "Love one another as I have loved you" (John 15:12); "love your enemy and do good. . . . You will rightly be called sons of the Most High, since he himself is good to the ungrateful and the wicked" (Luke 6:35). In these passages Jesus is alluding to a real capacity in human beings, to their ability to open up to others and to give of themselves to the utmost.

Now this love is really the grace of God becoming history in human beings. As Augustine put it: "Because you loved me first, you have made me lovable and capable of loving." The gratuitousness of love is the gratuitousness of grace itself: "Love is of God; everyone who loves is begotten of God and has knowledge of God" (1 John 4:7). Humanity has always glimpsed the fact that there is something divine in love. The Greeks did, even in the days of Homer or earlier. In Jesus Christ the truth of reality has been revealed to us: "God is love" (1 John 4:8). Indeed the author of this epistle goes a step further and suggests that it is through love that God becomes tangible to human beings: "No one has ever seen God. Yet if we love one another God dwells in us, and his love is brought to perfection in us" (1 John 8:12).

Perfect love is not a love that loves everyone and everything on account of God (propter Deum) or in God (in Deo). Perfect love is a love that loves everyone and everything because it discovers the lovableness of all as the concrete presence of God's own love. Every created reality is a locale for the encounter with God that shines through the depths of every being. Here we have the basis for the identity that is set up by the New Testament between love for neighbor and love for God (1 John 4:20; Luke 10:25–37; John 15:12 ff.; 17:22ff.). Whenever we love, we are in fact loving the supreme mystery present in every reality that makes it lovable. In loving another being, we are always loving the great Other, God.

By the same token, however, this sublime reality is ever threatened by egotism, by the historical inability of human beings to communicate themselves universally. Thus we encounter the two faces of love. On the one hand, it is a fundamental exigency of the human heart and human society. On the other hand, it is a lack which accuses all and which turns their attention toward the divine Love who can liberate our oppressed capacity for love.

As I have insisted repeatedly in these pages on many topics, love as the grace of God can never be interpreted in purely individualistic terms. Its structure is eminently social. The more a society creates real forms of human relationship, brotherhood, justice, and love among human beings and nations, the more it manifests grace as love in the world. The criminal lack of solidarity and love on the international level, where brothers oppress brothers, bears witness to the ability of human beings to prevent God's love from realizing itself manifestly in history. The thirst for love, particularly for the lowly and the weak who were the privileged objects of Jesus' love, can immerse human beings in the struggle for the transformation of society. This struggle will entail much conflict and perhaps even the sacrifice of one's own life. This perfect love (see John 15:13) is also the most perfect manifestation of liberating grace in the world; and the sacrifice of Jesus is its prototype (John 13:1).

The three virtues of faith, hope, and charity are mentioned as far back as the New Testament (1 Cor. 13:13; 1 Thess. 1:3; Gal. 5:6; Rom. 5:1–5). They have been examined as a triad by theological tradition in terms of salvation history, i.e., in terms of Father, Son, and Holy Spirit. In fact, however, they do not constitute three virtues. They are one single principle operating in three directions and in different embodiments. Humanity's basic openness and transcendence is historicized in its awareness of some absolute meaning which it accepts and to which it entrusts itself; that is faith. It then celebrates its presence as an encounter of two freedoms and two self-communications (i.e., of God and human beings); that is love. And finally it opens up to a history that still has a future, that has not yet arrived at its eschatological fulfillment; that is hope. One single divine dynamism pervades the dynamism of humanity at that focal point which constitutes the unity of human life.

But now I should like to consider some of the other manifestations of grace in the liberated human being, though quite briefly.

Grace as Friendship

Relating to God in openness and mutual acceptance (grace) establishes friendly relations. The Scriptures allude to the category of friendship quite often. We are told that Abraham was a friend of God and that God "used to speak to Moses face to face, as one man speaks to another" (Exod. 33:11). Jesus called his disciples "friends" (Luke 12:4; John 15:14). Such friendship with God implies intimate, familiar dealings. Paul goes so far as to say that Christians are "members of the household of God" (Eph. 2:19).

In his commentaries on Aristotle we find Thomas Aquinas analyzing this friendship in detail.[6] It presupposes some ontological root, a certain communion of life between God and human beings. Other elements involved are:

1. benevolent love, which goes beyond love based on mutual interests;
2. mutual love;
3. a love that is stable, constant, and consciously accepted;
4. personal interchanges and mutual participation in each other's lives, so that the life of God ends up in Incarnation and that of humans in adoptive divine sonship;
5. mutual presence, which creates a community of "we," a *koinonia,* so that love makes each resemble the other more and more. Humans become theomorphic (the image and likeness of God) while God becomes anthropomorphic (the image and likeness of humanity, Phil. 2:7).

Thus the human experience of friendship comes to symbolize the authentic friendship that is established between God and graced human beings.

Grace as Peace

The meeting of human beings and God in friendship and familiar intercourse generates peace. The Hebrew Bible's term for peace, *"shalom,"* is difficult to translate with any one term. The Septuagint, for example, uses about twenty-five different words to translate the concept into Greek. Basically, however, Hebrew *shalom* signifies a state of individual and communal well-being on both the material and the spiritual level (see Exod. 18:23; 1 Kings 5:4).[7] To live in peace is to feel oneself whole and complete (the original sense of *shalom*), no longer divided with oneself or with God and no longer threatened by anyone. In the language of Augustine, it is the tranquility of order based on justice.

The contrasting experience is that of division, rupture, and perdition. Peace implies salvation, reunification, wholeness shared with God, with others, and with the cosmos. Such peace is a gift from God. Christ himself is our peace (Eph. 2:14) insofar as he toppled the old barriers between human beings and created a single humanity: the new man (Eph. 2:14–18). Peace is the fruit of redemption and justification (Rom. 5:1), attesting to the presence of the Holy Spirit (Gal. 5:22). The graced human being lives in peace even when he or she is caught amid the conflict and suffering of this fallen world (see 2 Sam. 11:7), because he or she feels safe and completely at one with God.

This peace of reconciliation and salvation is not achieved without a struggle (John 16:33). It is a process of conversion. In the social arena grace as peace can be achieved only by overcoming the motives that create human conflicts. So long as there is no conversion of the oppressed and the oppressors, peace cannot be more than mere pacification. Pacification is not tranquility based on order; it is tranquility within a context of disorder that is imposed by the violence of the stronger over the weaker. That is not the peace of God nor the peace brought by Jesus Christ. To achieve the peace that is the fruit of justice, we must struggle to overcome the objective causes of divisiveness and injustice. It is the justice of this cause that determines the rightness of the struggle. Living in peace with God and other human beings, the graced person fights on with a new sense of purpose and without a spirit of vengeance. This is a form of love motivated by justice, and it is the real matrix of any authentic or lasting peace. To experience that profound peace which the world can neither give nor take away (John 14:27) is to experience the grace of God pervading one's heart and the world.

Grace as Joy

Serenity and joy are the fruits of a basic project wholly oriented toward God. As a gift of the Spirit (Gal. 5:22)[8] and an imperturbable feeling of the heart, joy is not the feeling of idiots who are happy without any good reason. Joy arises from loving and being loved, from feeling safe and pardoned by God, from knowing that there is a good end for all creation. Joy wells up from the indubitable certainty that in Jesus Christ God accepted us as we are: lowly, weak, and slow to respond. Joy springs from experiencing the fact that we are children of God and brothers and sisters of all creatures, that we live as brothers and sisters in the house of our Father.

Such joy is not a psychological stirring or a transient state of the soul. It is a real ontological situation for every human being inhabited by God, the God of our "gladness and joy" (Ps. 43:4). Even in the midst of tribulation and persecution human beings are sustained in this authentic, perfect joy as Paul was (2 Cor. 7:4; 6:10) or as the other apostles were: "Full of joy that they had been judged worthy of ill-treatment for the sake of the Name" (Acts 5:41; 4:12; Luke 24:46ff.; 1 Pet. 4:13).

Humble, day-to-day joy is enjoyed by the just in the happy circle of friends and loved ones, in their work, in the food that nourishes their existence, in creative activities, and in recreation. All these are sacraments of the perfect joy of the kingdom (see Isa. 62:5). Despite all the ambiguity they may contain, they are historical manifestations of grace as joy in human existence.

Grace as a Critical Spirit

One of the prime ways in which grace takes concrete shape in human beings is in their critical spirit and function, which is so urgently needed today. After all, we live in a world that is riddled with contradictory ideologies and hierarchies of value. In biblical terms a critical spirit is equivalent to wisdom and the discernment of spirits that constitute a gift from God. To criticize is not to destroy. It means knowing how to distinguish the true from the false, the good from the bad, in every concrete situation so that we always do what pleases the Father (John 8:29).[9] The critic looks about without illusions and detects the ideologies camouflaging reality (Prov. 13:7). He possesses good judgment (1 Sam. 25:33), tact (Prov. 11:22), and good sense (Prov. 26:16). The same call for sound criticism can be found in the New Testament: "Do not trust every spirit, but put the spirits to a test to see if they belong to God" (1 John 4:1); "test everything, retain what is good" (1 Thess. 5:21). Lacking a persistently critical spirit, people end up conforming to the spirit of their age (Rom. 12:2). Hence Paul urges them to "be transformed by the renewal of your mind, so that you may judge what is God's will."

Without the special work of grace human beings deceive themselves. They feel split in two because the desires of the flesh go counter to those of the spirit (Gal. 5:17–21). As Paul put it: "I cannot even understand my own actions. I do not do what I want to do but what I hate" (Rom. 7:15).

Jesus of Nazareth was an expert in using the critical spirit to liberate human beings from legalism, traditionalism, preconceptions, and false representations of God. He sought to make people more aware of God's concrete will as it manifests itself in history and their own activity.

Grace as a critical spirit manifests itself in uneducated people. Even though they may not be able to offer motives or to review the theoretical stages of their praxis, the Spirit guides them in such a way that they are quite capable of distinguishing truth from ideology and phoniness. Today the exercise of a critical spirit is clearly an outstanding way for us to experience the liberation and redemption brought by Jesus Christ. With it we can break the absolutism of systems closed to the future, whence God comes to summon human beings toward their eschatological fulfillment.

Grace as Courage

The grace of a critical spirit can and often should manifest itself as the grace to announce the truth and denounce human illusions with courage. Many passages in the New Testament make reference to this apostolic virtue. *Parrhesia* means speaking and acting courageously, but the courage in question comes from divine rather than human strength (see Acts 9:27–28; 14:3; 18:26; 19:8; 26:26; Eph. 6:19; Phil. 1:20; 1 Thess. 2:2).[10] It can endure obstacles, persecutions, and even physical liquidation.

There are times in life when the Christian conscience must denounce sin that betrays the truth of human beings and of Christ. Living in the midst of the world, Christians are called to bear witness to the sacred mystery of humanity that was assumed by God and to defend the divine right that is identified with the inviolable right of every human being to be respected as a person. To keep silent in the face of injustices and violations of the sacredness of every human being *(res sacra homo)* is to be an accomplice. Of course, it is easy and convenient. All sorts of reasons are invoked to justify absenteeism on our part: the need for good order, discipline, (false) unity, and noninvolvement in political questions, for example. But the grace of God leads us to brave danger, to assume the consequences of boldness, to overcome inhibiting fear, and to speak out boldly.

Today more than ever before, the hierarchy of the church is summoned to the prophetic task of annunciation and denunciation. It must speak out against the presumptive claims of the totalitarian state and the absolutism of ideologies, for in the name of the state all values are sacrificed and all rights are violated. By virtue of the moral authority it wields and the freedom it still enjoys, the ecclesiastical hierarchy cannot excuse itself from the evangelical duty that weighs upon the Christian conscience. All Christians, whatever their place in the social structure, should have the evangelical courage to bear witness to the critical truth of the gospel and Christ's project for human beings.

There may be situations where the Christian conscience has no choice but to denounce the existing state of affairs and follow Jesus Christ down the road to arrest, torture, and violent death. The wrath of God is gathering against the leaders and ideologists of totalitarian states for the crimes committed against prophets, the violent assaults on the free people who courageously defend the rights of their downtrodden brothers and sisters, and the offenses committed against the basic freedoms of humanity. They will be punished by the divine judge, and this punishment is already revealed in history insofar as their violence provokes violence against them in turn. For in these totalitarians we see "a heart deaf to the cries of human beings and a heart mute before God."[11]

Immersed in a context of repression and oppression, the Christian community can only echo the prayer of the persecuted primitive church community: "But now, O Lord, look at the threats they are leveling against us. Grant to your servants, even as they speak your words, complete assurance [*parrhesia*]" (Acts 4:29).

Grace as Humor

One of the most commonplace manifestations of grace is humor.[12] It has rarely been given consideration by "serious" theology, but its existence has been attested to by all true saints and mystics; and they are the only truly serious Christians. Humor is not synonymous with joking; there can be jokes without humor and humor without jokes. History is filled with humor and it retains its permanent aspect of grace. Human beings can take note of this humor time and again because their inner life needs this sparkle to retain its vitality.

Authentic humor can be understood only in terms of the inner depths of the human person,[13] which are ever oriented toward the unlimited and the utopian. In our inner depths the dark recesses outnumber bright spots, mysteriousness outweighs reality, and raw facts are less concrete than hope. On the other side of the coin we find the data of reality, elaborate reasons, human organizations and systems. They pose as reality pure and simple, as the serious and important thing that should be accepted and respected by human beings.

When human beings take note of the discrepancies and incompatibilities between these two realities—outside reality and their inner depths—then humor surfaces. Humor lightens the weight of life and its limitations. For a moment we feel free from fated history and natural necessity. Humor signals the transcendence of human beings, who can always go beyond any given situation. They need not allow themselves to be defined or circumscribed by any particular set of circumstances. In their innermost being they are free. They can look with humor on the systems that seek to box them in, the concepts that purport to define them, and the violence that seeks to tame them. As one philosopher has put it: "The secret essence of humor . . . lies in the force of the religious outlook. Humor sees human and divine things in terms of their inadequacy before God."[14] In the light of God's authentic seriousness, human beings smile at the aspects of human seriousness which pose as absolutely true and serious when they are not.

Graced human beings, whose lives are centered around God, can be the prototype of humor-filled beings. They relativize earthly kinds of seriousness. They are free vis-à-vis all occupations and preoccupations. They can retain their humor in the face of condemnation and death as did Thomas

More and St. Lawrence. The latter urged his executioners to turn him over on the spit because he was done on one side, and Ignatius of Antioch pleaded with the lions in the arena to hurry him up to heaven.

To maintain this serenity and humor is to view one's life from the standpoint of God. Rather than being a human effort, it is the grace of God liberating people from the burden of life and giving them a foretaste of total liberation.

Conclusion

We could write much more about the different manifestations of grace in the life of the just and the world they can create. For example, there are the charisms of the Spirit, which are special gifts given to particular people so that they may serve the community with them. Each receives his or her own charism for the common good (1 Cor. 12:7; 1 Pet. 4:10).[15] Then there are the gifts of the Holy Spirit. According to theology, they are self-communications of God designed to complete the virtues and make people even more perfect.[16] The fact that they are counted as seven has symbolic value. The number seven suggests the complete fullness of divine communication to human beings in order that they might become more and more divinized.

These virtues and charisms and gifts point up the fact that grace is not a static, ontological entity. It is a living dynamism that finds expression in many different forms. Yet it is also the unique grace of God and the saving dialogue between him and human beings. Further treatment could carry us far, but it would basically not tell us any more than we have already considered about God's revelation in human beings and the way they are altered by his grace.

CHAPTER 16

Sharers of the Divine Nature

The reflections in the previous chapter bring us very close to the theme of the divinization of human beings in their inner relationship with God. If we are members of the household of God (Eph. 2:19), made in his image and likeness (Gen. 2:16), then we are sharers in God. In what terms should we formulate and view this participation? At one point the New Testament makes an extremely bold statement, using an expression that is rooted in the surrounding Greek culture. The Second Letter of Peter says: "So that through these you . . . might become *sharers of the divine nature*" (2 Pet. 1:4).[1]

What does this expression mean in the New Testament and in the Hellenistic milieu. What is the underlying experience that prompted the writer to affirm such a bold and unheard-of reality? How was this revelation interpreted in Christian thought? How are we to translate it today in terms of the way we perceive the mystery of God and the problem of humanity?

Salvation Expressed in Hellenistic Terms

Today it is generally accepted that the Second Letter of Peter is a rather late document (around the end of the first century of the Christian Era) which was only attributed to the apostle Peter himself. The style and terms used bear witness to a strong Hellenistic influence. In any case here is the decisive section:

That divine nature of his has freely bestowed on us everything necessary for a life of genuine piety, through knowledge of him who called us by his own glory and power. By virtue of them he has bestowed on us the great and precious things he promised, so that through these you who have fled a world corrupted by lust *might become sharers of the divine nature* (2 Pet. 1:3–4).

The terms "divine nature" (*théios* and *physis*) are typical Greek ones. Besides nature, *physis* also denotes natural properties, the qualities of a nature.[2] Perhaps this meaning is imprinted on our text. It would then mean that human beings are called to share in the qualities of God's nature.[3] What are these qualities? How are we to understand this bold statement?

We must first situate it in its Hellenistic context. For the Greeks, human

175

salvation and liberation come about insofar as human beings get beyond their own nature. That nature has the following qualities. It is fragile, infirm, transitory, contingent, mortal, and ever dependent on God. By sharing in a nature that is immortal, necessary, eternal, and absolutely permanent, they feel redeemed and experience the total realization of their humanity.[4]

The passage of our epistle is framed in this very context. It sets up a contrast between two realities. In the world corruption reigns; Greek *ftora* signifies transitoriness and the corruption of death. Over against this corruption stands incorruption, which is a property of the divine nature. Sharing in the latter, Christians or other human beings share in its qualities of immortality and wholeness (i.e., salvation). As one eminent Catholic exegete puts it:

This participation in the divine nature . . . is nothing else but a participation in the imperishable life of God through the grace conferred at Baptism. Only in this sense can this passage be used in support of a theology of divinization.[5]

However, the expression "sharers in the divine nature" does not express something wholly new that is nowhere else articulated in the New Testament. It translates for the Greek mind what was put in other terms for the Hebrew mind, but the point remains the same: salvation implies liberation from death, introduction into the divine life, a transition to the realm of God. The author of this epistle is trying to bring out certain familiar themes of the Christian faith for his readers, but he is not trying to add anything new. The theme is not divinization, it is salvation: but salvation clearly implies divinization as a result. This theme is not treated as such in the New Testament, and that is not so surprising. The Greek word *theios* ("divine") in the expression "sharers in the divine nature" is never used elsewhere in the New Testament. For the Greek mind it expresses the fact that humans can be saved, immortal, and eternal. It does not mean that they become God; it means that they share in God and his divine attributes.

The idea of "sharing" or "participation" is expressed in the Bible with the term "image and likeness" (Gen. 1:26; 9:6). This suggests proximity on the one hand, but on the other hand it also clearly suggests distance and difference. The image and likeness will never be the original prototype. Ancient pagan belief held that humanity derived from the blood of a deity. The biblical texts of the Old Testament combat this idea, but they also preserve the original, underlying intuition: humanity lives in a unique relationship with God, that of father and child (Gen. 5:3); one shares in the atmosphere of the other. St. Paul clearly articulates the idea of mystical communion with Christ (1 Cor. 1:30; Rom. 8:10; 2 Cor. 13:5; Eph. 3:17). This mystique of union with Christ (*koinonia*) signifies participation in the mystery of his life, death, resurrection, and ascension into heaven. Christ is the firstborn among many brothers (Rom. 8:23), who reveals our own collective destiny. What was realized in him is now being realized in an anticipatory way in us (2 Cor.

1:22; 5:5; Eph. 1:14). All will attain their complete fulfillment when we too rise from the dead (Phil. 3:21; 1 Cor. 15:49).

At this point in their theological reflection Christians had not yet elaborated a theology of the incarnation of the Word. Such a theology could easily have talked about divinization; for in becoming human the Word divinizes humanity. In the New Testament, however, we find nothing of this. The reflection of later centuries would lead to a systematic explanation of what we find implicit in the statement that we are "sharers in the divine nature."

The Christian Theology of Divinization (2 Pet. 1:4)

The New Testament passage under consideration had a profound influence on Christian reflection, particularly in the Hellenistic cultural milieu. A whole theology concerning the divinization or deification (*theopóiesis*) of humanity was elaborated during the discussions about christological and trinitarian dogmas in the third and fourth centuries. The backdrop that makes this theme and its interest understandable is Hellenistic anthropology of Platonic inspiration. According to this anthropology, humans and other beings are to be viewed in terms of a *participation in God.* Everything shares in God, hence everything is a sacrament and an embodiment revealing divinity.

In this context grace signifies the most thorough assimilation to the deity, to the point where humanity becomes "consubstantial" with God. The task of human living is to make ourselves ever more similar to the deity, to the point where a real ontological mutation takes place in the human substance. From being mere humans we pass over into being divinized. Humans are fully human only when they go out of themselves and are elevated to the divine sphere. As many Greek fathers put it, humans were created human but were called to be God.

However, this divinization is not the result of any rational dialectics or mystagogical pathways or ritual initiations. It is a gift from God. Out of profound sympathy God bends down to humanity and assumes it to make it something it is not. This something else represents being at its utmost, i.e., divinization.

Since the time of St. Irenaeus it has been customary to distinguish between what is "image" and what is "likeness" in human beings. This tendency is much more evident in eastern theology than western theology, however. Humans are the "image" of God in their natural being, insofar as they are body and soul. This is not lost through sinfulness. They are the "likeness" of God insofar as they share in the deity who, according to the Greeks, are incorruptible and immortal. Human beings lost this participation in immortality and incorruptibility through sin. The redemption brought by Christ restored this likeness to us and brought it to its culmination. For he, as the Son of God and our brother, is the supreme image and likeness who is consubstantial with the Father and the Holy Spirit.

Against the backdrop of this anthropology Christians interpreted the mystery of God's Incarnation. This prolongs and brings to its final consummation a whole process of participation and likeness that was already present in creation. In Jesus Christ human beings are so like God and so share in God that it is God himself present in the world.

Thus he is the grace of God made visible in history. The original sense of the idea of Incarnation is not exhausted in its redemptive effects that liberate us from a situation of damnation. In intent the Incarnation aims at the divinization of humanity. Only by being more than human can humans be truly human. In other words, only by being God can they continue to be human beings. St. Irenaeus says this repeatedly, and this thought is picked up by other church fathers such as Athanasius, Cyril of Alexandria, and Augustine. In the Incarnation God came down to humanity so that humanity might be transformed into God[6]: "In his immense charity the Word became what we are so that we might be transformed into what he is."[7] Human flesh is *made the Word* (Athanasius, *Contra Arianos* 3.34; PG 26. 396) through the Incarnation of the Word; it thus becomes more suited to receiving divine grace and becoming more deeply like God.

The grace that comes to us through the Incarnation does not imply solely a new relationship vis-à-vis God. The new relationship is the consequence of a new reality inaugurated with the coming of the Word in the flesh. So we get a new ontological richness: the Word assumes something that it was not before (humanity) while humans receive what they did not have before (the eternal Word). God became human and humanity became divine. Thus we can say that grace, as the progressive assimilation of humanity to God, culminated in the Incarnation of the eternal Word in the world. After that event grace must be viewed as a prolongation of the Incarnation within human beings, conforming them more and more to Christ. As Cyril of Alexandria put it: "The same things that are in Christ flow down to us."[8] A real process of God's assuming of humanity is at work. Grace is a small-scale incarnation (*incarnatio diminuta, incarnatio brevis*). Clement of Alexandria goes so far as to say that the just are deities (*theoi*),[9] not just in eternity but already here in time.

In the light of these considerations the sacrament of the Eucharist acquires inestimable value. There human beings have material access to the deity, hence to deification and "consubstantiality" with God. The liturgy celebrates this ineffable fellowship and grace-filled mutual interchange (*commercium*).

The Meaning of Our Participation in the Divine Nature

It is not enough to refer to the data of the Bible and tradition. With the mind of faith we must make clear what it means to say that we are sharers in the divine nature. What is the point and message of this daring affirmation?

We would be superficial if we sought to sidestep the question by saying that divinization is a problem peculiar to the Greek way of experiencing and expressing humanity's relationship with God, that the matter is of no concern to us because we are not Greeks. The problem was expressed in Hellenistic terms, but the problem itself is a human one and hence it concerns us. The Greeks had a certain experience and articulated it in terms of a metaphysics of nature. Today we, too, are likely to have the same experience; and we will express it in a different key. What we must do now is recover the common motive force in both the Greeks and ourselves.

The basic intuition underlying the notion that we are "sharers in the divine nature" lies in the realization that human beings experience themselves as fully human only when they completely surpass themselves. They exist as a living transcendence, ever open and beyond themselves, ever moved by a passion for the infinite. They do not find their realization in the factual but in the totally utopian and transcendent.

The Greek spirit was extremely open and sensitive to this type of human experience. When it said that humans are summoned to divinization, that they can only be fully human in sharing the divine nature, they were trying to express their feel for this basic intuition and experience. Humanity can rest only in union with what is absolutely different from itself: God.

Living within our own culture today, we have the same basic experience but we do not appeal directly to talk about divinization. To be sharers in the divine nature is not one of the typical yearnings of contemporary human beings. The expression in the Second Letter of Peter might well mean little to them, for we would tend to express our infinite yearning for fulfillment in different terms. What we seek today is not divinization but the total humanization and the full realization of our personality. But once we explore the implications of this yearning, we run up against the whole problem of God. Human beings are human to the extent that they commune with something different from themselves. The more they move out of themselves, the more they reenact the experience of Abraham and relate to the other, the more they become persons. The more they relate to the absolutely Other, the more they are themselves. But the "totally Other" can be a name only for the mystery of God. Hence complete personalization implies the divinization of a human being, and we can again find meaning in Greek talk about being "sharers in the divine nature."

I shall pursue this point further in the remaining pages of this book, but first I want to review briefly what western theology had done to clarify what it means to be "sharers in the divine nature."[10] Here the road is quite intricate and complicated. For the sake of clarity let me say that the various attempts fluctuate between asserting too little and asserting too much.

J. Ripalda (d. 1648) maintains that the expression "sharers in the divine nature" must be understood as the ethical assimilation of human beings to the virtues of God himself.[11] The divine nature possesses a moral goodness that is essential and permanent. The more human beings become like the divine nature through grace, the more virtuous they are and the more they tend to do everything perfectly. Finally they attain to glory. There, united with the will of God, the supreme norm of all sanctity, they attain indissoluble unity. They do not do works. They are simply good in the fullest sense of the word, in the likeness of God, who is the only one who is good according to the New Testament (Matt. 19:17).

This interpretation is viewed as minimalist, as saying too little, because it stresses only the ethical aspect of grace. That aspect is real and important enough, but this view overlooks the main point, i.e., the ontological transformation of a human being who is in contact with the divine nature. New being precedes transformed doing. Ripalda's view does not give due consideration to question as to how the new being shares in, and is penetrated by, the divine nature.

The classic Thomist school and such neo-scholastics as R. Garrigou-Lagrange propose an extremely daring thesis.[12] They maintain that sharing in the nature of God means sharing in his very essence, which can only be known to God himself and which is completely beyond the capabilities of the human mind. Through grace the finite nature of human beings shares in the infinite nature of God, which represents the infinite and the plenitude of being. This implies a real divinization whereby humans know and love God as God knows and loves himself.

Such statements sin by excess. They cannot be checked or verified by any experience, even that of the most ardent mystics. They are deductions from a neo-scholastic metaphysics of supernatural being in which religious experience is replaced by logical deductions. Certain conclusions are derived from prior theses about the supernatural, and the latter is viewed as a totally other world which is accessible to human beings through purely verbal revelation. This view no longer recaptures the experience underlying the Greek phrase "sharers in the divine nature." It does not convey an experience of total union with the deity, to the point where we know and love as God knows and loves himself. Here we confront nothing but unconstrained wordiness and metaphors that go beyond the reach of any controlled theological discourse.

An intermediate solution is attempted by Suarez, a great Jesuit theologian of the sixteenth century (1548–1617).[13] For him grace produces such a transformation in the being of humans that they come to be capable of knowing God as he is. To know God as he is, it is necessary to share in God's nature. That will come about in a definitive way in heaven, through the beatific vision.

This doctrine is eminently logocentric, which is typical of western thought with a Greek bent. For such thought the highest happiness of humans lies in seeing or contemplating God (*theoria*). Our perception of reality here situates us within a much broader horizon, however. Human fulfillment is glimpsed in total encounter with God. That is not achieved solely in the glory of heaven, however. It also takes place in the process of mortal life, in the obscure journey of faith, in love, and in hope.

In the modern era theologians have stayed closer to the religious experience of grace and have offered a personalistic, all-embracing view of what it means to share in the divine nature.[14] To share in the divine nature is basically to share in Jesus Christ. This entails two things: (1) an ontic mutation of human beings which (2) enables them to live filially as Christ does (the personal element). It enables human beings to have the same sentiments as Christ (Phil. 2:5–11; 1 Cor. 2:16), to love as he loved the Father and human beings in union with the Holy Spirit. The category that comes to the fore here is that of friendship understood in the Aristotelian and Thomistic sense. Here the ontological aspect (mutual alteration of those who relate to each other as friends) takes precedence over the psychological and social aspects that are made possible by it. Divinization is no longer considered as participation in the divine nature or as a unity of essence but rather as personal communion with the three divine Persons. And thus we arrive at the theme of the indwelling of the Trinity in the lives of the just, which we shall consider in our final chapter.

Right now I should like to explore and develop this personalist, ontological line of thought, stressing the mutual insertion of humans in God and of God in humans to the point where it can be experienced by human beings.

As I have pointed out repeatedly, grace emerges only in the mutual opening-up of God and human beings. This interchange alters both: God becomes human and humanity becomes divine. The Incarnation is the prime expression of this mutual sympathy between the two: not only does God come to encounter humanity but humanity goes out continually to search for God. Jesus of Nazareth, God made human, represents the meeting of these two movements, the embrace of two loves that have been secretly searching for each other all the time. Of course the human search for God is the effect of God's search for humanity. God created human beings in such a way that they are always out looking for the Absolute. They are so structured in their innermost depths that real encounter with God constitutes their utmost hominization and realization.

So a certain agreement or suitability vis-à-vis the deity lies at the very roots of the human being. Human nature can be comprehended adequately only within the horizon of the divine nature. At some point, then, talking about humanity means talking about God. To forget God is to forget human beings in their most mysterious and fascinating aspects. For this reason we dare to assert that the expression "sharers in the divine nature" ultimately signifies the most secret essence of a human being. Without this participation in the very mystery of God historical human beings, human beings as they exist, never achieve their humanity. Grace is never something superfluous that can be dispensed with in the process of complete hominization, even though it is something that overflows (*super-fluo*) into humans. It is by virtue of this very gratuitousness that historical human beings were created as they are, i.e., as beings who become what they are (humans) only insofar as they share in what they are not (God).

What, then, is the nature of God that fulfills the nature of humanity? To ask about the nature of God is to ask about God's divinity, that which constitutes God as God. This cannot be grasped or learned *a priori,* for that would imply that there is something prior to God that serves as his reason for being. There is nothing prior or superior to God that would enable us to grasp who God is and what he means. God is the supreme reality, and we know only so much about God as he himself has made manifest in the history that he makes with human beings.

In the history of the Judeo-Christian experience—where the event decisive for anthropology took place (i.e., the resurrection)—God manifested himself as he is, i.e., as a being who exists only insofar as he is oriented outside himself, only insofar as he is eternal communication and permanent self-giving out of love. God is the total openness that moves out of itself and its absolute mysteriousness (Father), communicates itself fully (Son) and manifests itself in what is different from itself (creation in, for, with, and by the Logos), and returns to itself reuniting all in its primeval unity (Holy Spirit). In that sense, then, God is a living transcendence—*Deus semper maior*—which realizes itself and generates itself eternally and ever outside itself. In short, God is the love that created companions in love and that realizes its being (divinity) by loving and communicating itself to all that it created so that they might in turn accept it. In Jesus Christ God gave himself completely to the world, thus revealing himself as he truly is—i.e., as total self-giving.

For human beings, participating in God means being able to possess what in God is being: that is to say, it means being able to love radically, to give oneself permanently, and to commune openly with all things. It means being able to endure infinitely as God does, to possess the *cortesia* of God that was lived out so intensely by Francis of Assisi, to deal kindly and lovingly with all, even the unjust and the ungrateful (Luke 6:35).

Being a person means living in communion, opening up to others, being a living web of relationships. The more humans go out of themselves and commune with others, the more they enrich themselves and resemble the being of God himself. To love is to let God happen in one's life. To let God happen in one's life is to become divine and to allow God to become human. Divinization is not a miraculous process that lies outside our lives and cannot be experienced. It is the day-to-day process of love with its obscure but deep-rooted fidelity, the obstacles that it has to overcome, and the purifications it must go through. These are the things demanded by the careful attention and fine sensitivity of love. The process does not lack its great and small martyrs, nor its subtle moments of vibrant gratification amid the moments of anxiety and obligation that cannot be brushed aside.

In the course of life human beings are led to open themselves, to give of themselves and transcend themselves. Insofar as they do, they participate more and more in the nature of God, who realizes this openness in absolute, infinite, eternal form. Finally, in the definitive state of glory we are at home with the Lord (2 Cor. 5:8). We will no longer wonder what sharing in the nature of God means. Though we will preserve our personal identity, he will be all in all (1 Cor. 15:28). Knowing will give way to savoring once and for all.

To say that humans share in the nature of God is also to imply the reverse: God shares in the nature of humanity. Thus human beings are theomorphic and God is anthropomorphic. Real awareness of this point can lead to a truly mystical experience, in which we consciously live the reality of humanity being in God and God being in humanity. The latter implies that God, even as he generates himself, also gives birth to the Son and with him breathes out the Spirit within the good and just human being.

At this ineffable stage of mystery, where hallowed silence communicates more than wordy chatter, theological concepts lose their rigor and force. If statements are not to be mere deductions and applications of trinitarian ideas to the theme of grace, we must always stand on the firm ground of the experience of grace. In experiencing our own mysteriousness, our capacity for comprehension and communion, we glimpse what it means when we say that the Father subsists in his mysteriousness without origin and gives origin to everything, that the Son is the full understanding of this mystery, and that the Holy Spirit is their communion in love. In the depths of our own selves there is produced a pale reflection of the ineffable trinitarian process. It is the way in which the creature participates in the unique nature of God, who realizes himself in a trinity of persons. In experiencing ourselves wholly down to our very roots, we experience God.

So we must assume, then, that participation in the nature of God is a process of radical personalization. It is the person as a being for another and, ultimately, as a being for the absolutely Other, God. This being the case, it is clear that this reality cannot be reserved exclusively for Christians or for those who are aware of this reality. It is a standing offer to humanity. It is ever present in history insofar as human beings refuse to withdraw into them-selves and seek humanizing encounter in love, reconciliation, forgiveness, and the overcoming of obstacles that prevent people from being persons more and more. With St. Irenaeus we can say that supreme happiness in heaven is bound up with a pedagogical providence that slowly guides human beings to their total happiness, i.e., full participation in the nature of God. As Irenaeus made bold to say: "Humans were not created God from the begin-ning, but they were called to be God."[15] Perhaps it is here we must look for the roots of the ineradicable optimism of the Christian faith. When all is said and done, human beings are called to be more than human; they are sum-moned to oneness with God.

This interpretation salvages the theological aspect present in human exis-tence. We cannot interpret humans adequately if we view their lives merely with profane eyes. *"Res sacra homo"* [Humanity is a sacred reality]. Only in the horizon of the absolute sacredness of God do we really unveil the mystery of humanity, which is ultimately related and akin to the mystery of God.

CHAPTER 17

God's Children in His Son

Such themes as participation in the divine nature, the divine sonship of human beings, anointing by the Holy Spirit, and the indwelling of the Trinity in the lives of the just ultimately are attempts to express one and the same experience: the proximity of humans to God and of God to humans. So intimate is this proximity that the only way we can express it is to say that the human being is a relative of God, a child of God.

What experience underlies this statement? The task of this chapter is to rescue this original experience and to seek it out in our life today. The basic assumption, of course, is the one which I have made the theoretical cornerstone of this book. It is that talking about grace and the supernatural is not talking about some reality beyond the range of our experience. It is not as if we had access to it only through verbal and doctrinal revelation, as if we would have no experience of it except through revelation in abstract phrases. Our assumption here is quite the opposite. The verbal phrases and abstract propositions were presented to us because prior to them a divine reality was communicated to us and we were permitted to experience a divine reality.

When we are told that we are children of God in truth, not just in words, we are presented with a reality that is ever present in humans. It is a dimension of human life that is not for the privileged few, that structures the life of all. So the affirmation unveils for consciousness a reality that is ever there in life, that has been lived under different names and that has never been absent from human beings. It was the limited outlook of a clerical, ghetto-minded theology that restricted the life of grace and divine filiation solely to Christians. God does not practice that sort of discrimination and Jesus Christ always fought against such reductionism, either with reference to love of neighbor (Luke 10:29–37) or to love of God (Luke 6:35; Matt. 5:43–48). To say that we are children of God is to spell out and interpret the human experience of the Absolute in all its radicalness. It is not a piece of information coming from outside that would be otherwise inaccessible to us.

The Written Testimony

Among primitive peoples and in ancient cultures—e.g., Egypt, Babylonia, the Middle East—we find an awareness that humanity is the child of some deity.[1] Even proper names enshrine this conviction: Abibaal ("Baal is my father"), Abijah ("Jahweh is my father": 1 Sam. 8:2; 2 Chron. 13:20), Abiel ("the Lord is my Father": 1 Sam. 9:1), and Ben-Hadad ("son of the deity Hadad"). Divine filiation was attributed to chiefs, kings, and pharaohs in particular. Hence in the literature of imperial Rome we find the expression *divi filius* quite frequently.

In the Old Testament we find that Israel as a people believed that they were children of God, particularly for the special care he showed them when they were liberated from Egypt (Exod. 4:22; Hos. 11:1; Jer. 3:19). Later, members of the nation, particularly those who were upright, were called children of God (Isa. 63:8,16; 64:7). The king, a privileged member of the nation, felt he was a child of God through divine election and through his association with the destiny of the whole nation (1 Chron. 28:6; Ps. 89:28; Ps. 2:7). For a human being divine filiation means that he honors God in a special way, obeying him (Mal. 1:6) and imitating his way of acting (Sir. 4:10–11). God's paternity, in turn, is expressed in terms of a distinctive mercifulness (Ps. 103:12–13) and special protection (Ps. 27:10; Deut. 8:5; Sir. 51:10).

Thus in humanity we find a vague awareness of some underlying relationship to the deity. Paul pointed this out to the Athenians, echoing a phrase of the ancient poets: "for we too are his offspring" (Acts 17:28).

In the New Testament the term "son of God" is a key term in attempting to decipher the mystery of Jesus Christ and to describe the situation of humanity before God.[2] Jesus refers to God simply as Abba ("Dad"), and we see him using this term in all his prayers (Matt. 11:25–26; 26:42; Luke 10:21; 22:42; 23:34,46). He regards himself as son, indeed as *the* Son (Matt. 11:27; 24:36; 28:19; and fourteen times in John's gospel).[3] There is a mutual knowledge (Matt 11:25) and mutual agreement (Mark 1:11; 9:7) between him and the father, to the point where John's gospel will interpret it by putting these words in Christ's mouth: "The Father and I are one" (John 10:30). His sonship is unique (Mark 12:6). He distinguishes it from that of the disciples by talking about "my Father" and "your father" (Matt. 5:45; 25:34; Luke 24:49). He seems to suggest that other human beings become sons of God whereas he has always been that (Luke 2:49; see Matt. 5:44–45; Luke 20:36; John 1:1; 1:12–13). And other humans become children of God by adherence to Jesus (Matt. 8:10–12).

The child of God must imitate the Father, who is good and merciful (Matt. 5:45; Luke 6:45), who does not want any of his children to perish (Matt. 18:24), and who watches over the least thing with great care and providence (Matt. 6:8–32).

In the early church it was Paul who turned the divine filiation of humanity into a theological topic. For Paul, only Jesus Christ is the only begotten Son of God; humans are children of God through communion, grace, and adoption (*huiothesia*: Gal. 4:5; Eph. 1:5; Rom. 8:15–23). The term "adopted children" is not a happy one, since it seems to be framed in a juridical context.

Paul, however, does not attribute merely juridical significance to the divine filiation of humanity. Thanks to the fact that human beings are in Christ, their filiation is equivalent to a natural one. The noted Catholic specialist on Pauline theology, Lucien Cerfaux, has this to say:

In the Pauline sense "filiation" is always natural in the sense that it is not limited to a juridical act on God's part. Rather, it creates us in the spiritual order and truly glorifies us.[4]

In a series of close-knit affirmations Paul stresses our real divine filiation: "All of you who have been baptized into Christ have clothed yourselves with him" (Gal. 3:27). We have been predestined from all eternity to be the adopted children of God through Jesus Christ (Eph. 1:5). The Son was sent so that we might receive the character of God's children (Gal. 4:3–6). Because we are his children, God has sent the Spirit of his Son who cries out "Abba!" ("Father!"); and we are his children because we are moved by God's Spirit (Rom. 8:14; 2 Tim. 1:7). It is always the Spirit who enables us to take cognizance of our real situation as children of God (Rom. 8:15). We are truly children of God in his Son, Jesus (1 John 2:29 f.), and we are predestined to reproduce the image of God's only Son (Rom. 8:29).

Here we are not dealing with just another epithet to describe human existence. It is an ontological specification that is given great stress in the Joannine writings:

See what love the Father has bestowed on us in letting us be called children of God! Yet that is what we are. . . . We are God's children now; what we shall be later has not yet come to light (1 John 3:1–2).

As we have seen, this means really sharing the very nature of God (1 Pet. 1:4).

The Underlying Experience

Initially the term "son" or "child" translates an experience of profound natural intimacy with God, for which the father-child relationship serves as the prototype. It suggests a warm intimacy that dispels all fear and a clear linkup in the same sort of life. However, the notion of intimacy points even deeper, as we realize when we ask ourselves what it is grounded on.

Intimacy with God is born of a human being's intimacy with self, just as all true experience of God emerges from the deeper roots of human experience itself. Humans seem to be the only beings in creation who possess intimacy and an inner life. In the intimacy of their inner life they experience the mystery of their own selves. In the process of becoming persons we all go through a critical experience. We become a question mark for ourselves, as Augustine noted. Every individual is a challenging mystery to himself or herself. We must seek out and define our own ultimate meaning in our own unique way. And this mystery sets us thinking.

At the same time our perception of this intimacy with self opens us up to our frailty and our grandeur. We feel fragile because we sense that we have been sent and yet realize that our existence is a gratuitous gift. We did not ask to exist and yet we cannot basically resist existence either. On the other hand, we sense our grandeur because we can give and receive, because we can accept ourselves as we are and live a gracious life, enriching ourselves for the sake of another. Ever deeper and more courageous dialogue with these two dimensions of our inner life makes us more mature as human beings. It helps us understand and empathize with the mystery of other human beings.

In the horizon of this personal mystery there emerges the mystery of God as the One who creates, sustains, and sends out human beings unceasingly. Here we meet the pure, benevolent gratuitousness of God. God is more intimate to us than our own inner selves, as Augustine expressed it: *intimior intimo meo.*

Thus human intimacy and innerness brings the mystery of human beings closer to the supreme mystery which we call God. At its uttermost depths existence shows up as total openness, bottomless depth, and pure transcendence. In some vague, confused way humans have always sensed that they are a reality which is lost within the mystery of God. Human beings can only be contemplated adequately in the context of the divine. If their horizon were simply the human, then we would never know for sure what the human itself is. Only the divine deciphers the human, making the latter as mysterious and indecipherable as it itself is. Herein lies the grandeur and the sacred nature of the human. We share in the nature of God. We sense that we are the children of God. The term "child of God" alludes to this basic inner experience and expresses it.

Thus divine filiation is not the exclusive feature of a few privileged humans. It is the innermost structure of every human being. This experience was spelled out in exemplary and definitive form by Jesus of Nazareth. He experienced God as his Father and himself as the well-beloved Son of God: and he conducted himself as such. He went so far as to proclaim his divine identity with the Father. The Pharisees noted this, and then began to threaten him with death. Jesus felt that he had been sent by the Father. He lived on the most intimate terms with the Father, and they have been beautifully described in John's gospel (John 5:17,19,23,26; 6:46; 7:29; 10:15,28–30; 14:10–20; 17:5,10–12; 21:25). However, his behavior was not neurotically dependent or infantile. He took responsibility, fought for his ideas, and did his job as an adult son. Without the experience of filiation which Jesus went through, we would never enjoy the filial consciousness we possess today.

The dogmatics of the early church, both in the New Testament and in the decisions of the first Councils, did a fine job of interpreting Jesus' behavior. They saw it as the Incarnation of the eternal Son of the Father in the power of the Holy Spirit. But this Incarnation of the only begotten Son is not a curiosity in religious history. It reveals that God himself is for the world, and that our status is that of children of God in his Son. We are not merely creatures, condemned to live as such apart from God and marked out for nothingness. We are called to share in the eternal history of God as children of God in his Son. We are to be so close to the mystery of God that we will form one destiny with him (1 Cor. 15:28).

In the last analysis, then, human beings are not ultimately oriented toward human beings but toward God. We can remain ourselves only by transcending ourselves and penetrating the realm of God. That is what happened in the case of Jesus of Nazareth, through the effort and grace of the supreme, divine mystery.

To say that human beings are the children of God in his Son is to assert that their absolute destiny and vocation is to be with God, in God, for God, and of God, i.e., to be sharers in the divine nature.

Divine Filiation Revealed in Christ

If we are children of God in his Son, then his Son, Jesus Christ, is the place we must look to find out what our divine filiation means.

Various gospel passages tell us that *Jesus called his fellow humans "brothers"* (Mark 3:31–35; Matt. 18:15–21; 25:34–40; see Rom. 9:3; Acts 14:2; Luke 8:21). The Letter to the Hebrews tells us that he was not ashamed to call us "brothers" (Heb. 2:11). He became like us in all things except sin (Heb. 2:17). He is the first of many brothers and sisters (Rom. 8:29). Acting as Son toward the Father and as brother to other persons, he revealed the filial nature of all human beings.[5]

The resurrection happening made it clear to the primitive Christian community that the Jesus they knew, who had lived, died, and been resurrected, was the only begotten, eternal Son of God (Rom. 1:4; Heb. 1:6; John 3:16). In him they grasped the ultimate meaning of creation and the definitive design of God. Everything has something to do with him in some way (Col. 1:15–20; 1 Cor. 8:6) and converges toward him (Eph. 1:10). From all eternity human beings were predestined to be *children of God through Jesus* (Eph. 1:5), and to reproduce the image of the Son in themselves (Rom. 8:29). Hence we all can relate to the Father as he did (Rom. 8:14–17; Gal. 4:1–7; Heb. 2:10–14; 3:6; 4:16).

To say that we all are brothers of Christ and children of God along with him is to say that each of us in our own way are called to be what Jesus Christ was historically. And as we shall see further on, it means that we are to be this in the very bosom of the Trinity.

Because we are the brothers and sisters of Christ, *we share in his heritage,* i.e., divinization and the enjoyment of an absolute future (Rom. 8:17–29; Gal. 4:7; Titus 3:7; 1 Pet. 1:23). This heritage is not just a promise for the future. It is already concretely embodied in the present (Rom. 8:20–23). It is a life fleshed out in love, in freedom vis-à-vis death, in the liberty of the children of God who have reached the stage of mature adulthood (Gal. 4:1–7; 1 Cor. 3:1; 13:11; Rom. 8:15) and who therefore can manage the world.

The Incarnation inserted the Son into a world limited in space and time. The resurrection universalized his immersion in creation. When resurrected, he penetrated to the very heart of the world. He never abandoned the creation that he had assumed. He touches all human beings and all things at their very roots. This is the radical, eschatological import of the resurrection and it does not concern the historical Jesus alone: it concerns all creation. The resurrection anticipates the future, showing us what humanity and the cosmos will be in their definitive state, i.e., a total transfiguration in God. As the prolongation and fulfillment of the incarnation process, the resurrection created *a truly Christic atmosphere in which all human beings are immersed.* Pauline theology expressed the same idea by talking about "being in Christ" or "living in Christ." The idea must be taken quite concretely, in the strongest possible ontological terms. Humans and the world take on a new quality that was already accepted and assumed by God through the Incarnation of his eternal Son.

The human atmosphere is not the same as it was before the Incarnation and the resurrection. An ontological "plus" has appeared. Some latent possibility, as yet unexperienced, has become a reality for both God and the world. A new salvific situation has been created. Because of this new ontological atmosphere we can now have a christological mystique that is cosmic in character. That is what we find in such people as Paul, Saint Francis of Assisi, Maurice Blondel, Pierre Teilhard de Chardin, and others.[6] The Christian mystery is not experienced solely as mystical union in the person of Christ. It also becomes a new experience of the world, in which faith detects the cosmic presence of the risen Jesus bringing fulfillment to all reality and leading human beings to a filial way of life. It is grace in the world, which always possesses a christic and filial character.

This presence of the cosmic, risen Christ is sacramental in different ways and on different levels. It manifests itself in the world, in human beings, in the just, in Christians, in the community of the faithful, in the sacraments, in the sacred power of their leaders, and so forth. But it is always the same total Christ who shows up in these various surface appearances.

The real basis for the fact of divine filiation is to be found in reflection on the Trinity. Here we get beyond a merely juridical view of adoptive filiation and we glimpse its universal application to all human beings. As all paternity comes from the Father (Eph. 3:15; Acts 3:25), so all filiation comes from the Son. In going out of himself and revealing himself, the absolute mystery (the Father) is called the Son. The Son is the eternal and full expression of both the Father and creatures. And because all created things also reveal the absolute mystery, they too possess a filial character. In the very same movement in which the Father generates the Son as his complete expression he also generates—in him, with him, by him, and for him—all other possible beings as a derivative expression of himself. Cyril of Alexandria wrote: "Filiation comes through the Son because only he is the one, authentic, sovereign Son."[7] Augustine noted: "We are members of the only begotten Son of God";[8] "we are the children of God, we are the Son, because we are one in him even though we are many."[9] E. Mersch, a Catholic theologian, has done more than anyone in this century to pick up this great tradition and to stress our eternal and historical oneness with the Son. He wrote: "The two filiations constitute only one in him who is the principle of all."[10]

Obviously we are not to confuse the realities here.[11] The person of Christ is not the person of individual human beings. As is true in christological dogma, there is a union between Christ and his fellow humans that is "distinct, immutable, indivisible, and inseparable." Human beings are not children of God directly by virtue of their own person; they are so by virtue of the union of their person with the eternal person of the Son. That is why we say that we are "adoptive" children of God rather than his natural children as Christ is. However, this adoption must be interpreted ontologically rather than juridically. As the early fathers put it, it must be interpreted "physically" as a matter of truth and fact.[12] It is a real sharing in the natural and eternal filiation of the Son. To point up the nonjuridical character of this filiation, I should like to cite a passage written by Cyril of Alexandria:

Christ is simultaneously the unique Son and the only begotten Son. He is the unique Son as God. He is the only begotten son through the salvific union he established between himself and us. He became human that we might become children of God in him and by him. We are thus children of God by nature and by grace. We are so by nature in him, and in him alone. We are so by participation and grace through him in the Spirit. Just as the trait of only begotten became a property of humanity in Christ because it was united to the Word in the economy of salvation, so it became a property of the Word to be the firstborn among many brothers and sisters because he unites with flesh and blood.[13]

This passage brings out the essential link between the eternal filiation of the Son and our own filiation that is imbedded in it.[14] *Not only human beings but all things possess a filial character because they all were fashioned in and for the Son.* They all reveal both the Father and the Son in whom they were conceived and created. This is the basis for the fraternal character of all things. We are brothers and sisters in the house of the Father, who willed us to be his children. Living in this awareness, we develop a tender humanism and a universal confraternity with both the human and nonhuman world as Francis of Assisi so well exemplified.

The Incarnation deepened this filiation and fraternity with the Son. Already in eternity we were children of God in the Son. Now in history we express the import of this fact in time and space, in the flesh and in the spirit.

Becoming incarnate in Jesus of Nazareth, our Jewish brother, the Son somehow assumed all human beings and all things. In a bold formulation Athanasius states: "Through the Incarnation the Son turned all creation into children of God and thus leads it, as such, to the Father."[15]

So our divine filiation has its roots in eternity and the Trinity. Its revelation to us in Jesus made us aware of something that had always existed in human beings. From all eternity we were children of God in the Son; with the Christ-happening, the filial structure of human beings is brought to the level of historical awareness. It can now be celebrated, lived, and considered thematically in a way never possible before.

On the basis of this ontological foundation—i.e., creation in the Son and the universal project of Christ—we can talk without reductionism or exclusivism about divine filiation in the church through the sacrament of Baptism. Baptism is grounded on the divine filiation of the universe. It prolongs and deepens it because it immerses baptized people more deeply in the mystery of Christ. By the fact of creation every human being is a child of God in the Son. By the fact of universal redemption this filial quality is restored in its pristine nature, which had been violated by sin, and is brought to its fulfillment through a distinctive union with Christ. The crucified and risen Christ is present in the world and in the church. Baptism and the other sacraments virtually contained in it accomplish this specific and unique immersion of human beings into the divine filiation of the Son. The church, the community of the baptized, becomes the community par excellence of the children of God and the brotherhood that follows from it. This filiation and brotherhood are not exclusivist. They open out to the whole universe, where they find their nourishment and roots. All of us have been conceived, created, and loved in and for the Son so that we might make up the great family of the Father.

Being children of God is not merely a piece of information about our divine reality. *It entails a corresponding way of being and living.* When we say that we are children of God, we are basically talking about three realities.

First, no one is a child without a father. The two realities imply one another. In other words, to be a child is to be *from* another and *for* another. As one who receives life from another, the child is sent; he or she lives as a being related to, and graced by, another. The child is all the more child insofar as he or she senses having come from a father and nurtures this relationship with the father. The humanity of human beings is not really defined by the fact that they transcend the world and their various infrastructures (biological, psychological, social, and so forth) by moving toward another. It is defined much more by their immersion in the Father and their orientation toward him. As children of God, human beings carry the whole universe along with them and offer it to the Father from whom they have received everything.

Second, the child relationship expresses a personal relationship rather than a casual one. It is the existence of human beings as creatures that constitutes a casual relationship. Human beings are created by God. They recognize their point of origin and can relate to it humbly and thankfully. As creatures, their being comes *from* God and *through* God. The realization that they are children of God sets up a personal relationship in the framework of liberty. We are children to the extent that we know and recognize our Father and are known and recognized by him in turn. The more we open up to our Father, the more we become truly his children, so much the more do we become hallowed persons. Thus there are degrees of intensity in filiation. It is a dynamic rather than a static quality. It can grow and have a future. It involves the task of becoming children of God more and more by opening up to Him more and more.

Third, the term "child" (*huios* in Greek) does not signify the same thing as "youngster" (*teknon* in Greek). The child or son (*huios*) possesses independence and has come of age. The youngster (*teknon*) is a dependent minor. Thus humans as the children of God are free, adult beings before God. Their relationship with the Father is not a fated one but results from their act of accepting their filiation. It is an act of love, gratitude, and obedience that presupposes freedom. The children of God have received a task from their Father. They are to be his representatives in the world. The whole world is their inheritance and they, in God's name, are to be its responsible masters.[16] We are no longer in the situation described by Paul: "While we were not yet of age, we were like slaves subordinated to the elements of the world" (Gal. 4:3). The much debated expression "elements of the world" (*stoikeia tou kosmou*) probably refers to the social, political, and cultural order, i.e., the law.[17] Human beings are not slaves of the established order but free beings responsible for its order. They were set up by God their Father as free masters, as children responsible for his project of creation. Creation must be ruled in such a way that it is worthy of God's children and an honor to God himself.

The traits of the Father should appear in the activity of his children. According to the Judeo-Christian experience, those traits include kindness, mercy, love, and sensitive consideration of all things. We must also display the traits of the Son because we are children of God in him. Within the Trinity the Son is the intelligence and light of the Father as well as the receptivity, openness, and thankfulness ever centered on the Father. In the Incarnation the Son historicized these traits. He felt that he had been sent by the Father, that he had come *from* God *for* his brothers and sisters. He gave himself to the utmost in humility, love, and continual self-effacement. The more the children of God in the Son exemplify these traits in their lives and thus embody the ideal of humanity, the more they will reveal themselves to be children of God.

Being children of God is a challenge and a task to be faced day by day. If our human journey is faithful to this task, the traits of God's Son and the mysterious face of the loving Father will be revealed more and more.

CHAPTER 18

The Holy Spirit:
One Person in Many Persons

The themes discussed in the two previous chapters—participation in the divine nature and divine filiation—tell us of the intimacy and involvement of human beings with God. The theme of this chapter, the indwelling of the Holy Spirit, tells us of God's living and active presence in existence and the world. In the history of religions and in the Judeo-Christian experience this presence was experienced first as a vague, numinous force, then as the Spirit of Yahweh and the Spirit of Christ, and finally as a distinct reality of its own, the third person of the Blessed Trinity.

Human Experience of the Spirit

For the Greeks, the Spirit (*pneuma*) was an elementary, dynamic, life-giving reality that led people into states of enthusiasm or ecstasy.[1] It is present where life is in real motion, especially human life when it extrapolates from ordinary experience. Thus we find it in such phenomena as artistic inspiration, poetry, divination, and ecstatic experiences such as speaking in tongues and prophesying.[2] By virtue of its elementary nature which fills and penetrates everything, human beings cannot manipulate the Spirit; they can only open themselves to its mysterious power. For this reason the Greeks viewed it as a divine reality (*theion, theon, theou pneuma*).[3] The Pythagoreans and later the Stoics saw the Spirit as a reality surrounding and suffusing the whole universe and thus making it possible for there to be union and communion with all beings: deities, human beings, animals, and so forth.[4]

In the Old Testament the Spirit was experienced initially in the realm of history.[5] There was the sudden appearance of charismatic leaders who liberated the Hebrew people from oppression by their enemies: "The spirit of the Lord came upon him [Othniel], and he judged Israel. When he went out to war, the Lord delivered Cushan-rishathaim, the king of Aram, into his power" (Judg. 3:10); "the spirit of the Lord enveloped Gideon" (Judg. 6:34; 14:6). As a charismatic, liberating force it also descended on Saul (1 Sam. 11:6), Jephthah (Judg. 11:29), Joshua (Num. 27:18; Deut. 34:9), and David (1 Sam. 16:13). It was the Spirit that moved the prophets (Ezek. 48:16; Neh.

9:30; Mic. 3:8). It is present in the creative power of human beings, in their intelligence and their capabilities (Zech. 4:6; 6:8; Ezek. 31:3; 32:15; 35:31). On the basis of this sociopolitical and historical experience of the Spirit, Israel later came to experience the Spirit in nature and in the creative act of God. It is the creative principle that is operative in plants, animals, and nature as a whole (Gen. 1:2; 2:7; Job 33:34; 37:10; Ps. 29). Because the Spirit is ubiquitous, it embodies the proper mode of divine existence itself (Ps. 139:7). It fills and renews the face of the earth constantly.

As is the case in the Old Testament, in the New Testament the Spirit is not revealed first in creation but in the community's collective experience of God.[6] It manifests itself in numerous charisms, particularly in prophesying and in the general enthusiasm that takes hold of the whole church. It is at work in the community fostering energies, words, and deeds that would not otherwise be unleashed. The presence of the Spirit tends to make people break down conventional barriers and go beyond themselves. People moved by the Spirit say and do things that they ordinarily would not. They give themselves to others, straining themselves in the service of others. They seem to be "outside themselves."

Experience of the Spirit entails seeing and hearing things and then bearing witness to what has been seen and heard (Acts 2:33; 22:15). It is no more visible than breath or the wind (the original sense of "spirit": *ruah* in Hebrew, *pneuma* in Greek). Yet it can be seen and experienced in its impact and effects.[7] The experience of the Spirit takes place in an aura of fascination or enchantment. It envelops people and leaves a profound mark on them. The surprising and extraordinary aspects of the experience take hold of people and carry them beyond themselves. In both the mythical age and the modern age human beings intuit that something mysterious and alive pervades reality, giving life to things and sustaining all the varied manifestations of life. All the forms of fascination, including the most secularized ones (e.g., sports, art, technology, fan clubs, and so forth) reveal the glow of the Absolute. The element of fascination is bound up with something that seems unique and self-evident. The more fascinating something is, the more irreducible, intangible, and absolute it seems to be.[8]

Insofar as the Spirit is the force that pervades everything, we can say that it was always in the world. The world is the temple of the Spirit; from the first moment of creation it has been inhabited by the Spirit.

According to the New Testament, the advent of the Messiah, Jesus Christ, brought the full manifestation of the Spirit. In Luke's theology in particular, Jesus is presented as the bearer of the Spirit in all its fullness and in a permanent way (Luke 1:35; 4:18–21; Acts 4:27; see Matt. 1:18; Heb. 1:9; 2 Cor. 1:21; 1 John 2:22). In Jesus the Spirit becomes "incarnate," as it were. For this reason everything that Jesus says and does in life flows from his own strength and power. He is not led by the Spirit. Instead he pursues his course "in the Spirit" (Luke 4:14). Because the Spirit dwells in him, his actions exert a fascination over people. They seek him out time and again, as the evangelists point out repeatedly (Matt. 2:2; 5:41; 6:51; Matt. 7:28; 12:23; 13:54; 19:25; Luke 4:32; 9:43). Their admiration and surprise (Matt. 9:33; Mark 5:20; Luke 2:18; 4:22; Matt. 8:37; 15:31; 21:20) does not suggest a dry acquaintance with some mere information; it suggests a profound experience that moved them to their very depths. They experienced the fascination of Jesus' Spirit.

The resurrection revealed the full dimensions of the Spirit's presence in Jesus. Before the resurrection Jesus had possessed a carnal, fragile, mortal body. After the resurrection he came to possess a spiritual, incorruptible body full of divine energy (1 Cor. 15:44). The risen Christ was "transformed" into pure Spirit, as it were. Indeed Paul goes so far as to identify the risen Lord with the Spirit: "The Lord is the Spirit" (2 Cor. 3:17). This statement should not be understood in trinitarian terms. It should be taken in the Old Testament sense as a way of describing how the risen Jesus now exists and acts. He lives and acts in the manner of the Spirit: free from the fetters of the flesh, pervading the whole cosmos, and in the plenitude of power and communion.[9]

The Spirit fills the face of the earth, vivifying and leavening everything. In like manner the risen Christ fills everything, giving life and vigor. Paul draws an impressive parallel between the risen Christ and the Holy Spirit: Christ dwells in us (Gal. 2:20) and so does the Spirit (Rom. 8:10; 2 Cor. 3:18); we are justified in Christ (Gal. 2:17) and in the Spirit (1 Cor. 6:11); we are sanctified in Christ (1 Cor. 1:2) and in the Spirit (Rom. 15:16); we are sealed in Christ (Eph. 1:13) and in the Spirit (Eph. 4:30); Christ dwells in us (2 Cor. 13:13) and so does the Spirit (Rom. 8:9–11).

We possess the Spirit of Christ. He is operative in us as he was in Christ: "The proof that you are sons is the fact that God has sent forth into our hearts the spirit of his Son" (Gal. 4:6); "whoever is joined to the Lord becomes one spirit with him" (1 Cor. 6:17); "all who are led by the Spirit of God are sons of God" (Rom. 8:14). We are children of God in the Son, so the Spirit makes us aware of this fact and prompts us to call God our Father (Rom. 8:16).

The Holy Spirit is the enduring presence of the risen Jesus in the world until it reaches its consummation. Christ continues among us in the form of the Spirit. The Spirit lay hidden in the earthly Jesus behind his activities. Thanks to the resurrection, he emerges from hiding and shows *himself* as he really is. Once Jesus ascended into heaven, the epoch of salvation history became that of the Holy Spirit revealed in his own proper identity. That took place on Pentecost. However, the Spirit does not replace Jesus. Instead the Spirit makes his presence real and recalls his words to mind (John 14:26). He does not teach a different message, he simply teaches the fullness of Jesus' message (John 16:13): "He will have received from me what he will announce to you" (John 16:14).

The Spirit does not exist independently of Jesus. He is sent by the Father and the Son (John 14:26; 7:37–39). But in the temporal interim between Jesus' ascension and the Parousia, the Spirit makes his own history; it is the history of creation being sanctified and reunited eschatologically. Meditating on this distinctive activity of the Spirit of Jesus Christ, the Christian community gradually came to identify the Holy Spirit with a person of the Trinity who is distinct from the Father and the Son; and it also realized that the Spirit has his own personal mission in the history of salvation. He is to lead all creation to union with the Father through the Son. The era of the Spirit is the era that will see the definitive turn of creation back toward its creator.

Reflecting on the person of the Holy Spirit, Christians came to realize that divine grace, the experience of grace, the salvific force that pervades history, and the thrust of creation toward its ultimate destination are nothing but manifestations of the Holy Spirit making his presence and activity felt everywhere. The church is constituted as the sacrament of the Holy Spirit.[10] Over the centuries it makes visible his new presence in creation and the lives of human beings, particularly in the lives of the just. And this new presence is grounded on the Christ-event.

The Era of the Holy Spirit

By the "era of the Holy Spirit" I mean a time in salvation history that is characterized by the predominance of the Holy Spirit as the proper and enduring way to contemplate and live out God's relationship with humans and their relationship with God.[11] To say that we live in the era of the Holy Spirit is to say that the Spirit is the fontal reality from which our salvific situation is to be perceived and understood. The notion of an era of the Holy Spirit can be found as far back as the Letter to the Romans. In Chapters 5–7, Paul distinguishes three stages in the history of God's relations with human beings: a situation of sinfulness "before the law" extending from Adam to Moses (Rom. 5:13–14), a situation of sinfulness "under the law" extending from Moses to Christ (Rom. 6:14), and a situation of life in Christ "under grace" (Rom. 6:14). In the last we live under the law of the Spirit, which has freed us from the law of sin (Rom. 8:2). Sin reigned until Christ came; now grace reigns (Rom. 5:21).

These three stages entail both continuity and discontinuity. They are discontinuous because each embodies a distinctive form of interaction between God and human beings. Before the Mosaic Law there was sinfulness (Rom. 5:12). After the Mosaic Law was enacted, sin was consciously noted as rebellion against God (Rom. 7:7–24). Now grace and divine justification reign through faith in Jesus Christ. There is also continuity, however, because God's saving plan is realized in history despite everything. One era intermingles with another because the superabundant grace of Jesus Christ was also at work in Abraham (Rom. 4:1–25).

Thus the new situation does not mean that grace was never lacking to human beings. It simply means that grace is present in history in a new way, i.e., in the Spirit of Christ. As Paul puts it: *"Now* we have been released from the law—for we have died to what bound us—and we serve in *the new spirit,* not the antiquated letter"* (Rom. 7:6). The veil that hid the presence of the Spirit in the world has dropped. The Spirit has emerged to view and we now live under his sway. This era will not be superseded (Heb. 8:13) since the Spirit will be with us always (John 14:16). All the later epochs of history will come under the era of the Holy Spirit; they will be his historical embodiments and manifestations in the changing context of different cultural situations.

The personalization of the Holy Spirit. The era of the Holy Spirit began with the breaking-in of the Christ-event, when the eternal Son was made flesh in time. The Son was sent to free and fulfill human beings and the cosmos by taking on their very nature. Bound up with the sending (mission) of the Son was the sending of the Holy Spirit as the Spirit of the Son. It is not just that the Incarnation is the work of the Spirit. As St. Basil and Leo XIII's encyclical *Divinum illud munus*[12] put it, the Spirit is the unction of Christ, who always acted under the presence of the Spirit. Unction, "anointing," is the biblical term for sanctification. Here it refers to the fullness of grace and the divine presence in Jesus of Nazareth. Just as the Son entered history, so he also entered the Holy Spirit as his own Spirit.[13] The latter is not just the Spirit of God as such. He is the Spirit of Christ, associated with his work of redemption, sanctification, and consummation. The statement that "the Spirit became unction" [i.e., sanctification; grace] must be taken in the concrete, forceful sense we use when we say that the Word became flesh and dwelt amongst us (John 1:14). There is a process of *becoming* in the Spirit. He begins to be something that he was not before, inaugurating a new history with human beings in conjunction with Jesus Christ, the incarnate Son.

How might we characterize the specific mission of the Holy Spirit in salvation history? It is different from that of Jesus Christ, but it prolongs and continues the same process of union which he initiated. In the Incarnation all creation is somehow touched and assumed by the Son; for it was always envisioned and created in him, by him, and for him. In the sending of the Holy Spirit it is principally the world of persons that it touched and sanctified.[14] The Incarnation created an enduring and definitive situation for human beings and the world insofar as they were taken up into God. In like manner the sending of the Holy Spirit is an enduring and irreversible event; for he is the Spirit of Christ, who is an enduring and irreversible event.

The Spirit communicated himself totally in Jesus, who possessed the plenitude of the Spirit. The Spirit continues to communicate himself to the children of God in the Son, to the brothers and sisters of Jesus, and to the church. He does so as a grace that liberates and divinizes. If the Son became incarnate in nature, then the Holy Spirit has become personalized in the persons of the just. In the Trinity, for example, the Holy Spirit is one person from two persons: the Father and Son combine as a single principle to breathe the Holy Spirit. Much the same is true in the history of salvation: the Holy Spirit is one person in many persons,[15] who knits them all into one "mystical person." In his work of reintegration here and now, he anticipates the union of all redeemed creation in God when God will be "all in all" (1 Cor. 15:28).

The sending of the Spirit reaches its culmination when he inhabits people and spiritualizes them.[16] Paul uses the image of the temple: "Are you not aware that you are the temple of God, and that the Spirit of God dwells in you?" (1 Cor. 3:16); "you must know that your body is a temple of the Holy Spirit, who is within—the Spirit you have received from God" (1 Cor. 6:19). The notion of the indwelling of the Spirit in persons becomes clearer if we realize that "temple" in antiquity did not signify some hallowed community spot but the locus of God's presence. It was the place where God personally manifests himself in his glory and his grace, the place where he can be encountered and invoked. Now the temple is no longer the sacred building made by human hands but people themselves who are inhabited by the Spirit, in whom he becomes a person by spiritualizing them.

The Manifestations of the Holy Spirit. The Christ-event enabled people to reread and reinterpret the whole past history of salvation. They came to realize that all creation is bound up with him. He is the culmination of a process that began with God's act of creation; all creation was fashioned by him, for him, and in him.

The same sort of rereading was made possible by the Spirit-event, by his personalization in the Incarnation and his mission to the church and justified persons. All that is force, life, wisdom, and holiness in all times and places, in all persons and cultures, are so many more manifestations of the Holy Spirit. Through him people dreamed up myths that symbolized the meaning of life for human beings. Through him wise men thought their thoughts, prophets spoke their message, and both Christians and pagans were sanctified. Through him human beings remained open to the future of history, whence God approaches with his grace and salvation. Through his strength they were able to transform nature and society into more humane and habitable realities. Through his inspiration the spirit of liberation and renewal was never absent from human history, breaking down fetishistic attachment to ossified social and religious institutions.

Through the power of the Holy Spirit human beings have engaged in annunciation and denunciation in every age. They have spoken out for justice and condemned injustice, the overweening power of some, and the exploitation of the lowly and the poor. They have learned how to endure patiently persecution, torture, and death for the cause of justice. As Vatican II points out, the Holy Spirit is the Lord and fountainhead of life (LG 13). He directs the course of history and renews the face of the earth in its process of social development (GS 26). He brings salvation to non-Christians (GS 22) and prompts people to love God, the world, and other human beings (AA 27). In a word, history is pregnant with Jesus Christ and the Holy Spirit.

This rereading of human life in terms of the personalization of the Holy Spirit should not induce any false naiveté in us. We should not imagine that the presence of the Spirit is direct, epiphanic, or unmediated. Human action within the range of human freedom is not to be cast aside. It is through such action, though sometimes in spite of it, that the Spirit operates and makes our work both totally human and totally divine.

Viewed in terms of the era of the Holy Spirit, the Charismatic Renewal Movement takes on special relevance because of its global import.[17] Initiated in 1967 in the United States at Duquesne University, it spread to Notre Dame University, the University of Michigan, the whole country, and then the whole world. Its aim is not to split the church or to withdraw from the institutional embodiment of the church. Through prayer and faith in the Word of God, it asks God to flesh out in concrete life the gifts that the Christian people have already received. Through radical faith in the Holy Spirit it hopes to concretize his gifts and fruits in the lives of those who belong to Christ.[18]

This movement starts from the belief that the Spirit is ever present in the world and the church. Through the latter he is at work in the former: in the sacraments, the liturgy, theology, the authentic magisterium, institutional structures, and the lives of the faithful. But the work of the Spirit is not confined to these official channels of ecclesial organization and practice. He blows where he wills, stirring up special movements, e.g., popular missions after Trent, spiritual movements in eighteenth-century France, the Focolare movement in Italy in 1943, the Cursillo movement in Spain in 1949, and grass-roots ecclesial movements in Latin America since the Medellín Conference in 1968. The gifts of the Holy Spirit can also take many other forms, e.g., service to the poor, prayer services, healing, and speaking in tongues.

The Charismatic Renewal Movement is of particular relevance to the church because of its range. It marks a new epoch for the Christian faith, one which is characterized by a vivid realization of God's presence in the community and in daily life (1 Cor. 14:25). It heralds the end of the era that seems to have begun at the time of the later New Testament writings and to have become formalized in the era of Constantine. That era was characterized by the predominance of power, order, discipline, dogma, institutions, and the hierarchy. God was experienced primarily as an infinite being, as the cause of creation rather than a loving presence in our midst. Jesus Christ was experienced more as the juridical founder of his church than as its permanently living principle. In its extreme forms this outlook produced triumphalism, juridicism, dogmatism, and formalism. To be a Christian meant to insert oneself into an already defined and established religious universe. Experience of God was replaced by doctrine, and participation in community life was undermined by the clergy's excessive hold on all religious power.

Gradually, however, a new experience of God and his Spirit was taking shape. It was characterized by freedom, spontaneity, charismatic activity, and courageous public witness to the presence of God in the world. There were also new forms of praying, of being a church, of participating in community life, and of being a lay person or a priest. The Charismatic Renewal Movement does not seem to be an ahistorical leap back to the primitive church nor a display of frenetic, illogical enthusiasm. Rather it seems to be a vigorous manifestation of the Spirit himself, who wants a church with new features for the sake of human beings and himself.

Catholic Pentecostals refer to the concrete experience of the Spirit and his gifts as the "Baptism of the Holy Spirit." For Protestant Pentecostals it is a "new" work of grace. For Catholics it is an "old" work; but it is "new" because it signifies the newness of all things in connection with Christian initiation and its implications. In practice it is more an experience of reaffirmation than of initiation. For Catholics, the "Baptism of the Holy Spirit" is not a new sacrament or a substitute one. Akin to the renewal of baptismal promises, it is a renewal of faith and of our desire to be all that Christ wants us to be.[19] If these fruits are verified in reality, then we can say that the Spirit is truly and explicitly in our midst.

Too much emphasis should not be placed on the external signs or manifestations of this "Baptism of the Spirit." Speaking in tongues, prophecy, and other extraordinary manifestations may come from the Holy Spirit or from the human spirit. They always contain an element of ambiguity that makes discernment necessary. They are common experiences in past and present religious life, in other world religions and paganism. They may be a way in which the unconscious seeks to find integration, adaptation, and the underlying meaning of life amid ossified institutions and stereotyped religious acts. The charismatic movement can appeal to the Spirit on the basis of the fruits it produces, e.g., a growth in brotherly love, a deeper spirit of prayer, greater involvement in the ecclesial community, a sounder missionary spirit, and even awareness of institutional flaws.

How do we know that we are dealing with an authentic experience of the Holy Spirit rather than with something rooted in our own human spirit? Speaking in this context, Paul offers a decisive criterion: "All well and good, so long as everything is done with a constructive purpose" (1 Cor. 14:26). The Spirit's gifts and experiences are given "for the common good" (1 Cor. 12:7). If an appeal to the charisms leads to divisiveness and harms the church, then we can say that the human spirit of self-aggrandizement is at work. Paul also points out what the real fruits of the Spirit are: "love, joy, peace, patient endurance, kindness, generosity, faith, mildness, and chastity" (Gal. 5:22; Phil. 4:4–5). Today we might put it a slightly different way. If people are calm, understanding toward others who think differently, devoid of fanaticism and open to enlightenment, critical-minded, detached from their own charisms, and capable of humor, then we can believe that we are confronted with a manifestation of the Holy Spirit.

Above all the extraordinary charisms, however, stands the extraordinary reality of day-by-day love. Paul hymns its wonder in unforgettable terms (1 Cor. 13). The truthfulness of an extraordinary charism lies in one's ability to shoulder daily life with all its ambiguities and obscurities. Authentic faith does not see the workings of the Spirit solely in its extraordinary manifestations. It sees them in every human situation where people seek the good, practice virtue, live a life of love, respect human beings, and worship God. This may take place in ossified institutions, in formalized liturgy, or in a common gesture of familiar, individual prayer.

To conclude, then, we may say that the indwelling of the Holy Spirit has the following meaning. Those who live as just people live their lives on the same foundation that Jesus Christ did. The mysterious presence and power of God manifested in Jesus Christ was the Holy Spirit. That same Spirit is present in all just human beings, and particularly in the followers of Jesus Christ. It is the Holy Spirit who makes just people just, open to God, and open to all that comes from God. We are inhabited by a force that is the underlying strength of our own strength. No longer anonymous, that force is now called the Spirit of Christ, the Spirit of God. Together with all the just he constitutes a mystical person.

CHAPTER 19

The Indwelling of the Holy Trinity

Now let us move a step further and consider how just human beings, who are children of God in his Son and who are inhabited by the Holy Spirit, are related to the mystery of the Blessed Trinity. In Christian faith, relating to God always means relating to the Trinity because there is no God but the triune one.

As far back as the New Testament we find testimony about the indwelling of the three divine persons in the lives of the faithful. Many passages in the Joannine writings allude to the immanence of God in humans and of humans in God:

Those who keep his commandments remain in him and he in them (1 John 3:32).

The way we know we remain in him and he in us is that he has given us of his Spirit (1 John 4:13).

When anyone acknowledges that Jesus is the Son of God, God dwells in him and he in God (1 John 4:15).

God is love, and he who abides in love abides in God, and God in him (1 John 4:16; see also 1 John 2:6,24,27–28; 3:6; 5:20).

The union existing between Father and Son symbolizes the union that should exist between God and graced human beings:

I pray . . . that all may be one as you, Father, are in me, and I in you. I pray that they may be one in us, that the world may believe that you sent me (John 17:20–22; see John 14:20–21).

During his last discourse Jesus spells out this union more explicitly, at least as the evangelist understands it: "Anyone who loves me will be true to my word, and my Father will love him; we will come to him and make our dwelling place with him" (John 14:23). His Father will send the Son and the Holy Spirit to be with us forever (John 14:15–16; 16:7). Matthew's gospel alludes to this mutual indwelling when he writes that we are baptized in the name of the Father, the Son, and the Holy Spirit (Matt. 28:19).

All these assertions already represent advanced theological reflection and a late stage in the elucidation of Christology. Paul sums up this faith in the indwelling of the Trinity in felicitous phrase: "The proof that you are sons is the fact that God has sent forth into our hearts the spirit of his Son which cries out 'Abba!' ('Father')" (Gal 4:6).

Various Attempts at Theological Description

How are these assertions to be understood? It is not enough to cite and recite them. As understanding of the faith, theology must seek out their meaning, uncover the Christian experience that lies buried in them, and then articulate their content in conjunction with the other mysteries of faith insofar as that is possible. At bottom all these mysteries are merely explicitations of the one great mystery: the self-communication of God the Father, through the Son and in the Holy Spirit, to the hearts of human beings. So our concern is to give existential meaning to this mystery so that the average Christian can realize it in his or her own concrete existence.

Few theological questions are so much disputed as this one.[1] The level of abstraction and formalization in discussing this topic is so great that only the initiated can follow it. But the question is too basic to Christian living to be left solely to experts who cannot share their thoughts in such a way that they contribute to the life and understanding of the people of God. This prompts me to try to approach this central truth of faith in such a way that it may shed light on our Christian journey. We want to rescue the experience that underlies the New Testament statements of the Joannine school and Paul's reflections on Christ and the Spirit. At the same time we fully realize, as Pius XII pointed out in his encyclical on the Mystical Body (1943), that the indwelling of the Trinity is a profound mystery which cannot be seen "unveiled in this time of earthly exile."[2]

What is the task of reflection here? It should enable us to approach the mystery in such a way that we can echo the words of the Hebrews: "For what great nation is there that has gods so close to it as the Lord, our God, is to us whenever we call upon him?" (Deut. 4:7). We Christians have even more cause to voice that question and to offer a reply to others who ask it.

There are many different currents of theological thought. In one way or another they all try to answer various questions that might be raised about the indwelling of the Trinity. What is the nature of their presence in the lives of the just? Is it merely a reduplication of their presence as exemplified in creation and their omnipresence? Is it a special kind of indwelling? Is it merely an intensification, on the level of the individual good person, of the trinitarian presence in creation? And what is the nature of the presence of the just person in the Trinity? Do the just relate to each person of the Trinity individually, or to the Trinity as such? In this section I want to offer a brief overview of several currents of theological thought.[3]

The indwelling as a process of assimilation. The first school of thought is based on a general axiom of theology framed in the context of classical metaphysics: "God is present where he is operative."[4] God is at work in all creation, so God is omnipresent in all things. In the lives of the just, who are oriented to love and union with God, God is at work in a very special way: he himself is the grace present in them that makes them more and more like the Trinity. In other words, God is the efficient and exemplary cause of the indwelling. He produces the presence of the Trinity in the just, and they become more and more assimilated to the Trinity.

This assimilation is a dynamic reality. Theologians describe it in terms of a process of engraving applied to a very fluid or malleable substance. Suppose a mold is applied to very soft wax. If we want the mold to persist on the wax, we must keep applying it; if it is taken away, the wax will return to its formless shape. The indwelling is also compared to water in a glass that takes the shape of the glass. If the water is spilled or the glass breaks, then the water will lose that particular shape. Much the same is true of the presence of the Trinity in the just. If this presence is to endure, then the Trinity must be present continuously and thus keep on producing its divinizing presence.[5] It is a form of generation in which God shares his own life with that of the just person. God impresses his own trinitarian image on the person. This image (*sigillatio*) is that of the divine essence which is identical in the three persons of the Trinity. According to this line of thought there is no assimilation to the individual persons of the Trinity as such. For in their activity relating to creation, the three persons of the Trinity share a common action; in this area everything is common to all three.

This theological theory focuses on the process of human divinization and describes it in very plastic terms. However, it adheres to an intrasystemic axiom which it does not compare with the data of the New Testament and theological tradition itself. According to that data, each divine person has his own proper action both in the work of creation and in the work of divinization.[6]

God not only is present but also inhabits our faculties. This second line of thought combines the universal presence of God in creation with his very special presence in the lives of graced human beings. In a famous passage Thomas Aquinas says:

There is a *common way* by which God is in all things with his essence, power, and presence as a cause is present in the effects that share its goodness. Besides this common way, there is also *another very special way* that belongs to a rational nature alone. In the latter God is present as an object known is present in the knowing subject and as a loved person is present in the lover. With its activities of knowing and loving, the rational creature attains God himself. By virtue of this special way, God is present in the rational creature only insofar as he dwells in it as in his temple.[7]

In this view the indwelling of the Trinity does not merely duplicate God's presence in creation. It extends that presence by deepening it and giving it a distinctive embodiment. For in this case we are dealing with a rational creature who is capable of knowing and loving God. When the rational creature knows and loves God, God is present in that creature in a very special way.

Since human beings are creatures, God is already present in them and in their faculties of knowing and loving. However, when they take cognizance of this presence and choose to know and love God, then God is not just objectively present; he also becomes subjectively present in an intimate way and inhabits them.

It is more or less like friendship.[8] The indwelling establishes a very intimate friendship between God and human beings. Friendship presupposes a union between two people in feelings and values, and this union is nurtured by their presence and nearness to each other. Because the friendship between God and a human being is divine, it is the most perfect type of friendship and union.[9] In this case the intimate presence of God in the life of a human being means that the triune God as such comes to dwell in the just human being.

In this line of thought there is no unnecessary duplication or rupture. There is oneness between human life and its activities of knowing and willing on the one hand and divine indwelling on the other. In the concrete act of knowing and loving God, human beings are inhabited by the triune God. It is God who makes possible their activity of knowing and loving, triggers it, and enables it to enjoy authentic experience of God.[10]

The indwelling makes humans deiform. A third line of thought is based on a datum that we find consistently in the New Testament and tradition.[11] It suggests that the difference between a person living in God's grace on earth and one enjoying the beatific vision in heaven is only accidental or secondary. Both are living one and the same unique reality but in different situations. The former's situation is that of a wayfarer (*homo viator*) on earth; the latter's is that of a person who has attained glory (*homo comprehensor*). The indwelling of the Trinity on earth prepares and anticipates the beatific vision, and the latter is the prolongation of the former. As Cardinal Newman put it, grace is glory in exile and glory is grace arrived at its homeland (see 2 Cor. 1:22; 5:5; Rom. 8:2; Eph. 1:13).

In the beatific vision we have the most intimate imaginable union between the Trinity and the just person. There the just person knows, loves, and enjoys God as he exists triunely. But no creature as such can unite with God as God exists in himself. So God unites with a human intelligence and will, enabling them to exercise a type of knowing and loving which is truly divine even while remaining truly human. The human being becomes deiform.

This basic transformation precedes and makes possible all concrete acts of knowing and loving. Here, obviously, we are not talking about a new incarnation of God in the intellectual life and the lovelife of the just human being. That would imply that God somehow became an accident or even a substance in the makeup of a created reality. Here we are dealing with a very special kind of activity on God's part. It is a *quasi-formal* union, a union in the nature of a formal cause. In this kind of union the effect possesses the same nature as the cause because the cause enters its makeup in such a way as to confer its own characteristics on it. This, then, is what happens in the union between the Trinity and the just person. The just person shares in the inner life of God, in the knowledge whereby the Father generates the Son and in the love whereby both jointly breathe the Spirit.

Just as in the beatific vision there are distinctive relationships with each of the three divine persons, so there are distinctive relationships with them in the indwelling of the Trinity. Each of the divine persons is present and operative in accordance with his own notional properties.[12] The Father is present as the absolute mystery from which everything comes and to which everything returns. The Son is present as knowledge and truth. And the Holy Spirit is present as love and union.

Here and now, in the obscure darkness of the present day, human beings begin to live what will someday be their definitive state in the glory of heaven, i.e., a face-to-face vision of God and love without any mediating factors.

The indwelling as friendship with the Father, through the Son, in the Holy Spirit. However relevant the above descriptions may seem to be, they all suffer from a terrible amount of metaphysical abstractionism. They overlook the wealth of data to which the Scriptures bear witness. Furthermore, their treatment prescinds completely from the function of Christ and his prolongation in history, the church.

A fourth line of thought was developed to describe the reality of indwelling more concretely.[13] It sought to make use of the intuitions derived from the personalist approach. The key category in trying to shed light on the mystery here is that of *friendship*. Right away that implies a dialogic dimension with each one of the three divine persons. To be real friendship, it must entail a richer knowledge of God than what we get from contemplating the works of creation. It presumes a knowledge of God as he revealed himself in Jesus Christ and is actualized through the church. Perfect friendship, then, is articulated in the realm of Christology and ecclesiology. God makes himself present through these privileged historical mediations that he himself chose, and he is present in such a way that he effects an ontological elevation in human beings.

From this standpoint the indwelling can be spelled out in such terms as the following:

The Father, the Son, and the Holy Spirit admit human beings to their own inner life, giving themselves to human beings as one person gives himself to another. In this communion there is an order. The Father invites human beings to his friendship through the Son that is made flesh. In turn the Son sends the Holy Spirit who is the oneness of love between the Father and the Son. The Holy Spirit is given as the "soul of the church" (LG 7). Uniting themselves in a mysterious way with human beings, they turn them into members of the salvific community who are capable of living a filial life.[14]

This line of thought takes advantage of a whole range of data which is part of the experience of friendship: presence, dialogue, and mutual self-giving with all the intellectual, emotional, immanent, and transcendent qualities that are characteristic of love. It is not only vision but also enjoyment, fruition, communication, and fulfillment; for all true friendship implies these things. This kind of loving relationship with each of the three divine persons has its own stages in life and involves ways of relating to them, until it reaches its full measure in the glory of heaven.

A Personal Attempt

The various lines of thought described above attempt to spell out traditional concepts (the beatific vision, grace as *assimilatio* or *sigillatio Trinitatis*, trinitarian operations *ad extra,* and so forth) or the statements of Holy Scripture. However, they tend to forget that those concepts and statements are an attempt to translate a Christian experience. They themselves are already an interpretation of something more fundamental and pristine. True understanding does not mean simply interpreting interpretations; it involves recovering the original datum and expressing it in the context of our own time with its different ideas and points of view. It is awfully hard for us to get any existential feel for the various viewpoints described above. The "indwelling" of the Trinity strikes us as an alien superstructure of little relevance for our lives. We find it hard to grasp and get a clear picture of something that supposedly affects our whole life and is the key to salvation or damnation.

Faith does not create new realities. In the light of God it makes explicit the realities experienced in actual existence. It draws various dimensions of human life out of the shadows and, by moving beyond a merely naturalistic viewpoint, restores their sacred character to them. They possess such a character because they are linked by an umbilical cord to the sacred mystery of God.

The expression "the indwelling of the Trinity" (Father, Son, and Holy Spirit) is meant to be the translation of the most basic and profound Christian experience. Obviously it is not an experience like any other, as if God could be just another object in our daily world. Because it has to do with the most sublime and mysterious reality of the Christian faith, it must also relate to the most radical and ineffable reality of human life. Such depth is not to be found in the intricacies of conceptual reflection but in the transparent simplicity of daily life. We can approach this level only with halting words and groping hands. In attempting to describe the mystery of the indwelling, Teresa of Ávila begins with the respect and confusion that the sacred always provokes:

O great God! Surely a creature as miserable as I must tremble to treat of anything so far beyond what I deserve to understand. And indeed I have been in a state of great confusion and have wondered if it will not be better for me in a few words to bring my account of this Mansion to an end. I am so much afraid it will be thought that my knowledge of it comes from experience, and this makes me very much ashamed; for, knowing myself for what I am, such a thought is terrible.[15]

In any case we must admit that the revelation of the mystery of the Trinity does not come to us in abstract phrases. It is not gotten across when we say that God is one in nature and triune in persons—Father, Son, and Holy Spirit—though we cannot know how three can be one and one three. Such a statement is an intellectual translation, within a particular conceptual horizon, of the experience of the God's mysteriousness in salvation history. God revealed himself, and was experienced by humans beings, as the absolute mystery. God did not remain inside himself. God ever showed an incredible sympathy toward human beings. He gave himself in love, in understanding, in hope, in the maintenance and support of all.

This God that lives inside us, insofar as he is the mystery of mysteries that gives rise to everything, is called Father. Insofar as he opens up and reveals the truth of himself, communicates himself to human beings and is reflected in all his potential imitations, goes out in search of them and establishes a covenant, this God is called Son. Insofar as he calls all back to himself and gathers them together into the undivided union of love, this God is called Holy Spirit. Viewed in terms of the history of salvation, the Trinity is not a speculative curiosity. It is an explication of the Christian experience under the banner of Jesus Christ. For Jesus is the incarnate Son who made room for such a revelation of the Trinity and its attendant experience.[16]

Because the Trinity revealed itself thus in salvation history, it is intimately bound up with the reality of human beings. It was for our salvation that it communicated itself and entered human history. Even before it was revealed as Trinity, it was already there, filling human existence with light, grace, and life. That is why it could be proclaimed as Trinity later on. But how was it there? How has it ever been there as a presence in the historical life of human beings? The function of reflection and analysis is to shed light on the mystery of the Trinity that is prior to the mystery of the Incarnation and the church and interior to the mystery of humanity itself. Indeed it is the mystery of the Trinity that gives to the mystery of humanity its authentic dimension. Let us consider this point briefly.

Speaking genetically and epistemologically from our standpoint (*quoad nos*), we can say that the mystery of humanity precedes the mystery of God. Once the mystery of God emerges on the scene, however, it takes on ontological priority. It is that mystery which grounds human existence, which enables us to think, will, love, know, and pose the problem.

Human beings emerge as a great mystery to themselves. As Augustine put it: *"Mihi factus sum quaestio magna."* The human being presents itself as a basic, fontal unity that is fleshed out in many varied manifestations. It is a unity that knows and thinks, that opens itself up to understanding itself and the world, and that can relate to everything in self-giving. It is a personal unity that is communicated as self-awareness, that dialogues and opens up to others, and that turns back in on itself to work on a synthesis with all the different realities it has encountered. This personal unity does not merely have knowledge of its experiences with different realities and try to work up synthesis. It also seeks communion with them. It fashions *community,* relating to others in love and self-giving. It can even go so far as to sacrifice itself. It is not only truth but love as well.

Now this original unity of person, manifesting itself as truth and giving itself in love, discovers that it itself is gratuitous. It is not grounded on itself. It finds itself in existence without ever having asked anyone to exist. No necessity dictates its existence. It is here as a reality supported in some way and related to Someone, to a Mystery. Thus it feels itself to be the manifestation of Something that is not itself. It calls for some ontological ground to justify it. It is a mystery within some supreme Mystery. Hence its truth is the manifestation of another great Truth and its love is the concrete embodiment of another love.

Granting all that, let us ponder a few questions. Did we not say that the Father signifies God precisely insofar as God is the absolute mystery who gives origin to everything without having any origin himself? Doesn't that correspond to the mystery of the human person? Doesn't the human person communicate self in truth and love, in an intelligence that sees and a will that loves? But the human person is never exhausted in any concrete communication. It transcends every specific act and remains ever available for something more. Everything is its manifestation. It itself is a mystery that extrojects its thoughts, actions, and love into things.

Did we not say that the Son (the Word, or logos) is that which exists as knowable and intelligible in the Father? Doesn't that correspond to human truth and understanding insofar as these reveal the truth and intelligibility of the person and the world?

And did we not say that the Holy Spirit is the love of two different persons, the Father and the Son, restoring all in oneness to the unfathomable mystery of God? Doesn't that correspond to the human love that inserts someone different into the bosom of our personal mystery, thereby creating community and unifying everything?

In its radical manifestations of truth and love the human person symbolizes the mystery of God. But note this point well: the Trinity is not deduced from an analysis of human reality; it only seems that way from a genetic standpoint. In reality analysis reveals the reference point which the human person must maintain to gain clarity about itself. It is the absolute reference point that we call God. Truth and love, too, are symbolic. They mirror another Love and

another Truth that historicizes us in the world and reveals its own communication.[17] Thus human beings arise to view as inhabited by the Trinity.

What we are trying to express here constitutes the objective presence of
the Trinity in human thinking, willing, and living. However, it does not
depend on human willing. Even those who do not live in the grace of God
reflect the Trinity in their rational being. As Teresa of Avila put it:

> We think that within our soul there is some kind of darkness. Of the soul that is not in
> grace, I grant you, that is true—not, however, from any defect in the Sun of Justice,
> Who is within it and is giving it being, but because . . . this soul is not capable of
> receiving the light.[18]

Thus human beings are so structured that they are ever bathed in the
reflection of the Trinity. It is the presence in essence, power, and immensity
of which Thomas Aquinas spoke in the text cited earlier.

It is in this framework that we must ponder the indwelling of the Trinity.
Piux XII suggested as much in *Mystici Corporis Christi:*

> We say that the divine persons inhabit us insofar as they are present in beings
> endowed with intelligence in some inscrutable way and the latter, through knowledge
> and love, are established in a wholly intimate and singular relationship with them that
> transcends every created nature.[19]

But there is also the subjective presence of the Trinity. Just people, whose
life project is open to God and who focus on the mystery of God, allow
themselves to be taken over by the objective presence of the Trinity. The
more just people are, the more they live the right way vis-à-vis God and
themselves and the more the reality which inhabits them is allowed to
surface. Their understanding is more and more oriented by the supreme
Truth, and their will by pure Love. In short, they are more and more
assimilated to the Trinity.

Grace and the indwelling of the Trinity are not a mere duplication of the
presence of the Father, Son, and Holy Spirit in the lives of the just. They
intensify a process that is *already* present and they can lead it more and more
to its fulfillment, to its culmination in heavenly glory.

In the eyes of those human beings who live a life of love grounded on the
mystery of God (the just), all reality is transfigured. They do not contemplate
it profanely in and for itself. Instead they contemplate it religiously, insofar as
it is relinked with its ultimate foundation: God. They feel that they are
inhabited by Someone greater. This someone is not a blind force or a
nameless Mystery. It is the Son who, as the eternal truth of the Father, is
given in human truth. It is the Holy Spirit who, as the love of Father and Son,
is historicized in human love. It is God the Father who, as the absolute

mystery, reveals himself in the mystery of personal existence. There is the Light by which we see the light!

Insofar as human beings are led to open up to the mystery of themselves, they are also led by the supreme mystery to an intimate encounter with the Trinity. The generation of truth in us reflects the eternal generation of the Truth of the Father: the Son. Our love, through which we communicate with others, reflects the eternal flow of the Father's and Son's mutual love: the Holy Spirit. Here and *now* we are *already* assimilated into the trinitarian process. We are no longer outside it. We have been made sharers of the very nature of God as it truly exists, i.e., in a Trinity of persons.

The Council of Florence (1439–45) taught that glory and heavenly delight consist in "open contemplation of God, one and triune, as he is in himself" (DS 1305). The encyclical *Mystici Corporis Christi* (1943), whose doctrinal formulation clearly carries the weight of authority, has this to say about the beatific vision. Speaking in the context of the indwelling of the Trinity, it says that the beatific vision will enable people:

to contemplate the Father, the Son, and the Holy Spirit and to take part for all eternity in the processions of the divine persons. The just will be inundated with a joy akin to that which constitutes the happiness of the blessed and undivided Trinity (DS 3815).

That, of course, is an eschatological reality. But precisely because it is eschatological, it is anticipated here in history. It is initiated here on earth in the mystery of the just human being; it will reach its culmination in heaven, where the human mystery will be immersed forever in the divine Mystery.

My remarks on the indwelling in terms of the mystery of the human person must also be taken up in terms of the community of persons. The Trinity is community. The mystery of the Trinity is reflected in human community, which lives by truth, keeps seeking more truth, finds its nourishment in love, and works constantly for social relations based on greater love and brotherhood. What kind of conversion on the personal level and social revolution on the community level must take place if those levels are to be places where the mystery of the Trinity is concretely articulated in time?

By way of conclusion I should like to cite the experience of Teresa of Avila, that great mystic, with regard to the Trinity. Here knowledge becomes pure savoring, thanks to the grace and work of the divine Mystery itself:

It [the soul] is brought into this Mansion by means of an intellectual vision, in which, by a representation of the truth in a particular way, the Most Holy Trinity reveals itself, in all three Persons. First of all the spirit becomes enkindled and is illumined, as it were, by a cloud of the greatest brightness. It sees these three Persons, individually, and yet, by a wonderful kind of knowledge which is given to it, the soul realizes that most certainly and truly all these three Persons are one Substance and one Power and one Knowledge and one God alone; so that what we hold by faith the soul may be said here to grasp by sight, although nothing is seen by the eyes, either of the body or of the soul, for it is no imaginary vision. Here all three Persons communicate Themselves to the soul and speak to the soul and explain to it those words which the Gospel attributes to the Lord—namely, that He and the Father and the Holy Spirit will come to dwell with the soul which loves Him and keeps His commandments.

Oh, God help me! What a difference there is between hearing and believing these words and being led in this way to realize how true they are! Each day this soul wonders more, for she feels that they have never left her, and perceives quite clearly, in the way I have described, that They are in the interior of her heart—in the most interior place of all and in its greatest depths. So although, not being a learned person, she cannot say how this is, she feels within herself this Divine companionship.

This may lead you to think that such a person will not remain in possession of her senses but will be so completely absorbed that she will be able to fix her mind upon nothing. But no: in all that belongs to the service of God she is more alert than before; and, when not otherwise occupied, she rests in that happy companionship.[20]

Here is what it means in day-to-day life when we say that the Mystery of the Trinity is dwelling intimately in the mystery of human beings.

Conclusion

The Catholic treatment of grace is certainly one that is burdened with the heavy weight of various heterodox doctrines and responses to them. The tract on grace is filled with disputes, heresies, and condemnations. This only underlines the importance that reflection on grace holds for Christian experience. Serious efforts were made to probe into the mystery of grace in a personally committed way, for the issue of salvation versus damnation is the most decisive one in human life. Study of these disputes cannot and should not be limited to historians. We must salvage the existential dimension that lies hidden behind the various abstract theories that do not dovetail with our own modern outlook.

My reflections here have not aimed primarily to spell out all that has been thought and learned in the past. Their chief aim was to ponder and explicate what was really at stake in what theological tradition has thought and said about this matter. What was and is and always will be at stake is *the presence of God and his love in the world and the corresponding human experience.* This presence is called grace. How does it appear today? How does it visit us? In what concrete forms of our personal and social life does it reveal itself? What demands does it impose on us?

The aim of my theoretical effort was to lay hold of some basic perspectives on the basis of which we might be able to take cognizance of grace and its presence in the world, broaden our horizons, and hence accept it in a more liberative sense. On the basis of this theoretical effort we must then structure a truly concrete praxis. Such a praxis, entailing concrete, practical exercises, should enable us to show how grace makes its presence felt in the basic functions of life. I hope I have helped the reader to realize that various human endeavors and relationships—e.g., sports, carnivals, personal encounters, authentic human relationships, and so forth—are not merely human realities. While they possess a solidity of their own, they also symbolize another reality that makes its presence felt in the beauty, gratuitousness, depth, and goodness they display. That other reality is the grace of God. A carnival does not cease to be a carnival, a feast of fools celebrating the gratuitousness of life. A soccer match does not cease to be a soccer match, with all its hidden undercurrents of personal ambition and monetary gain. Human love as embodied in family life does not cease to be human love with all its dark spots and bright spots. At the same time, however, all these things are also parables about another Love, another Festivity, another Fascination. They are so many different ways in which the grace of God reaches us in the world. It mingles with profane realities without losing its own identity—leavening here, purifying and straightening there, and leading all to the definitive encounter with God.

The aim of my reflections was to sharpen people's vision and fine-tune their antennas for the here-and-now reality of our lives. We must seek, for only the seekers are allowed to find and enjoy. We can seek, find, and enjoy only if we live our lives as an active commitment and as an opportunity to fashion something definitive and eternal. Living means something more than simply not dying. We live to realize some meaning and to fashion a project with the help of God and his grace. That project is to stretch beyond the boundaries of this mortal life and endure in eternity.

If my reflections here were of any help to the reader, then the credit must go to the grace of God rather than to me.

I began this book with a parable, and I should like to conclude it with a similar parable. The first parable tried to set people thinking. This final parable is meant to confirm the basic line of thought set forth here. The main point is that divine grace ever takes priority over human initiatives. The superabundance of grace always prevails over human sins, however abundant they may be. Though sin can perpetuate itself, it can never succeed in frustrating the divine design of love. What is more, grace does not thrive on the decline or subversion of nature. It is not the strength of God designed to take the place of human weakness. Rather, it is the ultimate strength of our strength, and it is meant to give added strength to ours. Those who accept it and follow its impulses and rhythms are more than human beings, are deities in miniature. Though we are not God, we are called to be with God.

*   *   *

Once there was a man who could do everything. I don't know whether he lived in an era when magic was real or whether he was simply a human being who had attained everything that could be attained on earth. He was simply called the-man-who-could-do-everything.

One day the-man-who-could-do-everything grew disgusted with the hubbub of his own metropolis and sought out a solitary spot where he might be able to hear the silence and enjoy some tranquillity and rest. After being there for a few days he began to reflect, and soon he was troubled again. He suddenly realized that he was not at rest at all. He was turning at the rate of 1,700 kilometers per hour, for that is the rate at which the earth turns around its own axis. He grew disgusted at the earth for dragging him around with it.

The man-who-could-do-everything decided to abandon the ground of earth and so he transferred to the tranquil silence of the moon. It, too, was rotating around its axis, but not as fast as the earth was. Then one day his heart jumped when he realized that his flight had not been to any avail. With the earth and all the beings under its attraction he was moving around the sun at the rate of 107,000 kilometers per hour.

He tried to think of some way out that would guarantee him tranquillity. Finally he decided to move completely beyond the orbit of earth and its sway, so he transferred himself beyond the orbit of Jupiter. He was not there long when he found himself in deep distress. Though he could escape the earth, he could not escape the sun. With the sun and all the other planets in the solar system he was moving around the center of our galaxy at the rate of 774,000 kilometers per hour.

The man-who-could-do-everything decided to move beyond the frenetic velocity of the solar system. Then one day he realized he was still moving at a horrendous speed. With our galaxy he was moving around the center of a conglomerate of 2,500 neighboring galaxies at the rate of 2,172,000 kilometers per hour. Since he could do everything, he decided to start walking in the opposite direction to this motion; at least then he could feel that he was slowing down a bit. But soon he realized that he and all the other bodies in the universe were galloping at the rate of 579,000 kilometers per hour away from a point in space where the universe had its origin billions of years ago.

The man-who-could-do-everything suddenly realized that he could do nothing more. No matter how much he might run away, he could not succeed. He was being carried by something greater that enveloped him. To look for absolute rest and tranquillity was to lose it.

The man-who-could-do-everything gave up his name and his pretensions. He returned humbly to his earth, his land, and his own house. He sat down tranquilly on his veranda and learned how to contemplate the tranquillity of all things. Though they all are subjected to those terrible rates of speed, they do not grow enraged or revolt. Instead they seem to be quite still in the tranquil serenity of nature. To accept all that was to find the tranquillity and grace in all things.

*   *   *

Isn't grace something like that? It penetrates and envelops all. To accept it is to gratify oneself; to flee from it is to damage oneself without managing to escape from its presence. Grace in all its gratuitousness does not change. Only human beings can change; only they can be either grace or dis-grace. Grace itself is simply grace always. The author of Psalm 139 caught the omnipresence of God and his grace in moving terms:

> O Lord, you have probed me and you know me;
> You know when I sit and when I stand;
> You understand my thoughts from afar. . . .
> Behind me and before, you hem me in
> And rest your hand upon me.

Such knowledge is too wonderful for me;
Too lofty for me to attain.

Where can I go from your spirit?
From your presence where can I flee?
If I go up to the heavens, you are there;
If I sink to the nether world, you are present there.
If I take the wings of the dawn,
If I settle at the farthest limits of the sea,
Even there your hand shall guide me,
And your right hand hold me fast.
If I say, "Surely the darkness shall hide me,
And night shall be my light"—
For you darkness itself is not dark,
And night shines as the day.
Darkness and light are the same.

Truly you have formed my inmost being;
You knit me in my mother's womb.
I give you thanks that I am fearfully, wonderfully made;
Wonderful are your works (Ps. 139:1–14).

Notes

Chapter 1

1. Leonardo Coimbra, *A alegria, a dor e a graça* (Porto, 1916), p. 173.
2. Augustine, *En. in psal. 70:21*, PL, 36:891: "Every human is Adam, every human is Christ."

Chapter 2

1. Simone Weil, *La pesanteur et la grâce* (Paris: Plon, 1948), p. 151; Eng. trans., *Gravity and Grace* (New York: Putnam, 1952).

Chapter 5

1. See my comments in the anthology *Experimentar Deus hoje* (Petrópolis: Ed. Vozes, 1974), pp. 126–34.
2. See A. S. Kessler, A. Schöpf, and C. Wild, "Erfahrung," in *Handbuch Philosophischer Grundbegriffe* (Munich, 1973), 2:373–86; S. Kambartel, "Erfahrung," in *Historisches Wörterbuch der Philosophie* (Basel, 1972), 2:610–23; F. Alquié, *L'expérience,* Initiation Philosophique 10 (Paris, 1970).
3. Aristotle, *Metaphysics* 980b, 28 ff.; *Analytica Posteriora,* 100a, 4 ff.
4. Thomas Aquinas, *Summa Theol.* 1, q. 54, a. 5.2: *"Experientia fit ex multis memoriis";* Thomas Hobbes, *Leviathan* 1:2: *"Memoria multarum rerum experientia dicitur."* G. W. F. Hegel, *Phänomenologie des Geistes,* Ed. Hoffmeister, Philosophische Bibliothek 114, p. 73: "The dialectical movement of consciousness upon itself, or its knowledge, or its object, insofar as the new authentic object arises in it, is what is properly called experience."
5. Forcellini, *Thesaurus totius latinitatis* 2:367a.
6. See the extended compilation of texts in *Thesaurus linguae latinae,* 5:1651–54.
7. For all this see ibid., 1660–90.
8. See Ernout-Meillet, "Experientia" in *Dictionnaire étymologique de la langue latine.*
9. Ortega y Gasset, *La idea de principio en Leibniz y la evolución de la teoría deductiva,* in *Obras completas,* 8:177; idem, *El hombre y la gente,* ibid., 7:188 ff.
10. G. de Mello Kujawski, "Experiência e perigo," in *Introdução à metafísica do perigo* (S. Paulo: Ed. Convívio, 1974), pp. 52–64, especially p. 57.
11. See Henri de Lubac, *Le Surnaturel* (Paris: Aubier, 1946).
12. For the whole issue of the relationship between the natural and the supernatural see G. Muschalek, "Criação e aliança como problema de natureza e graça," in *Mysterium Salutis* 2/2:131–42; H. Mühlen, "Gnadenlehre," in *Bilanz der Theologie im 20. Jahrhundert* (Freiburg, Basel, and Vienna, 1970), 3:163–78.
13. F. Diekamp, *Katholische Dogmatik,* 2:47.
14. Older tradition says "stripped of the supernatural and wounded in the natural," whereas the neo-scholastic tradition ends with "wounded in the *preternatural.*" The "preternatural" refers to things that are relatively rather than absolutely supernatural insofar as they exceed the nature of a given being. Thus immortality is a relatively supernatural gift for human beings; but it is not absolutely supernatural because we can imagine a being who might be immortal by its very nature.
15. This kind of analysis is masterfully developed by Henri de Lubac, *Le Surnaturel* (Paris, 1946); *Le mystère du surnaturel* (Paris: Aubier, 1965); Eng. trans., *The Mystery of the Supernatural*

(New York: Herder and Herder, 1966). Also see Karl Rahner, *Geist in Welt* (Munich, 1964); idem, *Hörer des Wortes* (Munich: Kösel-Verlag, 1963).

16. Henri de Lubac, *Le mystère du surnaturel,* p. 106.

17. Romano Guardini, *Welt und Person* (Würzburg: Werkbund-Verlag, 1962), p. 113.

18. Hans Urs von Balthasar, *Karl Barth: Darstellung und Deutung seiner Theologie* (Cologne: Hegner, 1951), Eng. trans., *The Theology of Karl Barth* (Holt, Rinehart & Winston and Doubleday and Company, Anchor Books, 1971–72), Part Four, Ch. 3, "Nature as a Theological Concept." Also see Hans Urs von Balthasar, "Der Begriff der Natur in der Theologie," *Zeitschrift für katholische Theologie* 75 (1953): 452–64.

19. See H. Mühlen, "Gnadenlehre," in *Bilanz,* p. 174.

20. M. Flick and Z. Alszeghy, *Fondamenti di una antropologia teologica* (Florence: Libreria editrice fiorentina, 1970), p. 433.

21. J. Alfaro, "El problema teológico de la transcendencia y de la inmanencia de la gracia," in *Cristología y antropología* (Madrid, 1973), pp. 227–343; idem, *Persona y gracia,* pp. 345–66.

22. Charles Péguy, *Nota conjunta sobre Descartes y la filosofía cartesiana,* Spanish trans. (Buenos Aires, 1946), cited by Juan Luis Segundo, *Grace and the Human Condition,* Eng. trans. (Maryknoll, N.Y.: Orbis Books, 1973), p. 6.

23. See data compiled by E. J. Fortman, *Teología del hombre y de la gracia* (Santander, 1970), pp. 34–38.

24. See J. L. Segundo, *Grace and the Human Condition,* pp. 15–16.

25. See the outstanding and valuable study of J. Comblin, "A missão do Espírito Santo," in *REB (Brazilian Ecclesiastical Review)* 35 (1975): 288–325.

Chapter 6

1. These remarks on science and technology are deeply indebted to the lectures and books of J. Ladrière: *La science, le monde, la foi* (Paris: Casterman, 1972); *Vie sociale et destinée* (Gembloux: Duculot, 1973); *L'articulation du sens: Discours scientifique et parole de la foi* (Paris: BSR, 1970), Eng. trans., *Language and Belief* (Notre Dame, Ind.: University of Notre Dame Press, 1972). See also: G. Thils, *La fête scientifique: d'une praxéologie scientifique à une analyse de la décision chrétienne* (Paris: BSR, 1973); A. N. Whitehead, *Science and the Modern World* (New York: Free Press, 1925); L. Lakatos and A. Musgrave, *Criticism and the Growth of Knowledge* (Cambridge, 1970); J. Haberman, *Erkenntnis und Interesse* (Frankfurt am Main: Suhrkamp, 1968), especially pp. 146–48 on science and technology as ideology; Eng. trans., *Knowledge and Human Interests* (Boston: Beacon Press, 1971); H. Rombach, *Substanz, System, Struktur: Die Ontologie des Funktionalismus und der philosophische Hintergrund der modernen Wissenschaft,* 2 vols. (Freiburg and Munich: K. Alber, 1966). The last cited book, in my opinion, remains the most profound and pertinent treatment of the points brought up in this chapter. Also important is P. Roqueplo, *L'énergie de la foi (Science-foi-politique)* (Paris: Cerf, 1973).

2. Vatican II, *Gaudium et Spes* 59. All citations from conciliar documents are taken from Walter M. Abbott, S.J., ed., *The Documents of Vatican II* (New York: Guild Press, 1966).

3. See J. Ladrière, "Intégration de la recherche scientifique dans la vie chrétienne," in *La science, le monde, la foi* (Tournai: Casterman, 1972), pp. 35–53, especially pp. 37–38; idem, "Les sciences humaines et le problème du fondement," in *Vie sociale et destinée,* pp. 198–210.

4. L. Wittgenstein, *Schriften* (Frankfurt am Main, 1969), 1:82.

5. Ibid., p. 84.

6. See H. de Lima Vaz, "O ethos da atividade científica," in *REB (Brazilian Ecclesiastical Review)* 34 (1974): 45–73.

7. See the highly relevant reflections in J. Ladrière, "Fonction propre de la grâce à l'égard de la science," in *La science, le monde, la foi,* pp. 45–53.

8. See J. Ratzinger, "Gratia supponit naturam," in *Dogma und Verkündigung* (Munich and Freiburg: Wewel, 1973), pp. 161–82.

Chapter 7

1. There is an immense bibliography on this subject, and Brazilians have distinguished themselves in this area, e.g., Fernando Henrique Cardoso, Floristán Fernández, Celso Furtado, and Hélio Jaguaribe. For a good introduction see G. Arroyo's two papers for the El Escorial

meeting: "Pensamiento latino-americano sobre el subdesarrollo y dependencia externa," and "Consideraciones sobre el subdesarrollo de América Latina," in *Fe cristiana y cambio social en América Latina* (Salamanca: Sígueme, 1973), pp. 305–22 and 323–34. Also see J. Comblin, *Théologie de la pratique révolutionnaire* (Paris: Ed. Universitaires, 1974), pp. 118–27; R. Poblete, "La teoría de la dependencia: análisis crítico," in *Liberación: Diálogos en el CELAM* (Bogotá, 1974), pp. 201–20.

2. See Gustavo Gutiérrez, *A Theology of Liberation,* Eng. trans. (Maryknoll, N.Y.: Orbis Books, 1973). Also L. Boff, "Teologia da libertação," in *Grande Sinal,* 1974: ten essays on the matter.

3. Hugo Assmann, "The Political Dimension of Faith: Man's Liberation in History," in *Theology for a Nomad Church,* Eng. trans. (Maryknoll, N.Y.: Orbis Books, 1976), pp. 29–40.

4. See R. A. Cobian, "Factores económicos y fuerzas políticas en el proceso de liberación," *Fe cristiana y cambio social,* pp. 33–64.

5. Celso Furtado, *O mito do desenvolvimento econômico* (Rio de Janeiro: Ed. Paz e Terra, 1974), p. 34.

6. Ibid., p. 38, fn. 21.

7. J. J. Llach, "Dependencia cultural y creación de cultura en América Latina," in *Stromata* 30 (1974): 5–23.

8. Fernando de Bastos de Ávila, "A missão social da Igreja hoje," in *Missão da Igreja no Brasil* (São Paulo: Ed. Loyola, 1973), p. 159.

9. See C. G. Langoni, *Distribuição da renda econômica do Brasil* (Rio de Janeiro: Ed. Expressão e Cultura, 1973), p. 64; H. Jaguaribe, *Brasil: crise e alternativas* (Rio de Janeiro: Zahar, 1974), pp. 52–66.

10. See J. Comblin, "Movimientos e ideologías en América Latina," in *Fe cristiana y cambio social,* pp. 101–27, especially pp. 111–13.

11. E. Dussell, "Historia de la fe cristiana y cambio social en América Latina," in *Fe cristiana y cambio social,* pp. 65–99.

12. B. de Las Casas, *Brevísima relación de la destrucción de las Indias* (Buenos Aires: Editorial Universitaria de Buenos Aires, 1966), p. 36; Eng. trans., *Tears of the Indians* (Williamstown, Mass.: J. Lilburne, 1970).

13. See E. Hoornaert, *Formaçao do Catolicismo Brasileiro 1550–1800* (Petrópolis: Vozes, 1974); H. E. Wetzel, "O condicionamento histórico étnico-cultural da Igreja no Brasil," in *Missão da Igreja no Brasil,* pp. 27–47.

14. In *REB (Brazilian Ecclesiastical Review)* 34 (1974): 976.

15. See E. Hoornaert, *Formação do Catolicismo Brasileiro,* pp. 98–136.

16. Idem, "A tradição lascasiana no Brasil," in *REB* 35 (1975).

17. J. H. Rodrigues, "O Clero e a Independência," in *REB* 32 (1972): 309–20, especially p. 309.

Chapter 8

1. See the whole issue 1/2 of *Stromata* (1974) on the topic of cultural dependence and cultural creation in Latin America.

2. J. Comblin, *Théologie de la pratique révolutionnaire* (Paris: Ed. Universitaires, 1974), p. 65.

3. Ibid., p. 127.

4. See A. Alonso, "Una nueva forma de hacer teología," in *Iglesia y praxis de liberación* (Salamanca: Sígueme), pp. 50–88; R. Vidales, "Cuestiones en torno al método de la teología de la liberación," *MIEC-JECI Document* 9 (Lima, 1972), Eng. trans., "Methodological Issues in Liberation Theology," in *Frontiers of Theology in Latin America* (Maryknoll, N.Y.: Orbis Books, 1979); E. Dussel, *Método para una filosofía de la liberación* (Salamanca: Sígueme, 1974); I. Ellacuría, "Tesis sobre la posibilidad, necesidad y sentido de una teología latino-americana," in *Teología y mundo moderno* (Madrid: Ed. Cristiandad, 1975), pp. 325–50; L. Boff, "Que é fazer teología a partir da A. Latina em cativeiro," in *Teología do cativeiro e da libertação* (Lisbon, 1976), pp. 26–56.

5. See J. C. Scannone, "La liberación latinoamericana, ontología del proceso auténticamente liberador," in *Stromata* 28 (1972): 107–50; also in *Teología de la liberación y praxis popular* (Salamanca: Sígueme, 1976), pp. 133–86.

6. See G. Gutiérrez, "Liberation Praxis and Christian Faith," in *Frontiers of Theology in Latin America.*

7. For an overview of this whole issue in Latin American theology see *Panorama de la teología latinoamericana,* 2 vols. SELADOC study team (Salamanca: Sígueme, 1975); *Frontiers of Theology in Latin America; Concilium* 96 (New York: Seabury Press, 1974); J. L. Segundo, *The Sacraments Today* (Maryknoll, N.Y.: Orbis Books, 1974); idem, *The Liberation of Theology* (Maryknoll, N.Y.: Orbis Books, 1976); H. Assmann, *Theology for a Nomad Church* (Maryknoll, N.Y.: Orbis Books, 1976).

8. L. Gera, "Cultura y dependencia a la luz de la reflexión teológica," in *Stromata* 30 (1974): 169–93; idem, "La Iglesia frente a la situación de dependencia," in *Teología pastoral y dependencia* (Buenos Aires: Ed. Guadalupe, 1974), pp. 18–19.

9. See C. Mesters, "O futuro do nosso passado: O que deve ser, tem força," in *REB* 35 (1975).

10. See L. Gera, "Cultura y dependencia," *Stromata* 30 (1974): 174.

11. See E. Hoornaert, *Formação do catolicismo brasileiro 1500–1800* (Petrópolis: Ed. Vozes, 1974), pp. 98–136.

12. See R. Falla, "La conversión desde la antropología política," in *Teología y mundo contemporáneo,* pp. 393–418.

Chapter 9

1. For the major works on this subject see Romano Guardini, *Freiheit, Gnade Schicksal* (Munich: Kösel-Verlag, 1948), pp. 125–89; Eng. trans., *Freedom, Grace and Destiny* (Westport, Conn.: Greenwood Press, 1975); idem, *Unterscheidung des Christlichen* (Mainz: Matthias-Grünewald-Verlag, 1935), pp. 335–60: "Die Glaube an die Gnade und das Bewusstsein der Schuld"; B. Langemeyer, "Die Frage nach dem gnädigen Gott heute," in *Geist und Leben* 43 (1970): 125–35; idem, "Das Phänomen Zufall und die Frage nach der göttlichen Vorsehung," in *Geist und Leben* 45 (1972): 25–41; P. Fransen, "Pour une psychologie de la grâce divine," in *Lumen Vitae* 12 (1957): 209–40; W. W. Meissner, *Foundations for a Psychology of Grace* (New York: Paulist Press, 1965); H. D. Lewis, *Our Experience of God* (London: Allen and Unwin, 1959); O. Rabut, *L'expérience mystique fondamentale* (Tournai: Casterman, 1969); J. Maréchal, "A propos du sentiment de présence de Dieu chez les profanes et chez les mystiques," in *Etudes sur la psychologie des mystiques* (Bruges, 1929) 1:69–129, Eng. trans., *Studies in the Psychology of the Mystics* (Albany, N.Y.: Magi Books, 1964); L. Boff, *A atualidade da experiência de Deus* (Rio de Janeiro, 1974).

2. K. Rahner, "Über die Erfahrung der Gnade," in *Schriften zur Theologie* (Einsiedeln, 1964) 4:105–09. This multivolumed series is translated into English as *Theological Investigations* and now published by Seabury Press, New York.

3. See the relevant remarks of Langemeyer, "Das Phänomen Zufall"; also see J. Monod, *Chance and Necessity* (New York: Alfred A. Knopf, 1971); the anthology edited by G. Eder, W. Wickler, and W. Kern, *Gesetzmässigkeit und Zufall der Natur* (Würzburg, 1968); J. Mussard, *Gott und der Zufall,* 3 vols. (Zurich, 1970).

4. In English see Ludwig von Bertalanffy, *General System Theory: Essays on Its Foundation and Development* (New York: Braziller, 1969); see also C. W. Churchman, *Design of Inquiring Systems: Basic Concepts in Systems Analysis* (New York: Basic Books, 1972).

5. J. P. Sartre, *L'imaginaire: Psychologie phénoménologique de l'imagination* (Paris: Gallimard, 1940), Eng. trans., *Imagination: A Psychological Critique* (Ann Arbor, Mich.: University of Michigan Press, 1962); Roy L. Hart, *Unfinished Man and the Imagination* (New York: Herder and Herder, 1968); W. F. Lynch, *Christ and Apollo: The Dimensions of the Literary Imagination* (Notre Dame, Ind.: University of Notre Dame Press, 1975); M. T. Kelsey, *Dreams: The Dark Speech of the Spirits: A Christian Interpretation* (New York, 1968); idem, *God, Dreams and Revelation: A Christian Interpretation of Dreams* (Minneapolis: Augsburg, 1974); H. Cox, *Feast of Fools: A Theological Essay on Festivity and Fantasy,* paperback edition (New York: Harper and Row, 1972); R. Alves, *Tomorrow's Child: Imagination, Creativity and the Rebirth of Culture* (New York: Harper and Row, 1972).

6. See Cox, *Feast of Fools.*

7. Ibid.; also see J. Pieper, *In Tune with the World: A Theory of Festivity,* Eng. trans. (New York: Harcourt, Brace, Jovanovich, 1965); R. Caillois, *L'homme et le sacré* (Paris, 1950), pp. 121–62; for a fuller bibliography see L. Boff, *A oração no mundo secular* (Petrópolis: Ed. Vozes, 1975), pp. 41–44.

8. Pieper, *In Tune with the World,* pp. 17–18.

9. J. Chrysostom, *De sancta Pentecostes,* hom. 1, *PG* 50. 455.

10. L. Coimbra, *A alegria, a dor e a graça* (Porto, 1916), p. 170.

11. See O. F. Bollnow, "O encontro," in *Pedagogia e filosofia da existência* (Petrópolis: Ed. Vozes, 1974), pp. 139–204: "Every encounter is a gift befalling man as a chance occurrence. Expressing it in religious terms, Buber said that every encounter is a grace. We cannot find the Thou simply by seeking it. We encounter it through grace" (p. 143).

12. See H. Assmann, *Teología desde la praxis de la liberación* (Salamanca: Sígueme, 1973), pp. 67–70, Eng. trans., *Theology for a Nomad Church* (Maryknoll, N.Y.: Orbis Books, 1976).

13. Dionysius the Areopagite, *De divinis nominibus* 15.180.

14. Augustine, *Sermo* 368.5: *PL* 39.1655.

15. Idem, *Confessions* 13.9.

16. This is the basic thesis of Josef Pieper's important work *Über die Liebe* (Munich: Kösel, 1972).

17. *Die Laune des Verliebten,* sc. 5.

18. Dante, *Vita Nuova,* chap. 2.

19. In *Cherubinischer Wandersmann* the same basic thought was well expressed by Angelus Silesius: "I know that the nightingale does not criticize the song of the cuckoo. If I do not sing as you, why should you ridicule my song?"

20. See the remarks of D. Grings, *A força de Deus na fraqueza do homem* (Porto Alegre: Livraria Sulina, 1975) on the character of the priest in Graham Greene's novel *The Power and the Glory:* "In a state of sin and in the midst of religious persecution, a priest longs to cross the Mexican border and go to Confession. In his flight he becomes a real angel of mercy for all he meets. He does not manage to escape because he puts the salvation of others first. Thus a life that seems to be lost in moral and Christian terms by human standards proves to be suffused with the presence of God" (p. 151). To be suffused with the presence of God is to live in Paradise already. As Angelus Silesius put it so aptly: "If Paradise were not already in you, O human being, then believe me, you would never have a chance of entering it at all" *(Cherubinischer Wandersmann).*

Chapter 10

1. See H. M. Dion, "La prédestination dans saint Paul," *Revue des Sciences Religieuses* 53 (1965): 5–43; K. Koch, "Zur Geschichte der Erwählungsvorstellung in Israel," *ZAW* 67 (1955): 205–26; H. H. Rowley, *The Biblical Doctrine of Election* (London, 1950).

2. See Murphy-O'Connor, "Péché et communauté dans le Nouveau Testament," *RB* 74(1967): 161–93. The *Sitz im Leben* (the real-life situation in which the text was composed) seems to have been the Judeo-Christian community in Palestine. Great efforts were made to convert the Jews. That they failed to recognize the Messiah is pardonable. But that they would return to Judaism after becoming Christians, and thus betray their free profession of faith, seemed unpardonable.

3. Several other passages might be considered here. Consider Heb. 6:4–6: "For when men have once been enlightened and have tasted the heavenly gift and become sharers in the Holy Spirit, when they have tasted the good word of God and the powers of the age to come, and then have fallen away, it is impossible to make them repent again, since they are crucifying the Son of God for themselves and holding him up to contempt." Here we are dealing with the subjective dispositions of the sinner, not with the impossibility of objective pardon on God's part. Nothing more can really make an impression on someone who had so utterly rejected the light. Repentance seems impossible so long as such attitudes endure. See J. Ramos-Regidor, *El sacramento de la penitencia* (Salamanca, 1975), pp. 164–65.

Another passage is in 1 John 5:16: "Anyone who sees his brother sinning, if the sin is not deadly, should petition God, and thus life will be given to the sinner. This is only for those whose sin is not deadly. There is such a thing as a deadly sin; I do not say that one should pray about that." Here a "deadly sin" would be an extremely serious sin meriting exclusion from the community (1 John 2:19; 4:4–5; 5:12; see R. Schnackenburg, *Die Johannesbriefe,* Freiburg, 1963, p. 227 f.). The gospel writer does not say that such a sin is unforgivable. He says that the prayer of the community of brethren, which ordinarily obtains the pardon of sins, is not effective here. By virtue of the gravity of the sin, not of the ineffectiveness of the prayer, we must assume that the proper dispositions of repentance are missing and hence there is no forgiveness. See Murphy-O'Connor, "Péché et Communauté": 171–72; M. G. Cordero, "Las diversas clases de pecados en la Biblia: Pecados irremisibles?" in *XVIII Semana Bíblica Esp.* (Madrid, 1959), pp. 70–75.

4. *Deus omnipotens omnes homines sine exceptione vult salvos fieri (1 Tim. 2:4), licet non omnes*

salventur. Quod autem quidam salvantur, salvantis est donum; quod autem quidam pereunt, pereuntium est meritum.

5. The bibliography on the subject is enormous. Here I mention only a few of the more notable titles: M. Flick and Z. Alszeghy, *Il Vangelo della Grazia* (Florence: Libreria Editrice, 1964), pp. 251–319; J. Auer, *Das Evangelium der Gnade* (Regensburg: F. Pustet, 1970), pp. 41–70; 240–54; J. Rabeneck, "Grumdzüge der Prädestinationslehre Molinas," *Scholastik* 31 (1956): 351–69; H. Rondet, "Prédestination, grâce et liberté," in *Essais sur la théologie de la grâce* (Paris: Beauchesne, 1964), pp. 201–41; A. Trapé, "A proposito di predestinazione: S. Agostino ed i suoi critici moderni," *Divinitas* 7 (1963): 234–84. F. J. Coute, *Hoffnung im Unglauben: Zur Diskussion über den allgemeinen Heilswillen Gottes* (Munich: F. Schöningh, 1973); P. Maury, *La prédestination* (Geneva: Labor et Fides, 1957); H. Ott, *Die Antwort des Glaubens* (Stuttgart, Berlin: Kreuz-Verlag, 1972), pp. 199–206; T. Simonin, "Prédestination, préscience et liberté," in *Nouvelle Revue Théologique* 85 (1963): 711–30; M. Löhrer, "Gotes Gnadenhandeln als Erwählung des Menschen," in *Mysterium Salutis* 4/2 (Einsiedeln, 1974): 773–827; M. J. Farrelly, *Predestination, Grace and Free Will* (Westminster, Md.: Newman Press, 1964).

6. For a critique of the systems see Löhrer, "Gottes Gnadenhandeln," *Mysterium Salutis* 4/2: 783–89; Auer, *Das Evangelium der Gnade*, p. 246–49; Flick-Alszeghy, *Il Vangelo della Grazia*, pp. 309–19; Farrelly, *Predestination, Grace and Free Will*, pp. 28–37; G. Ferreras, "Sobre la gracia y su teología," in *Naturaleza y gracia* 22 (1975): 59–90, which provides the most lucid critique of the presuppositions underlying the traditional tracts.

7. See L. Boff, *Experimentar Deus hoje* (Petrópolis: Vozes, 1974), pp. 126–90.

8. Flick-Alszeghy, *Il Vangelo della Grazia*, p. 317.

9. For this whole question see J. Heilsbetz, *Fundamentos teológicos das religiões não-cristãs*, Quaestiones Disputatae 33 (São Paulo, 1970); G. Thils, *Propos et problèmes de la théologie des religions non chrétiennes* (Tournai: Casterman, 1966), especially pp. 146–54, 186–96; L. Boff, "Die Kirche als universale sacramentum salutis und die Religionen der Erde," in *Die Kirche als Sakrament im Horizont der Welterfahrung* (Paderborn, 1972), pp. 426–41.

10. See L. Boff, *Die Kirche als Sakrament.*

11. See L. Boff, *Vida para além da morte* (Petrópolis: Ed. Vozes, 1974), pp. 34–45; idem, *A ressurreição de Cristo e a nossa ressurreição na morte* (Petrópolis: Ed. Vozes, 1974), pp. 92–102.

Chapter 11

1. For works in the same vein see P. Fransen, "Der Gnandenstand," in *Mysterium Salutis* 4/2 (Einsiedeln, 1975): 954–64; idem, "Pour une psychologie de la grâce divine," *Lumen Vitae* 12 (1957): 209–40; Flick and Alszeghy, *Il Vangelo della Grazia* (Florence, 1964), pp. 143–67, 191 ff., 342–55; idem, "L'opzione fondamentale della vita morale e la grazia," *Gregorianum* 41 (1960): 593–619; H. Reiners, *Grundintention und sittliches Tun* (Quaestiones Disputatae 30) (Freiburg, 1960), pp. 47–74; R. Blomme, *Widerspruch in Freiheit* (Limburg: Lahn-Verlag, 1965), pp. 115–22; J. B. Libanio, *Pecado e opção fundamental* (Petrópolis: Ed. Vozes, 1975).

2. See R. Dahrendorf, "Homo sociologicus," in *Ensaios de teoria da sociedade* (Rio de Janeiro, 1974), pp. 32–107, especially pp. 59f. and 73f.

3. See Bertalanffy, *Teoria Geral dos Sistemas,* Portuguese trans. (Petrópolis: Ed. Vozes, 1975), p. 81, Eng. edition, *General System Theory: Essays on its Foundation and Development* (New York: Braziller, 1969).

4. See the works listed above in n. 1. For a more detailed treatment see J. B. Libanio, *Pecado e opção fundamental,* pp. 42–69.

5. See J. Ladrière, *Vie sociale et destinée* (Gembloux: Duculot, 1973), especially pp. 66–78.

6. See J. Ramos-Regidor, "El pecado como acción humana," in *El sacramento de la penitencia* (Salamanca, 1975), pp. 99–103.

7. *Met.* 5.20, 1022b 4; *S. Theologica,* 1/2, q. 50, a. 1. P. Bourdieu defines habits as "systems of durable dispositions, structured structures that are inclined to function as structuring structures" (p. 175); or again a habit is "a system of durable and transferable dispositions which integrates all past experiences and functions at every moment as a matrix of perceptions, evaluations and actions, thus allowing for the execution of infinitely differentiated tasks" (p. 178; *Esquisse d'une théorie de la pratique,* Geneva and Paris: Droz, 1972).

8. See *Mysterium Salutis* 4/2 (Einsiedeln, 1975): 977–82; D. Grings, *A força de Deus na fraqueza do homem* (Porto Alegre, 1975), pp. 100–09; J. Auer, *Das Evangelium der Gnade* (Regensburg, 1970), pp. 215–38; O. H. Pesch, "Die Lehre vom Verdienst als Problem für

Theologie und Verkündigung," in *Wahrheit und Verkündigung* (Munich, 1967), pp. 1865–1907.

9. Flick-Alszeghy, *Il Vangelo della Grazia*, p. 667.

10. Trent, Session 6, chap. 16: DS 1545–1582, especially 1582.

11. See J. Rivière, "Sur l'origine des formules ecclésiastiques 'de condigno' et 'de congruo,'" in *Bulletin de littérature ecclésiastique* 28 (1927): 75–83.

12. See M. Schmaus, *Der Glaube der Kirche* (Munich: Hueber, 1970), 2:651.

13. See J. Auer, *Das Evangelium der Gnade*, pp. 174–84, with his bibliography. He poses the problem along lines that are fundamentally different from mine here.

14. Karl Rahner, *Der Leib und das Heil* (in collaboration with A. Görres) (Mainz: Matthias-Grunewald-Verlag, 1967), pp. 29–44.

15. See F. Vering, *De certitudine status gratiae in Concilio Tridentino*, Ph.D. diss., Rome, 1953; E. Stakemeier, *Das Konzil von Trient über die Heilsgewissheit* (Heidelberg: F. H. Kerle, 1947).

16. See F. Vering, *De certitudine*; J. Alfaro, "Certeza de la gracia y certeza de la esperanza," in *Esperanza cristiana y liberación del hombre* (Barcelona: Herder, 1972), pp. 71–100.

17. See J. Alfaro, ibid., p. 73; F. Vering, *De certitudine*, pp. 19–59. At Trent Costacciarius, a well-known Scotist theologian, defended the certainty about grace in syllogistic form: "Whoever does all in his power is certain of his grace; but the justified person can know that he has done all in his power; therefore he can be certain, with the certainty of faith, of having acquired grace" (Vering, *De certitudine*, p. 99).

18. Luther and Trent agreed on this point, among many others. Luther did not affirm any intellectual certitude. He talked about a "certitude lived in confident surrender to the love of God, a certitude grounded in God rather than in man" (J. Alfaro, "Certeza de la gracia," p. 92).

19. Ibid., p. 109.

Chapter 12

1. See J. B. Libanio, *Pecado e opção fundamental* (Petrópolis: Ed. Vozes, 1975), including the bibliography.

2. See P. Bonnetain, "Grace actuelle," in *DBS* 3, 1195–1205; M. Schmaus, *Der Glaube der Kirche*, vol., 2 pp. 539–65; *Mysterium Salutis* 4/2 (Einsiedeln, 1975), p. 964 ff.; A. Perego, *La gracia* (Barcelona, 1963), pp. 93–250, including the extensive bibliography; J. H. Nicolas, *Les profondeurs de la grâce* (Paris: Beauchesne, 1969), pp. 184–226.

3. Karl Barth railed against the fragmentation of grace in Catholic theology and dogma: "One need hardly believe that Catholics in fact live with a grace so horribly fragmented as that of their dogmatic theology. On the contrary we have every reason to believe that they, like we, live in the one, undivided grace of Jesus Christ" (*Kirchliche Dogmatik*, IV/1, Zurich, 1953, p. 93; Eng. trans., *Church Dogmatics*, Naperville, Ill.: Allenson, 1936–69). See H. Küng, *Rechtfertigung: Die Lehre Karl Barth's und eine Katholische Bessinung* (Einsiedeln, 1957), pp. 198–203; Eng. trans., *Justification: The Doctrine of Karl Barth and a Catholic Reflection* (New York: Nelson, 1964).

4. Every manual has its own division. For example, see the detailed arrangement of Aloisio Arias, *Gratia christiana* (Madrid: Ediciones Religión y Cultura, 1964), p. 160f.

5. See J. Fuchs, *Situation und Entscheidung* (Frankfurt am Main: J. Knecht, 1952).

6. See Flick-Alszeghy, *Il Vangelo della Grazia* (Florence, 1964), pp. 117–200.

7. See against Hus, DS 1216; against the figures of the Reformation, DS 1557; against Baius (who said that "all the deeds of the infidels are sins and all the virtues of the philosophers are vices"), DS 1925; against Jansen (who taught that "everything is sin that is not done out of supernatural Christian faith operating through love"), DS 2311 and also DS 2308; against Quesnel (who asserted that "the prayer of the sinner is a sin, and his fear of punishment is again a sin"), DS 2445, 2451–67.

8. For the history of this maxim see J. Rivière, "Quelques antécédents de la formule 'Facienti quod in se est,'" in *Revue des Sciences Religieuses* 7 (1927): 93–97; A. M. Landgraf, *Dogmengeschichte der Frühscholastik* 1/1 (Regensburg: F. Pustet, 1952), pp. 249–64. There is a detailed commentary in Flick and Alszeghy, *Il Vangelo della Grazia*, pp. 236–42.

Chapter 13

1. See J. L. Segundo, *Grace and the Human Condition*, chap. 1, Clarification III ("The Social Dimension of Grace and Sin"), Eng. trans. (Maryknoll, N.Y.: Orbis Books, 1973), pp. 37–39. Also see P. Fransen, "Die personale und gemeinschaftliche Struktur der menschlichen Exis-

tenz," in *Mysterium Salutis* 4/2 (Einsiedeln, 1975): 939–51; M. Schmaus, *Die göttliche Gnade,* vol. 3 of his *Katholische Dogmatik* (Munich: Max Heuber, 1956), 3:389–99; J. Ladrière, "Fonction propre de la grâce à l'égard de la science," in *La science, le monde, la foi* (Paris: Casterman, 1972), pp. 45–53.

2. See M. Theunissen, *Der Andere: Studien zur Sozialontologie der Gegenwart* (Berlin: De Gruyter, 1965). An older book that remains highly pertinent is by D. von Hildebrand, *Metaphysik der Gemeinschaft* (Augsburg, 1930). Also see P. Demo, "Problemas sociológicos da 'comunidade,'" in *Comunidades: Igreja na base,* CNBB Studies 3 (São Paulo, 1975): 67–110.

3. See J. L. Segundo, *Grace and the Human Condition,* p. 38; R. Lourau, *A analise institucional* (Petrópolis: Ed. Vozes, 1975), pp. 118–43.

4. See R. Dahrendorf, "Homo sociologicus," in *Ensaios de teoria da sociedade* (Rio de Janeiro, 1974), pp. 32–107, especially p. 74; Eng. edition, *Essays in the Theory of Society* (Stamford, Calif.: Stamford Univ. Press, 1968); idem, "Sociologia e natureza humana," ibid., pp. 109–110. Also see this author's work in English: *Homo Sociologicus* (London: Routledge and K. Paul, 1973).

5. See P. Bourdieu, *Esquisse d'une théorie de la pratique* (Geneva and Paris, 1972), pp. 175–78.

6. For relevant reflections from a Latin American standpoint see J.C. Scannone, *Hacia una pastoral de la cultura,* MIEC-JECI Documentation 16 (Lima, 1976); idem, "Transcendencia, praxis liberadora y lenguaje: Hacia una filosofía de la religión postmoderna y latinoamericanamente situada," in *Nuevo Mundo* (1973) 1:221–45 or in *Panorama de la teología latinoamericana* (Salamanca: Sígueme, 1975), 1:83–117; idem, "La liberación latinoamericana: Ontología del proceso liberador," in *Stromata* 28 (1972): 107–50; L. Boff, *Teologia do cativeiro e da libertação* (Lisbon, 1976), pp. 103–33; R. Alves, *Tomorrow's Child: Imagination, Creativity and the Rebirth of Culture* (New York: Harper & Row Publishers, 1972).

7. See Scannone, *Hacia una pastoral de la cultura,* p. 39.

8. See J. Ladrière, "Le volontaire et l'histoire," in *Vie sociale et destinée* (Duculot, 1973), pp. 66–78, especially pp. 76–77; H. Ott, "L'herméneutique de la société, Le problème de l'historicité collective," in *Ermeneutica e Escatologia,* E. Castelli ed. (Rome, 1971), pp. 255–74.

Chapter 14

1. See L. Boff, "O que é propriamente processo de libertação?" in *Teologia do cativeiro e da libertação* (Lisbon, 1976), pp. 83–102, with a bibliography focusing on liberation theology in Latin America.

2. See my more detailed study, "Elementos de una teología de la crisis," in *Nuevo Mundo* (1971) 1:205–28, with a full bibliography.

3. See O. F. Bollnow, "A crise," in *Pedagogia e filosofia da existência* (Petrópolis: Ed. Vozes, 1970), pp. 37–65; P. Furter, "As diversas acepções da noção de crise," in *Educação e vida* (Petrópolis: Ed. Vozes, 1975), pp. 69–92.

4. Augustine, *En. in psalm.* 70. 2, 1; *PL* 36. 891.

5. See L. Boff, "O sofrimento que nasce da luta contra o sofrimento," in *Concilium,* no. 9 (1976).

6. See the important study of G. Greshake, *Gnade als konkrete Freiheit: Eine Untersuchung zur Gnadenlehre des Pelagius* (Mainz: Matthias-Grünewald-Verlag, 1972). He shows that Pelagius was badly misunderstood by Augustine because their languages and idioms were different. Augustine spoke the idiom of Platonic ontology while Pelagius was using the idiom of historical Christian experience. "For Augustine . . . the grace event is an event carried out above and beyond history. It is unconditionally linked to human history only through the work of Christ (and in a weaker sense through the saving community known as the church). For Pelagius . . . grace is an activity of God that touches humanity in many different ways in history. It is a concrete force, which can be experienced and verified, and which also frees human beings for freedom" (p. 228).

Modern discussions of Pelagianism offer a reworking of the historical figure of Pelagius and his optimism. Some offer a view of his position that would dovetail perfectly with our understanding of the faith today. See P. Fransen, "Augustin und der Pelagianismus," in *Mysterium Salutis* 4/2 (Einsiedeln, 1975): 646–63; G. I. Bonner, "How Pelagian was Pelagius? An Examination of the Contentions of Torgny Bohlin," in *Studia Patristica* 9, 94 (1966): 350–58, a critique of Bohlin's book, *Die Theologie des Pelagius und ihre Genesis* (Uppsala: Lundequistska Bokhandeln, 1957).

7. In contrast to this tradition, but in a different vein from this book also, see the following: H. Rondet, "La grâce libératrice," in *Essais sur la théologie de la grâce* (Paris, 1964), pp. 39–74; V.

Capágana, *Agustin de Hipona* (Madrid: BAC, 1974), pp. 106–8 ("la gracia de la liberación"). See Augustine, *En. in psalm. 64*, 1, *PL* 36. 772: "We must first come to know our *captivity*, and then our *liberation.*"

8. The most serious study is that of H. Küng, *Rechtfertigung: Die Lehre Karl Barths und eine katholische Besinnung* (Einsiedeln, 1957): Eng. trans., *Justification* (New York: Nelson, 1964). Also see O. H. Pesch, *Theologie der Rechtfertigung bei Martin Luther und Thomas von Aquin* (Mainz: Matthias-Grünewald-Verlag, 1967); there is an excellent resumé in *Mysterium Salutis* 4/2 (Einsiedeln, 1975): 831–920.

9. See S. Gonzalez, "El proceso de la conversion a la luz del Concilio de Trento," in *Revista de espiritualidad* 5 (1946): 56–73; E. Schillebeeckx, "O decreto tridentino sobre a justificação em nova perspectiva," in *Concilium* 5 (1965): 141–45; English edition published by Paulist Press.

10. In the debates over chapters 5 and 6, concerning the "preparation for grace" (within the "Decree on Justification," DS 1525–26), there was heated debate between the Augustinian-Franciscan school on the one hand and a late scholastic school on the other. The former espoused a more evolving and process-oriented point of view; the latter espoused a more formal and ontological view of justification. The former position tied its process-oriented thought to the whole experience of conversion and the gradual assimilation of divine grace. On all this see E. Stakemeier, "Die theologischen Schulen auf dem Trienter Konzil während der Recht-fertigungsverhandlungen," in *Theologische Quartalschrift* 117 (1936), pp. 188–207, 322–50; idem, *Der Kampf um Augustin auf dem Tridentinum* (Paderborn, 1937), pp. 151–60; H. Jedin, *Geschichte des Konzils von Trient* 2 (Freiburg, 1957), pp. 213–14, 241–42; *Mysterium Salutis* 4/2 (Einsiedeln, 1975): 718–20.

11. See L. Boff, *Vida para além da morte* (Petrópolis, 1973), pp. 15–33.

12. This is the way that liberation theology would phrase the expression *simul iustus et peccator.* See W. Joest "Paulus und das lutherische simul justus et peccator," in *Kerygma und Dogma* 1 (1955): 269–320; Hans Küng, *Rechtfertigung*, pp. 231–42; Karl Rahner, "Gerecht und Sünder zugleich," in *Schriften zur Theologie*, 6, pp. 262–76, Eng. trans., *Theological Investigations* (New York: Seabury Press); O. H. Pesch, "Simul iustus et peccator," in *Mysterium Salutis* 4/2: 886–91.

13. This formulation should not be misinterpreted. The terms *in re* and *in spe* are not in opposition; there is merely a shift in emphasis. A person *liberatus in spe* is one who is not yet totally liberated but who has hopes of being so liberated. To that extent he is also *liberatus in re* insofar as he participates in liberation; but since he is not completely liberated, he still remains *oppressus in re* as well.

Chapter 15

1. See P. Fransen, "As virtudes teologais como dinamisme ativo do estado de graça," in *Mysterium Salutis* 4/2 (Einsiedeln, 1975):918.

2. Cited by J. Pieper, *Über das christliche Menschenbild* (Munich, 1950), p. 8.

3. In scholastic theology it was Bonaventure who asserted that habitual grace is one single reality whose ramifications flower into a variety of virtues, gifts, and fruits. The basis of this is the oneness of the soul whose faculties are distinct only formally and not in real life. See his *Breviloquium*, pars. 5, chaps. 4–6. Also see A. Briva Mirabent, *La gloria y su relación con la gracia según las obras de San Buenaventura* (Barcelona, 1957).

4. On the virtues see the still classic works of the following: L. Billet, *De virtutibus infusis* (Rome, 1905); H. Lennerz, *De virtutibus theologicis* (Rome: Apud Aedes Universitatis Gregorianae, 1947); J. B. Alfaro, *Fides, Spes, Caritas* (Rome: Pontificia Universitas Gregoriana, 1974); T. Soiron, *Glaube, Hoffnung und Liebe* (Regensburg, 1934); *Mysterium Salutis* 4/2:938–64; H. Rondet, "Grâce, vertus, mérites," in *Essais sur la théologie de la grâce* (Paris, 1964), pp. 75–106; O. F. Bollnow, *Wesen und Wandel der Tugenden* (Frankfurt am Main: Taschenbücher-Verlag, 1958); K. H. Schelkle, "Virtud y Virtudes," in *Teología del Nuevo Testamento* (Barcelona, 1975), 3:301–08; Eng. trans. *Theology of the New Testament* (Collegeville, Minn.: Liturgical Press, 1971–).

5. E. Bloch, *Das Prinzip Hoffnung*, 2 vols. (Berlin: Aufbau-Verlag, 1954–59); J. Moltmann, *Theology of Hope*, Eng. trans. (New York: Harper & Row, 1967); J. Alfaro, *Esperanza cristiana y liberación del hombre* (Barcelona: Herder, 1972); G. Gutiérrez, *A Theology of Liberation*, Eng. trans. (Maryknoll, N.Y.: Orbis Books, 1973).

6. Aquinas, *In Ethicam ad Nicomachum*, Books 8 and 9; *S. Theol.*, 2/2, q. 23, a. 1.

7. J. Comblin, *Théologie de la paix*, 2 vols. (Paris: Editions Universitaires, 1960).

8. K. H. Schelkle, "La alegría," in *Teología del Nuevo Testamento*, 3:222–32.

9. See J. B. Libanio, *A consciencia critica do religioso* (Rio de Janeiro, 1974).

10. See H. Schlier, "Parrhesia," in *Theologisches Wörterbuch zum NT,* 5:869–84; Eng. trans., *Theological Dictionary of the New Testament,* 10 vols. (Grand Rapids, Mich.: Eerdmans, 1964). Also see Karl Rahner, "Parrhesia," in *Schriften zur Theologie,* 7:252–58; Eng. trans., *Theological Investigations* (New York: Seabury Press).

11. See P. Roqueplo, *La foi d'un mal-croyant ou mentalité scientifique et vie de foi* (Paris: Cerf, 1969), p. 310.

12. See J. M. Carretero, "Sobre el humor y la ascética," in *Manresa* 38 (1966): 13–32; L. Boff, "A função do humor na teologia e na Igreja," in *Vozes* 64 (1970): 570–72, with a bibliography; H. Baggio, "O bom humor na vida religiosa," in *Grande Sinal* 28 (1974): 83–99.

13. H. Lützeler, "Der Humor und der 'Naturgrund' des Menschen," in *Philosophie des Kölner Humors* (Peters, Honnef Rh., 1954), pp. 9–11; see chap. 6 on "Der Humor und die Freiheit des Menschen," pp. 66–72.

14. T. Lersch, *Philosophie des Humors* (Munich, 1953), p. 26.

15. G. Hasenhüttl, *Charisma, Ordnungsprinzip der Kirche* (Freiburg, Basel, Vienna: Herder, 1969), pp. 129–244.

16. *Mysterium Salutis* 4/2:963–64.

Chapter 16

1. M. Lot-Borodine, *La déification de l'homme selon la doctrine des Pères grecs* (Paris, 1970); E. des Places, "Divinisation, pensée religieuse des grecs," in *Dictionnaire de Spiritualité Ascétique et Mystique,* 3:1370–75; H. Rondet, "La divinisation du chrétien, Mystère et problèmes," in *Essais sur la théologie de la grâce* (Paris, 1964), pp. 107–54, 155–200; J. H. Nicolas, *La grâce et la gloire: Appelés au partage de la vie divine* (Paris, 1971); idem, *Les profondeurs de la grâce* (Paris, 1969), pp. 400–14; Yves Congar, "La déification dans la tradition spirituelle de l'Orient," in *Vie Spirituelle* 43 (1935): 93–106.

2. See W. Bauer, *Wörterbuch zum Neuen Testament* (1952), p. 1578; Eng. trans., by W. F. Arndt and F. W. Gingrich, *A Greek-English Lexicon of the New Testament* (Chicago: Chicago University Press, 1957).

3. F. Mussner, "Die neutestamentliche Gnadentheologie in Grundzügen," in *Mysterium Salutis* 4/2 (Einsiedeln, 1973), p. 624.

4. We find similar expressions frequently in the Greek fathers. "God became mortal to free us from mortality" (see Basil of Caesarea, *Ep. 8.* 5). See M. Lot-Borodine, *La déification de l'homme,* pp. 52–66: "Le Theós Anthropos et la recapitulatio."

5. F. Mussner, *Mysterium Salutis* 4/2:624.

6. *Adversus haereses* 3.19, 1: *PG* 7. 939.

7. Ibid., 1. 5, Prol: *PG* 7. 1120. St. Athanasius: *Verbum Dei homo factus est ut nos deificaremus (Or. de Incarnatione Verbi* 8). St. Augustine: *Ille Filius qui cum esset Filius Dei, venit ut fieret filius hominis, donaretque nobis, qui eramus filii hominis, filios Dei fieri (Ep. 140; ad Honoratum* 3. 9). Then there is the often cited sentence of St. Cyril of Alexandria: "God became human so that humans might become God" (*Rm. hom.* 9.3).

8. *Thesaurus* 24, *PG* 75. 333: *Quaecumque enim Christo insunt, eadem in nos derivantur.*

9. *Stromata* 1. 7, c. 10: *PG* 9. 480.

10. The theme of divinization is not exclusively eastern. It is very much present in the thought of St. Augustine. See V. Capágana, "La deificación en la soteriología augustiniana," in *Augustinus Magister* (Paris, 1954), 2: 745–54.

11. *De ente supernaturali,* disp. 32, sect. 9, n. 15.

12. "La grâce, est-elle une participation de la déité telle qu'elle est en soi?" in *Revue Thomiste* 36 (1936): 470–85.

13. *De gratia,* 1. 7, c. 1.

14. Flick-Alszeghy, *Il Vangelo della Grazia* (Florence, 1964), pp. 557–60; or in *Fondamenti di una antropologia teologica* (Florence, 1969), pp. 295–98.

15. *Adv. haer.* 4. 38. 2–4; 4. 20. 7. See A. Verriele, "Le plan du salut d'après Saint Irénée," in *Revue des Sciences Religieuses* 24 (1934): 493.

Chapter 17

1. For the general literature on the theme in religions see G. Mensching and H. J. Kraus, "Vatername Gottes," in *Die Religion in Geschichte und Gegenwart* (Tubingen: Mohr, 1957), 6:

1232–34; G. Kruse, "Pater," in Pauly-Wissowa, *Realencyclopädie der classichen Altertumswissenschaft*, 36:2120–21; W. Koppers in F. König, *Christus und die Religionen der Erde* (Vienna, 1951), 2: 146f.; M. J. Lagrange, "La régénération et la filiation divine dans les mystères d'Eleusis," in *Revue Biblique* 38 (1928): 201–14.

2. On the theme of divine adoptive sonship some of the essential works are J. Jeremias, *Abba: Studien zur neutestamentlichen Theologie und Zeitgeschichte* (Göttingen: Vandenhoeck and Ruprecht, 1966), pp. 15–82; R. M. Grant, *The Early Christian Doctrine of God* (Charlottesville, Va.: University Press of Virginia, 1966); F. Büchsel, "Monogenesis," in *Theologisches Wörterbuch zum NT*, 4:745–50; Eng. trans., *Theological Dictionary of the New Testament* (Grand Rapids, Mich.: Eerdmans, 1964); M. W. Schoenberg, "St. Paul's Notion on the Adoptive Sonship of Christians," in *The Thomist* 28 (1964); E. Mersch, "Filii in Filio: la Trinité vivifiant les hommes," in *La Théologie du corps mystique* (Paris, 1949) 2: 9–68, Eng. trans., *Theology of the Mystical Body* (St. Louis: Herder, 1951); A. García Suarez, "La primera persona trinitaria y la filiación adoptiva," in *XVIII Semana Española de Teología* (Madrid, 1961), pp. 69–114; S. Dockx, *Fils de Dieu par grâce* (Paris, 1948); H. P. C. Lyons, "The Grace of Sonship," in *Ephemerides Theologicae Lovanienses* 27 (1951): 438–66.

3. This is not the place to consider the question as to whether Jesus of Nazareth called himself the "Son of God" or not, or to consider the development of this epithet in the theology of the various early-church communities. Here we need only rely on the basic dogma of Christian faith which holds Jesus Christ to be the only begotten Son of the Father who was sent into the world. See the consideration of this question in H. Küng, *Christ sein* (Munich and Zurich, 1974), pp. 427–34; Eng. trans., *On Being a Christian* (New York: Doubleday, 1977).

4. L. Cerfaux, *Le chrétien dans la théologie paulinienne* (Paris: Cerf, 1962), p. 299; Eng. trans., *The Christian Theology of St. Paul* (New York: Seabury Press, 1967).

5. J. Ratzinger, *Christliche Brüderlichkeit* (Munich: Kösel, 1966), Eng. trans., *Open Circle: The Meaning of Christian Brotherhood* (London: Sheed and Ward, 1966); idem, "Erwägungen über die christliche Brüderlichkeit," in *Katholisches Caritasverband* (Munich, n.d.), pp. 42–68.

6. L. Boff, *O evangelho do Cristo cósmico* (Petrópolis: Ed. Vozes, 1970).

7. *In Johan.* 2, 1: *PG* 73. 213; *De SS. Trinitate Dialogus 5; PG* 75. 749.

8. *In Johan.* 110. 111, *PL* 35 (1923, 1929).

9. *In Ps.* 123, *PL* 37. 1634.

10. See E. Mersch, "Filii in Filio," p. 42.

11. St. Augustine describes the distinction between Christ the Son and us as the children of God in these terms: *"Ille unicus, nos multi; ille unus, nos in illo unum; ille natus, nos adoptati; ille ab aeterno genitus per naturam, nos a tempore facti per gratiam (In Ps. 88 7, PL 37. 1124).*

12. See, for example, St. Cyril of Alexandria, *In Johan.* 1, *PG* 73. 156.

13. *De recta fide ad Theodosium* 30, *PG* 76. 1177. For an exegesis of the passage see Mersch, "Filii in Filio," pp. 39–40.

14. From this perspective there is much sense in the famous phrase of Meister Eckhart, the great German mystic: "God generates me as his child." Eckhart's works are being published in English now by the Paulist Press in New York.

15. *Ad Serapionem* 1. 25, *PG* 26. 589.

16. This idea was given systematic form by the German theologian, F. Gogarten in his book, *Der Mensch zwischen Gott und Welt* (Stuttgart: Friedrich Vorwerk Verlag, 1956), especially p. 329f.

17. See L. Scheu, *Weltelemente beim Apostel Paulus (Gal. 4:3.9; Col. 2:8.20)* (Washington, 1933); H. Schlier, *Mächte und Gewalten im Neuen Testament*, Quaestiones Disputatae 3, (Freiburg: Verlag Herder, 1953), Eng. trans., *Principalities and Powers in the New Testament* (New York: Herder and Herder, 1961).

Chapter 18

1. See H. Kleinknecht, "Pneuma en grec," in *Esprit (Dictionnaire biblique Gerhard Kittel)* (Geneva, 1971), p. 42.

2. Literary evidence is abundantly provided in Kleinknecht, ibid., pp. 23–40, especially pp. 28–29.

3. Ibid., p. 13.

4. Texts in Kleinknecht, ibid., pp. 41–48, especially p. 42.

5. See Baumgärtel, "Esprit dans l'Ancien Testament," ibid., pp. 56–74; H. Cazelles, Paul Evdokimov, and Albert Greiner, *Le mystère de l'Esprit Saint* (Paris: Mame, 1968).

6. See J. Comblin, "A missão do Espirito Santo," in *REB* 35 (1975): 288–325; E. Schweizer, "Esprit: Le Nouveau Testament," in *Esprit (Dictionnaire biblique Gerhard Kittel)*, pp. 127–242; B. Froget, *De l'habitation du Saint-Esprit dans les âmes justes* (Lethielleux, 1937), Eng. trans., *The Indwelling of the Holy Spirit in the Souls of the Just According to the Teaching of Saint Thomas Aquinas* (New York: Paulist Press, 1921). E. Bardy, *Le Saint-Esprit en nous et dans l'Eglise d'après le Nouveau Testament* (Albi, 1950); H. Mühlen, *Der Heilige Geist als Person* (Münster: Aschendorff, 1963); idem, *Una mystica persona: Eine Person in vielen Personen* (Munich, Paderborn, and Vienna: F. Schöning, 1964); the anthology edited by A. R. Guimarães, *O Espirito Santo: Pessoa, Presença, Atuação* (Petrópolis: Ed. Vozes, 1973); F. Urdánoz, "La inhabitación del Espíritu Santo en el alma justa," in *RET* 6 (1946): 513–33; G. Philips, "Le Saint-Esprit en nous," in *ETL* 24 (1948): 127–35.

7. See H. Mühlen and C. Heitmann, *Erfahrung und Theologie des Heiligen Geistes* (Hamburg: Agentur des Rauhen Hauses, 1974), pp. 83–100, especially p. 84.

8. See H. Mühlen, *Die Erneuerung des christlichen Glaubens: Charisma-Geist-Befreiung* (Munich: Don Bosco-Verlag, 1976), pp. 108–37.

9. The great exegete G. A. Deissmann wrote that the Spirit constitutes, as it were, the matter of the Lord's resurrected body (see 1 Cor. 15:35ff); G. A. Deissmann, *Die neutestamentliche Formel "in Christo Jesu"* (Marburg, 1892), pp. 89–90.

10. For a more detailed treatment see L. Boff, "A Igreja, sacramento do Espirito Santo," in the anthology *O Espirito Santo*, pp. 108–25.

11. See L. Boff, "A era do Espirito Santo" in the same anthology, pp. 145–57; H. Mühlen, "Der beginn einer neuen Epoche der Geschichter des Glaubens," in *Die Erneuerung des christlichen Glaubens*, pp. 21–68.

12. *A.A.S.* 29 (1896–97): 648; St. Basil, *De Spirito Sancto* 16. 39, *PG* 32. 140c.

13. This thesis was offered by such figures as Peter Lombard (Sent. I, dist. 17), the great dogmatic theologian Petau (*Dogmata theologica* 8, c. 6, n. 8, col. 486a), Scheeben (*Dogmatik* 3, sect. 276, n. 1612), and quite persuasively in recent times by H. Mühlen (*Una mystica persona*, sect. 8, 44–48. 69).

14. See J. Auer, *El Evangelio de la gracia*, Spanish trans. (Barcelona, 1975), p. 128.

15. See C. Baumgartner, *La grâce du Christ* (Tournai: Desclée, 1963), p. 193. As he explains it, the communication of the hypostasis (i.e., the person) can be understood in two different ways. In one case the hypostasis is the substantial principle of a human nature itself. In a second case the hypostasis is the principle and term of knowledge and love. Communication of the hypostasis in the first sense is true of Christ alone. It is communicated in the second sense to the just.

16. This expression is taken from Petau, a theologian of the eighteenth century who is considered the father of the history of dogmas. He says that although indwelling unites the just *substantially* to the Holy Spirit, it does not make them the Holy Spirit; instead it makes them "spiritual." See his *Dogmata theologica* 8, c. 7, n. 13, col. 494 (Ed. Vivès, 1865), vol. 3. Petau knew the fathers of the church well. His theory that the Holy Spirit is in us as the Word was in the humanity of Jesus of Nazareth was securely grounded on the thinking of St. Cyril of Alexandria. According to Cyril, the Holy Spirit acts on his own in us, sanctifying us, uniting us to himself, and making us sharers in his divine nature. Here we find the Greek term *housiodos* (Lat. *substantialiter*). The Holy Spirit unites himself *substantially* to the just (Petau, *Dogmata theologica* 8, c. 4, col. 459). We are made gods by grace, not by nature. Christ, to be sure, is God by nature; we, however, are divine. We are not the Spirit, though he is the constitutive form of our sanctification and union with God; we are spiritual. Just as the Son gives us a filial character, so the Spirit makes us spiritual.

Along the same lines see Scheeben, *Die Mysterien des Christentums*, sect. 26–27. Also see T. de Régnon, *Études de théologie positive sur la sainte Trinité*, Étude 27 (3rd series) 3:551–52; H. Ronder, *De gratia Christi* (Paris: Beauchesne, 1948), pp. 329–39: "Petau, Scheeben et l'inhabitation du Saint-Esprit: Retour aux Pères grecs."

17. See A. Abreu, "Católicos pentecostais e outros carismáticos nos Estados Unidos," in *Atualização* (August 1972): 341–61, with a full bibliography; Kevin and D. Ranaghan, *Católicos Pentecostais* (Rio de Janeiro, 1972); Eng. version *Catholic Pentecostals* (Paramus, N.J.: Paulist, 1970); F. A. Sullivan, "The Pentecostal Movement," in *Gregorianum* 53 (1972): 237–66; R. Laurentin, *Pentecostisme chez les Catholiques* (Paris: Beauchesne, 1975), Eng. trans. *Catholic Pentecostalism* (Garden City, N.Y.: Doubleday, 1977), an overall view of the phenomenon in the church and a consideration of the major theological problems involved.

18. Kevin and D. Ranaghan, *Católicos pentecostais*, pp. 181–82.

19. Ibid., p. 182.

Chapter 19

1. For the basic bibliography see C. Colombo, "Grazia e inabitazione della SS. Trinità," in *Problemi e Orientamenti di Teologia Dommatica* (Milan, 1957), 2:641–54, especially 648–54; P. de Letter, "Current Theology: Sanctifying Grace and the Divine Indwelling," in *Theological Studies* (1953) 14:242–72; J. Trütsch, *SS. Trinitatis inhabitatio apud theologos recentiores* (Trent, 1949); R. Verardo, "Polemiche recenti intorno all'inabitazione della SS. Trinità," in *Sapienza* (1954) 7:29–44; P. F. Chirico, *The Divine Indwelling and Distinct Relations to the Indwelling Persons in Modern Theological Discussion* (Rome: Pontificia Universitas Gregoriana, 1960); J. F. Dedek, *Experimental Knowledge of the Indwelling Trinity* (Mundelein, Ill.: St. Mary of the Lake Seminary, 1958); S. Dockx, "Du fondement propre de la présence réelle de Dieu dans l'âme juste," in *Nouvelle Revue Théologique* (1950) 72:673–89; J. Sittler, *Essays on Nature and Grace* (Philadelphia: Fortress Press, 1972); J. P. Mackey, *Life and Grace* (Dublin, 1966); I. Willig, *Geschaffene und ungeschaffene Gnade* (Münster: Aschendorff, 1964); P. Fransen, "Die Grundstrukturen des neuen Seins," in *Mysterium Salutis* 4/2: 927–82.

2. *A.A.S.* 35 (1943): 231; or in DS 3813.

3. Here I follow the best manual writers: A. Perego, *La gracia* (Barcelona) pp. 382–90; C. Baumgartner, *La grâce du Christ* (Desclée, 1963), pp. 183–89; Flick-Alszeghy, *Il Vangelo della Grazia* (Florence, 1964), pp. 485–98; idem, *Fondamenti di una antropologia teologica* (Florence, 1969), pp. 265–70; A. Turrado, *Dios en el Hombre* (Madrid: BAC 325, 1971), pp. 136–46.

4. This opinion is defended by G. Vázquez, in 1. q. 8, d. 30, c.3 nn. 11–12 (Lyon, 1631) 1:114; in modern times it has been defended by P. Galtier, *L'habitation en nous des trois Personnes* (Rome: Gregorinae, 1950); idem, *De SS. Trinitate in se et in nobis* (Paris: Beauchesne, 1933).

5. Galtier, *De SS. Trinitate,* nn. 456–58; idem, *L'habitation en nous,* p. 230.

6. There is an axiom in the tract on grace which says: *"Omnia sunt unum, ubi non obviat relationis oppositio."* Its point is that in the *ad extra* works of the Trinity, those relating to creation, all is shared by the three divine persons where there is no opposition from the relations which make them distinct from one another. This axiom has a real point to it. Otherwise we would have to say that there are three infinites, three creators, three divine providences, and so forth. What is debated is whether the work of sanctification and indwelling can be characterized as an *ad extra* work. In the natural order the three divine persons would act through their shared divine nature; in the supernatural order they would act as distinct persons, for between the life of grace and eternal life there exists a mysterious correspondence and a merely accidental difference (diverse situations of the *viatores* on the one hand and the *comprehensores* on the other hand). See H. Rondet, *De gratia Christi* (Paris,1948), p. 338.

7. See *S. Theol.,* 1, q. 43, a. 3; q. 8, a. 3 ad 4. See also the text in 1, d. 14, q. 2, a. 2.

8. See *S. Theol.,* 1/2, q. 28, a. 1.

9. This aspect is explored in great depth by Suarez, *De Trinitate* 12, 5, 13 (Ed. Vives) 1:811.

10. This dimension is discussed in detail by A. Gardeil, *La structure de l'âme et l'expérience mystique* (Paris, 1927), p. 60 f.

11. The most significant representatives are M. de la Taille, "Actuation créée par l'acte incréé: Lumière de gloire, grâce sanctifiante, union hypostatique," in *Recherches de Science Religieuse* 28 (1928): 253–68; Karl Rahner, "Zur scholastischen Begrifflickkeit der ungeschaffenen Gnade," in *Schriften zur Theologie* (Einsiedeln, 1954), 1:347–74, Eng. trans., *Theological Investigations* (New York: Seabury Press).

12. Notional properties, in trinitarian theology, are those that refer to the divine persons insofar as they are distinct from one another: e.g., the "generation" of the Son and the "aspiration" of the Spirit by both the Father and the Son.

13. This opinion is very staunchly defended by Flick-Alszeghy, *Il Vangelo della Grazia,* pp. 493–98; idem, *Fondamenti di una antropologia teologica,* pp. 269–70.

14. Flick-Alszeghy, *Fondamenti,* p. 270.

15. Teresa of Avila, *Interior Castle* (or *The Mansions*), trans., E. Allison Peers (New York: Doubleday, Image Books, 1961), "Seventh Mansion," p. 207.

16. See A. van den Berg, "A SS. Trindade e a existência humana, 2 parts, in *REB* (1973) 33:629–48, and (1976) 36:323–46.

17. See L. Boff et al., *Experimentar Deus hoje* (Petrópolis, 1974), pp. 173–80.

18. Teresa of Avila, *Interior Castle,* pp. 207–08.

19. *A.A.S.* 35 (1943): 232; or DS 3815.

20. Teresa of Avila, *Interior Castle,* pp. 209–10.

BIBLIOGRAPHY

ANTHOLOGIES

Guimarães, A. R., ed. *O Espírito Santo; Pessoa, Presença, Atuação*. Petrópolis: Ed. Vozes, 1973.

"Gottes Gnadenhandeln." *Mysterium Salutis* 4/2. Einsiedeln, 1973: 595–984.

AUTHORS

Alfaro, J. *Lo natural y lo sobrenatural*. Madrid, 1952.

―――. *Cristología y antropología*. Madrid, 1973.

―――. *Esperanza cristiana y liberación del hombre*. Barcelona: Herder, 1972.

Alonso, J. "Relación de causalidad entre la gracia creada e increada." *Revista Española de Teología* 6 (1946): 1–60.

Auer, J. "Um den Begriff der Gnade." *Zeitschrift für katholischen Theologie* 70 (1948): 314–68.

―――. *Die Entwicklung der Gnadenlehre in der Hochscholastik mit besonderer Berücksichtigung des Kardinals Matteo d'Aquasparta*, Teil 1–2. Frieburg i. B., 1942–1951.

―――. *Das Evangelium der Gnade* (Kleine Katholische Dogmatik 5). Regensburg: F. Pustet, 1972. Spanish trans., *El Evangelio de la gracia*. Barcelona, 1975.

Arias, A. *Gratia christiana*. Madrid: Ediciones Religion y Cultura, 1964.

Arias, L. "Boletín de teología dogmática: Teología de la gracia (1950–58)." *Salmanticensis* 6 (1959): 199–215.

Bartmann, B. *Teología dogmática 2: A graça*. São Paulo, 1964.

Baumgartner, C. *La grâce du Christ* (Le Mystère Chrétien: Théologie Dogmatique 10). Tournai: Desclée, 1963.

Beraza, B. *Tractatus de gratia Christi* (Cursus Theologicus Oniensis). Bilbao, 1929.

Boff, L. *A atualidade da experiência de Deus*. Rio de Janeiro, 1973.

―――. "A Igreja, sacramento do Espírito Santo." In *O Espírito Santo,* pp. 108–25.

―――. "A era do Espírito Santo." In *O Espírito Santo,* pp. 145–57.

Bouillard, H. *L'idée de surnaturel et le mystère chrétien* (L'homme devant Dieu). Paris, 1964.

Bouëssé H. "Du mode d'habitation de la trés Sainte Trinité dans l'âme du juste." *La Vie Spirituelle* 69 (1943): 225–40.

Bourassa, F. "Adoptive Sonship: Our Union with the Divine Persons." *Theological Studies* 13 (1952): 309–35.

―――. "L'habitation de la Trinité." *Sciences Ecclésiastiques* 8 (1956): 59–70.

―――. "Le Saint-Esprit, unité d'amour du Père et du Fils." *Sciences Ecclésiastiques* 14 (1962): 375–415.

Brinktrine, J. *Die Lehre von der Gnade*. Paderborn: F. Schöningh, 1957.

Coimbra, L. *A alegria, a dor e a graça*. Porto, 1916.

Colombo, C. "Grazia e inabitazione della SS. Trinità: Bibliografia." *Problemi e orientamenti di Teologia Dogmatica*. Milan, 1957, 2: 641–54.

Comblin, J. "A missão do Espírito Santo." *Revista Eclesiástica Brasileira* 35 (1975): 288–325.

Congar, Y. *Le mystère du temple ou l'Economie de la présence de Dieu à sa créature de la Genèse à l'Apocalypse* (Lectio Divina 22). Paris: Cerf, 1958.

Corti, M. *Viver em graça*. S. Paulo, 1961.

Cunningham, F. *The Indwelling of the Trinity: A Historico-Doctrinal Study of the Theory of S. Thomas Aquinas*. Dubuque, Iowa: Priory Press, 1955.

Daffara, M. *De gratia Christi*. Rome, 1950.

Davis, C. *La gracia de Dios en la historia*. Bilbao, 1970.

De La Taille, M. "Actuation créée par l'acte incréé: Lumière de gloire, grâce sanctifiante, union hypostatique." *Recherches de Science Religieuse* 18 (1928): 253–68.

———. "Théories mystiques à propos d'un livre récent." *Recherches de Science Religieuse* 18 (1928): 297–335.

De Letter, P. "Sanctifying Grace and the Divine Indwelling." *Theological Studies* 14 (1953): 242–72.

———. "Created Actuation by the Uncreated Act: Difficulties and Answers." *Theological Studies* 18 (1957): 60–92.

———. "Grace, Incorporation, Inhabitation." *Theological Studies* 19 (1958): 1–31.

———. "Divine Quasi-Formal Causality." *The Irish Theological Quarterly* 27 (1969): 221–28.

De Lubac, H. *Surnaturel*. Paris: Aubier, 1946.

———. *Le mystère du surnaturel*. Paris: Aubier, 1965.

Dedek, J. F. *Experimental Knowledge of the Indwelling Trinity: An Historical Study of the Doctrine of St. Thomas*. Mundelein, Ill.: St. Mary of the Lake Seminary, 1958.

———. "Quasi experimentalis cognitio: An Historical Approach to the Meaning of St. Thomas." *Theological Studies* 22 (1961): 357–90.

Dockx, S. *Fils de Dieu par grâce*. Paris, 1948.

———. "La présence réelle de Dieu dans l'âme juste." *Nouvelle Revue Théologique* 72 (1950): 673–89.

Dymek, L. *Das Hohelied der Gnade*. Immenstadt i. Allgäu, 1963.

Farrelly, M. *Predestination, Grace and Free Will*. Westminster, Md.: Newman Press, 1964.

Ferreras, G. "Sobre la gracia y su teología." *Naturaleza y Gracia* 22 (1975): 59–90.

Flick, M. and Alszeghy, Z. *Il Vangelo della Grazia: Un trattato dogmatico*. Florence: Libreria Editrice, 1964.

———. *Fondamenti di una antropologia teologica* (Nuova Collana di Teologia Cattolica 10). Florence: Libreria Editrice Fiorentina, 1969.

Fortman, E. *Theology of Man and Grace: Commentary*. Milwaukee: Bruce, 1966.

Fransen, P. *The New Life of Grace*. Eng. trans., New York: Seabury, 1972.

———. "Pour une psychologie de la grâce divine." *Lumière et Vie* 12 (1957): 209–40.

———. "How Should We Teach the Treatise on Grace?" In *Apostolic Renewal in the Seminary in the Light of the Vatican Council,* edited by J. Keller and R. Armstrong, pp. 139–63. New York, 1965.

———. "Dogmengeschichtliche Entfaltung der Gnadenlehre." In *Mysterium Salutis* 4/2: 631–75.

————. "Das neue Sein des Menschen in Christus." In *Mysterium Salutis* 4/2: 921–84.

Froguet, B. *De l'habitation du Saint-Esprit dans les âmes justes d'après la doctrine de Saint Thomas d'Aquin*. Paris, 1938.

Galtier, P. *De SS. Trinitate in se et in nobis*. Paris: Beauchesne, 1933.

————. *Le Saint-Esprit en nous d'après les pères grecs* (Analecta Gregoriana 35). Rome, 1946.

————. *L'habitation en nous des Trois Personnes*. Rome: Pontificia Università Gregoriana, 1950.

————. "Grazia e inabitazione della SS. Trinità." In *Problemi e orientamenti di Teologia dogmatica*. Milan (1957) 2: 610–40.

Gardeil, A. *La structure de la grâce et l'expérience mystique*, 2 vols. Paris, 1927.

————. *Le Saint-Esprit dans la vie chrétienne*. Paris, 1950.

————. "Comment se réalise l'habitation de Dieu dans les âmes justes." In *Revue Thomiste* (1923) 28: 3–42, 129–41, 328–60.

Garrigou-Lagrange, R. "L'habitation de la Sainte Trinité et l'expérience mystique." In *Revue Thomiste* (1928) 33:449–74.

————. *De Gratia*. Turin, 1946. Eng. trans., *Grace* (St. Louis: Herder, 1952).

Gerrish, B. *Grace and Reason: A Study in the Theology of Luther*. Oxford: Oxford University Press, 1962.

Gleason, R. *Grace*. New York: Sheed & Ward, 1962.

González, O. *Misterio trinitario y existencia humana: Estudio histórico-teológico en torno a San Buenaventura*. Madrid, 1966.

González. S. "De gratia Christi." In *Sacrae Theologiae Summa*. 3 (BAC, 62). Madrid, 1950.

Greshake, G. *Gnade und Konkrete Freiheit: Eine Untersuchung zur Gnadenlehre des Pelagius*. Mainz: Matthias-Grünewald-Verlag, 1972.

Grings, D. *A força de Deus na fraqueza do homem*. Porto Alegre: Livraria Sulina, 1975.

Guardini, R. "Die Gnade." In *Freiheit, Gnade Schicksal*. Munich: Kösel-Verlag, 1948, pp. 125–89. Eng. trans., *Freedom, Grace and Destiny*, 1961 reprint, Westport, Conn.: Greenwood Press.

————. "Der Glaube an die Gnade und das Bewusstsein der Schuld." In *Unterscheidung des Christlichen*. Mainz: Matthias-Grünewald-Verlag, 1935, pp. 335–60.

Gutiérrez, J. *El Espíritu Santo, Don de Dios: Estudio histórico de teología dogmática*. Mexico City, 1966.

Journet, C. *Entretiens sur la grâce*. Tournai: Desclée, 1959.

Joyce, G. *The Catholic Doctrine of Grace*. New York, n.d.

Júlio Maria. *A Graça*. Rio de Janeiro: Ed. ABC, 1897.

Kühn, U. *Natur und Gnade in der deutschen katholischen Theologie seit 1918*. Berlin, 1961.

Kuladran, S. *Grace: A Comparative Study of the Doctrine in Christianity and Hinduism*. London, 1964.

Küng, H. *Rechtfertigung: Die Lehre Karl Barths und eine katholische Besinnung*. Einsiedeln, 1964. Eng. trans., *Justification: The Doctrine of Karl Barth and a Catholic Reflection*. New York: Nelson, 1964.

Kunz, E. *Glaube-Gnade-Geschichte: Die Glaubenstheologie des Pierre Rousselot*. Frankfurt: J. Knecht, 1969.

234 BIBLIOGRAPHY

Ladrière, J. "Fonction propre de la grâce à l'égard de la science." In *La science, le monde, la foi*. Paris: Casterman, 1972, pp. 45–53.

Langemeyer, B. "Die Frage nach dem gnädigen Gott heute." In *Geist und Leben*. 43 (1970): 125–135.

——. "Das Phänomenon Zufall und die Frage nach der göttlichen Vorsehung." In *Geist und Leben* 45 (1972): 24–41.

Lennerz, H. *De gratia Redemptoris*. Rome, 1949.

Libanio, J. B. *Pecado e opção fundamental*. Petrópolis: Ed. Vozes, 1975.

Löhrer, M. Gottes Gnadenhandeln als Erwählung des Menschen." In *Mysterium Salutis* 4/2: 773–87.

Lonergan, B. *Grace and Freedom: Operative Grace in the Thought of St. Thomas Aquinas*. New York: Seabury Press, 1970.

Loossen, J. "Ekklesiologische, christologische und trinitätstheologische Elemente im Gnadenbegriff." *Theologie in Geschichte und Gegenwart* (Festschrift for M. Schmaus). Munich, 1957, pp. 89–102.

Lot-Borodine, M. *La déification de l'homme*. Paris, 1970.

Mackey, J. *Life and Grace*. Dublin and Melbourne, 1966.

——. *The Grace of God: The Response of Man*. New York: Magi Books, 1966.

Maréchal, J. "A propos du sentiment de présence de Dieu chez les profanes et chez les mystiques." In *Etudes sur la psychologie des mystiques*. Bruges, 1929, pp. 69–179. Eng. trans., *Studies in the Psychology of the Mystics*. New York: Magi Books, 1964.

Martho-Salin, "Función transcendente de la gracia en el problema social." In *Revista de Espiritualidad* 10 (1951): 279–88.

Martínez G. "El misterio de la inhabitación del Espíritu Santo." In *Estudios Eclesiásticos* 13 (1943): 287–315.

Meisner, W. *Foundations for a Psychology of Grace*. New York: Paulist Press, 1965.

Menéndez Reigada, J. "Inhabitación, dones y experiencia mística." In *Revista Española de Teología* 6 (1946): 61–101.

Mersch, E. : "Filii in Filio." In *La Théologie du Corps Mystique*. Tournai: Desclée, 1949, 2: 9–68. Eng. trans., *Theology of the Mystical Body*. St. Louis: Herder, 1951.

——. "Le Surnaturel." Ibid.: 165–92.

——. "La Grâce sanctifiante." Ibid.: 333–66.

——. "La Grâce actuelle." Ibid.: 367–99.

Moeller, C. and G. Phillips, *Grâce et Ecuménisme*. Chevetogne, Belgium: Ed. de Chevetogne, 1957.

Molari, C. "Ordine soprannaturale: Attuazione o Quasi-Informazione." In *Divinitas* 6 (1962): 385–406.

Mühlen, H. *Der Heilige Geist als Person: In der Trinität, bei der Inkarnation und im Gnadenbund (Ich-Du-Wir)*. Münster: Aschendorff, 1964.

——. *Una mystica persona: Eine Person in vielen Personen*. Munich, Paderborn, and Vienna: F. Schöning, 1964.

——. *Die Erneuerung des christlichen Glaubens: Charisma-Geist-Befreiung*. Munich: Don Bosco-Verlag, 1976.

——. "Gnadenlehre." In *Bilanz der Theologie im 20. Jahrhundert*. Freiburg i. B., 1970, 3: 148–92.

Mullard, R. *La grâce* (St. Thomas d'Aquin, Somme Théologique). Paris, 1920.

Nicolas, J. *Le mystère de la grâce*. Liège, 1950.

————. *Les profondeurs de la grâce.* Paris: Beauchesne, 1969.

Oman, J. *Grace and Personality.* Folcroft, Pa. (Folcroft Library Editions), 1919.

Penido, M. "La valeur de la théorie psychologique de la Trinité." In *Ephemerides Theol. Lovanienses* 8 (1931): 5–16.

Perego, A. *La gracia.* Barcelona, 1964.

Pesch, O. "Die Lehre vom Verdienst als Problem für Theologie and Verkündigung." In *Wahrheit und Verkündigung* (Festschrift for M. Schmaus). Munich, 1967: 1865–1907.

————. "Gottes Gnadenhandeln als Rechtfertigung des Menschen." In *Mysterium Salutis* 4/2: 831–920.

Philips, G. "De ratione instituendi tractatum de gratia nostrae sanctificationis." In *Ephemerides Theol. Lovanienses* 29 (1953): 355–73.

Puntel, B. L. "Deus na teologia hoje." In *Perspectiva Teológica* (1969): 1:15–24.

Rahner, K. *Graça divina em abismos humanos.* Portuguese edition. São Paulo, 1968.

————. *O homem e a graça.* Portuguese edition. São Paulo, 1960.

————. *Grace in Freedom.* New York: Seabury Press, 1960.

————. "Zur scholastischen Begrifflichkeit der ungeschaffenen Gnade." In *Schriften zur Theologie.* Einsiedeln, 1954, 1: 347–75. Eng. trans., *Theological Investigations.* New York: Seabury Press.

————. "Natur und Gnade." Ibid. 4:209–326.

————. "Über den Begriff des Geheimnisses in der katholischen Theologie." Ibid. 4: 51–99.

————. "Über das Verhältnis zur Natur und Gnade." Ibid. 4: 323–45.

Ratzinger, J. "Gratia supponit naturam: Erwägungen über Sinn und Grenze eines scholastischen Axioms." In *Einsicht und Glaube* (Festschrift for J. Söhngen). Freiburg i. Br., 1962: 135–49; also in the following listing.

————. *Dogma und Verkündigung.* Munich and Freiburg: Wewel, 1973, pp. 161–82.

Rito, H. *Recentioris theologiae quaedam tendentiae ad conceptum ontologico-personalem gratiae.* Rome: Herder, 1963.

Rivière, J. "Sur l'origine des formules ecclésiastiques 'de congruo' et 'de condigno'." In *Bulletin de Littérature ecclésiastique.* 1927, 28:75–83.

Rondet, H. *Gratia Christi: Esquisse d'une histoire de la théologie de la grâce.* Paris: Beauchesne, 1948.

————. *Essais sur la théologie de la grâce.* Paris: Beauchesne, 1964.

Ruini, G. *La transcendenza della grazia nella teologia di San Tommaso d'Aquino* (Analecta Gregoriana 180). Rome: Università Gregoriana, 1971.

Ryelandt, I. *The Life of Grace.* Eng. trans., Dublin and London: Clommore and Reynolds, 1964.

Schauf, H. *Die Einwohnung de H. Geistes.* Freiburg i. Br., 1941.

Scheeben, M. *As maravilhas de graça divina.* Portuguese edition. Petrópolis: Ed. Vozes, 1977.

————. *Die Mysterien des Christentums.* Freiburg i. Br., 1951.

————. *The Holy Spirit.* Eng. trans., Westminster, Md. (Christian Classics), 1974.

Schmaus, M. *A fé da Igreja; A justificação individual.* Petrópolis: Ed. Vozes, 1977.

————. "Die göttliche Gnade." In *Katholische Dogmatik* 3/4. Munich: Max Hueber, 1956.

Segundo, J. L. *Grace and the Human Condition* (A Theology for Artisans of a New Humanity, 2). Eng. trans. Maryknoll. N.Y.: Orbis Books, 1973.

Simon, P. *La littérature du péché et de la grâce, 1880–1950.* Paris: Librairie A. Fayard, 1957.

Simonin, T. "Prédestination, prescience et liberté." In *Nouvelle Revue Théologique* 85 (1963):711–30.

Sittler, J. *Essays on Nature and Grace.* Philadelphia: Fortress Press, 1972.

Smith, C. *The Bible Doctrine of Grace.* London: Epworth Press, 1956.

Stevens, G. *The Life of Grace.* Engelwood Cliffs, N.J.: Prentice-Hall, 1963.

Stoeckle, B. *Gratia supponit naturam: Geschichte und Analyse eines theologischen Axioms unter besonderer Berücksichtigung seines patristischen Ursprungs, seiner Formulierung in der Hochscholastik und seiner zentralen Position in der Theologie des 19. Jahrhundrts.* Rome: Herder, 1962.

Terrien, J. *La grâce et la gloire,* 2 vols. Paris, 1948.

Theodorou, A. "Die Lehre von der Vergöttung des Menschen bei den griechischen Kirchenvätern." In *Kerygma und Dogma,* 1961, 7:283–310.

Thils, G. *Sainteté chrétienne* (Précis de théologie ascétique: Assimilation à la Sainte Trinité). Tielt (Belgium), 1958, pp. 46–82.

Trütsch, J. *SS. Trinitatis inhabitatio apud theologos recentiores.* Trent, 1949.

Turrado, A. *Dios en el hombre: Plenitud o tragedia.* Madrid: Editorial Católica, BAC 325, 1971.

Urdánoz, T. "La inhabitación del Espíritu Santo en el alma del justo." In *Revista Española de Teología* (1946), 6:465–534.

———. "Influjo causal de las divinas personas en la inhabitación en las almas justas." Ibid. (1948), 8:141–202.

Vaz, H. de Lima. "A experiência de Deus." In *Experimentar Deus hoje.* Petrópolis: Ed. Vozes, 1976, pp. 74–89.

Vering, F. "De certitudine status gratiae in Concilio Tridentino." Ph.D. dissertation, Rome, 1953.

Volk, H. "Gnade und Person: Gott alles in allem." In *Gesammelte Aufsätze.* Mainz: Matthias-Grünewald-Verlag, 1961, 113–29.

Watson, P. *The Concept of Grace.* London: Epworth Press, 1959.

Weil, S. *La pesanteur et la grâce.* Paris: Plon, 1948.

Willig, I. *Geschaffene und ungeschaffene Gnade: Bibeltheologische Fundierung und systematische Erörterung.* Münster: Westfalen, Aschendorff, 1964.

Other Orbis books . . .

THE MEANING OF MISSION

José Comblin

"This very readable book has made me think, and I feel it will be useful for anyone dealing with their Christian role of mission and evangelism." *New Review of Books and Religion*

ISBN 0-88344-304-X CIP   *Cloth $6.95*

THE GOSPEL OF PEACE AND JUSTICE

Catholic Social Teaching Since Pope John

Presented by Joseph Gremillion

"Especially valuable as a resource. The book brings together 22 documents containing the developing social teaching of the church from *Mater et Magistra* to Pope Paul's 1975 *Peace Day Message on Reconciliation*. I watched the intellectual excitement of students who used Gremillion's book in a justice and peace course I taught last summer, as they discovered a body of teaching on the issues they had defined as relevant. To read Gremillion's overview and prospectus, a meaty introductory essay of some 140 pages, is to be guided through the sea of social teaching by a remarkably adept navigator."

National Catholic Reporter

"An authoritative guide and study aid for concerned Catholics and others." *Library Journal*

ISBN 0-88344-165-9   *Cloth $15.95*
ISBN 0-88344-166-7   *Paper $8.95*

THEOLOGY IN THE AMERICAS

Papers of the 1975 Detroit Conference

Edited by Sergio Torres and John Eagleson

"A pathbreaking book from and about a pathbreaking theological conference, *Theology in the Americas* makes a major contribution to ecumenical theology, Christian social ethics and liberation movements in dialogue." *Fellowship*

ISBN 0-88344-479-8 CIP   *Cloth $12.95*
ISBN 0-88344-476-3   *Paper $5.95*

THE CHURCH AND POWER IN BRAZIL

Charles Antoine

"This is a book which should serve as a basis of discussion and further study by all who are interested in the relationship of the Church to contemporary governments, and all who believe that the Church has a vital role to play in the quest for social justice." *Worldmission*
ISBN 0-88344-062-8   *Paper $4.95*

HISTORY AND
THE THEOLOGY OF LIBERATION

Enrique Dussel

"The book is easy reading. It is a brilliant study of what may well be or should be the future course of theological methodology."
Religious Media Today
ISBN 0-88344-179-9   *Cloth $8.95*
ISBN 0-88344-180-2   *Paper $4.95*

DOM HELDER CAMARA

José de Broucker

"De Broucker, an internationally recognized journalist, develops a portrait, at once intimate, comprehensive and sympathetic, of the Archbishop of Olinda and Recife, Brazil, whose championship of political and economic justice for the hungry, unorganized masses of his country and all Latin America has aroused world attention."
America
ISBN 0-88344-099-7   *Cloth $6.95*

THE DESERT IS FERTILE

Dom Helder Camara

"Camara's brief essays and poems are arresting for their simplicity and depth of vision, and are encouraging because of the realistic yet quietly hopeful tone with which they argue for sustained action toward global justice." *Commonweal*
ISBN 0-88344-078-4   *Cloth $3.95*

MARX AND THE BIBLE

José Miranda

"An inescapable book which raises more questions than it answers, which will satisfy few of us, but will not let us rest easily again. It is an attempt to utilize the best tradition of Scripture scholarship to understand the text when it is set in a context of human need and misery."

Walter Brueggemann, in Interpretation

ISBN 0-88344-306-6   *Cloth $8.95*
ISBN 0-88344-307-4   *Paper $4.95*

BEING AND THE MESSIAH

The Message of Saint John

José Miranda

"This book could become the catalyst of a new debate on the Fourth Gospel. Johannine scholarship will hotly debate the 'terrifyingly revolutionary thesis that this world of contempt and oppression can be changed into a world of complete selflessness and unrestricted mutual assistance.' Cast in the framework of an analysis of contemporary philosophy, the volume will prove a classic of Latin American theology." *Frederick Herzog, Duke University Divinity School*

ISBN 0-88344-027-X CIP   *Cloth $8.95*
ISBN 0-88344-028-8   *Paper $4.95*

THE GOSPEL IN SOLENTINAME

Ernesto Cardenal

"Upon reading this book, I want to do so many things—burn all my other books which at best seem like hay, soggy with mildew. I now know who (not what) is the church and how to celebrate church in the eucharist. The dialogues are intense, profound, radical. *The Gospel in Solentiname* calls us home."

Carroll Stuhlmueller, National Catholic Reporter

ISBN 0-88344-168-3   *Vol. 1 Cloth $6.95*
ISBN 0-88344-170-5   *Vol. 1 Paper $4.95*
ISBN 0-88344-167-5   *Vol. 2 Cloth $6.95*

THEOLOGY FOR A NOMAD CHURCH

Hugo Assmann

"A new challenge to contemporary theology which attempts to show that the theology of liberation is not just a fad, but a new political dimension which touches every aspect of Christian existence."

Publishers Weekly

ISBN 0-88344-493-3   *Cloth $7.95*
ISBN 0-88344-494-1   *Paper $4.95*

FREEDOM MADE FLESH

The Mission of Christ and His Church

Ignacio Ellacuría

"Ellacuría's main thesis is that God's saving message and revelation are historical, that is, that the proclamation of the gospel message must possess the same historical character that revelation and salvation history do and that, for this reason, it must be carried out in history and in a historical way." *Cross and Crown*

ISBN 0-88344-140-3   *Cloth $8.95*
ISBN 0-88344-141-1   *Paper $4.95*

THE LIBERATION OF THEOLOGY

Juan Luis Segundo

"It is a remarkable book in terms of its boldness in confronting the shortcomings of the Christian tradition and in terms of the clarity of vision provided by the hermeneutic of liberation. Segundo writes with ease whether dealing with the sociological, theological, or political roots of liberation. His is a significant addition to the recent work of Cone, Alves, Moltmann, and Gutiérrez because it compels the movement to interrogate its own theological foundations. A necessary addition, in one of the more fruitful directions of contemporary theology, it is appropriate for graduate, undergraduate, or clerical readers." *Choice*

"The book makes for exciting reading and should not be missing in any theological library." *Library Journal*

ISBN 0-88344-285-X CIP   *Cloth $10.95*
ISBN 0-88344-286-8   *Paper $6.95*

CHRISTIANS, POLITICS
AND VIOLENT REVOLUTION

J.G. Davies

"Davies argues that violence and revolution are on the agenda the world presents to the Church and that consequently the Church must reflect on such problems. This is a first-rate presentation, with Davies examining the question from every conceivable angle."

National Catholic News Service

ISBN 0-88344-061-X   *Paper $4.95*

CHRISTIAN POLITICAL THEOLOGY
A MARXIAN GUIDE

Joseph Petulla

"Petulla presents a fresh look at Marxian thought for the benefit of Catholic theologians in the light of the interest in this subject which was spurred by Vatican II, which saw the need for new relationships with men of all political positions." *Journal of Economic Literature*

ISBN 0-88344-060-1   *Paper $4.95*

THE NEW CREATION:
MARXIST AND CHRISTIAN?

José María González-Ruiz

"A worthy book for lively discussion."

The New Review of Books and Religion

ISBN 0-88344-327-9 CIP   *Cloth $6.95*

CHRISTIANS AND SOCIALISM

Documentation of the Christians for
Socialism Movement in Latin America

Edited by John Eagleson

"Compelling in its clear presentation of the issue of Christian commitment in a revolutionary world." *The Review of Books and Religion*

ISBN 0-88344-058-X   *Paper $4.95*

THE CHURCH AND
THIRD WORLD REVOLUTION

Pierre Bigo

"Heavily documented, provocative yet reasonable, this is a testament, demanding but impressive." *Publishers Weekly*

ISBN 0-88344-071-7 CIP   *Cloth $8.95*
ISBN 0-88344-072-5   *Paper $4.95*

WHY IS THE THIRD WORLD POOR?

Piero Gheddo

"An excellent handbook on the Christian understanding of the development process. Gheddo looks at both the internal and external causes of underdevelopment and how Christians can involve themselves in helping the third world." *Provident Book Finder*

ISBN 0-88344-757-6   *Paper $4.95*

POLITICS AND SOCIETY
IN THE THIRD WORLD

Jean-Yves Calvez

"This frank treatment of economic and cultural problems in developing nations suggests the need for constant multiple attacks on the many fronts that produce problems in the human situation."
The Christian Century

ISBN 0-88344-389-9   *Cloth $6.95*

A THEOLOGY OF LIBERATION

Gustavo Gutiérrez

"The movement's most influential text." *Time*

"The most complete presentation thus far available to English readers of the provocative theology emerging from the Latin American Church." *Theological Studies*

"North Americans as well as Latin Americans will find so many challenges and daring insights that they will, I suggest, rate this book one of the best of its kind ever written." *America*

ISBN 0-88344-477-1   *Cloth $7.95*
ISBN 0-88344-478-X   *Paper $4.95*